BEYOND BARTMAN, CURSES, & GOATS:
104 REASONS WHY IT'S BEEN 104 YEARS

BEYOND BARTMAN, CURSES, & GOATS
104 REASONS WHY IT'S BEEN 104 YEARS

Windy City Publishers
2118 Plum Grove Rd., #349
Rolling Meadows, IL 60008

www.windycitypublishers.com

Published in the United States of America

ISBN#:
978-1-935766-76-6

Library of Congress Control Number:
2013933606

Windy City Publishers

CHICAGO

BEYOND BARTMAN, CURSES, & GOATS:
104 REASONS WHY IT'S BEEN 104 YEARS

BY CHRIS NEITZEL

ABOUT MY SOURCE(S)
FOR THIS BOOK

Baseballreference.com—that is really all I need to say. All of the research (unless notated in a particular *Reason*) was found on baseballreference. com. I cannot thank baseballreference.com enough for its totality of baseball information. If you ever hoped to obtain a book, which has all of the baseball information you could ever need, I suggest you go to baseballreference.com. Every season, every player, every *game* you will find on baseballreference.com.

Therefore, as you enjoy the journey through my 104 reasons of Cubs' futility, and you begin to wonder, *Where did he get all of this information?* The answer is simple…baseballreference.com.

AND A VERY IMPORTANT "THANK YOU"

This book would have never been written without the influence of Brett Taylor and *Bleacher Nation*. If you are a Cubs' fan and are NOT aware of *Bleacher Nation*, you are sorely missing out. Growing up as a Cubs' fan, I would search every day in the *Chicago Tribune* and *Chicago Sun-Times* for a morsel of information regarding baseball and the Cubs. Now, a fan can get his Cubs' fix daily with one stop to Brett's blog. There are many Cubs' blogs to choose from; but for professionalism, quality of information, humor, and just a cool place for Cubs' fans to congregate online, *Bleacher Nation* is the place. If you are looking for a blog that gives credence to every silly rumor and proposes wild, unrealistic Cubs' trades…*Bleacher Nation* is NOT for you. If you wish to learn about the Cubs, laugh along the way, and be kept updated to the second on anything breaking in the Cubs' universe…*Bleacher Nation* is for you.

I had always felt there was a writer inside of me (which this book may prove to be true or false), and writing pieces on the *Bleacher Nation* message board stoked my thoughts even more. When Brett would link my message board writings to the main page…I had a sense of fulfillment I had never felt… the feeling that I could inform and entertain. The idea that even hundreds of people were reading my contributions was extremely rewarding.

In June of 2012, as I was lying in bed deciding on what I was going to write on the message board that morning…an idea hit me. As I drifted in and out of sleep, a title then came to my mind…and I realized that this was more than what I could write on the blog…and I had to do this. This "spark" would have never happened without the *Bleacher Nation* blog and Brett Taylor. I have no idea how many people will ever read this book…but I accomplished something I never thought possible.

For that, I am eternally grateful.

To my wife Krista, the love of my life,
and the English teacher who helped edit this project.

To my kids, Kara, Olivia, and Scotty, who let Dad
spend countless hours on the computer.

Once again to Brett Taylor of *Bleacher Nation*,
who helped inspire me to do this.

To my high school English teachers, Karla Hoinkes and Donna Barnes.
These educators did something right because when I got to college,
I wasn't the best student...yet I got As on all of my papers
while others were struggling

To the nameless man who randomly chose me to be batboy for a day,
whoever you are...wherever you are...

To the amazing team at Windy City Publishers.

And to the Chicago Cubs...
for giving me more than enough examples of futility
to fill a book with 104 reasons...

FOREWORD

by Brett Taylor

Founder of the Top Chicago Cubs Blog

Bleacher Nation

I used to dictate the outcomes of Chicago Cubs games.

A child of the *X-Men*, like so many before me who thought themselves able to fly or turn invisible or shoot lasers from their eyes, I had a power. No, I didn't change the scores of Cubs' games or strike down opponents with lightning—don't be ridiculous. I merely caused the Cubs to hit home runs, frequently at key moments in games, thus ensuring a win that was otherwise out of reach. That August 19, 1990, two-run home run by Hector Villanueva in the bottom of the eighth inning to beat the Braves? Yeah. You're welcome.

The power was a sensitive one, though. I could use it only when I had "the feeling"—a tickle in my belly suggesting the conditions were right for me to cause a home run. I couldn't misuse the power, you understand, or it would lose its effect. So, when the Cubs didn't homer, even after I'd gotten "the feeling," I was sure it was my fault. I had misinterpreted things. I had tried to will the home run to happen. And that's what made it not happen.

I'm sure I wasn't unique in my childish beliefs. Hell, if you're wearing your lucky underwear today, I would imagine I'm not alone in my adult beliefs, either.

Cubs' fans are drawn to these explanations because they give us some measure of control. The Cubs didn't lose today because they sucked. They lost because I wore the wrong socks. More importantly, if I just figure out the right outfit combo, they'll finally win.

Were it not so—were the Cubs to win and lose on the actual merits of their play (and a little bit of luck swinging in each direction)—our fandom would be reduced to that of helpless spectators, doomed to sit on our hands while our gladiators are eaten by tigers. Unfortunately, the rational mind—something of an oxymoron when speaking of fanatics—must accept that we are much closer to helpless spectators than we are to *X-Men*.

The truth is, the odds against your team "winning it all" are, by the very nature of sport, stacked against you. In professional baseball, "your" team is but one of 30 vying for the title, leaving 29 fan bases to be bathed in disappointment come October. In professional football, the winner is just one in 32. In college football, your team is likely to be one of 119 losers (as of 2012). And God help you if you're a college basketball fan in a non-power conference.

Sometimes, losing is just a matter of probabilities.

Still, the Chicago Cubs' bad luck appears to be rather extreme. Using an admittedly amateur, back-of-the-napkin calculation, consider this. Even if you assume that every team in baseball has equal odds of winning a World Series in a given season (a conservative assumption when talking about a large market team like the Cubs), the chances that a team would go 104 years in MLB without winning a World Series are quite slim.

From 1909 until 1960, there were 16 teams in MLB, meaning that, under this modest mathematical scheme, the Cubs had a 1 in 16 chance of winning a World Series each season during that fifty-two-year stretch. In 1961, two teams were added, leaving the Cubs with a 1 in 18 chance of winning it all. In 1962, two more teams were added, yielding a 1 in 20 chance until 1969, when another four teams came on board (1 in 24 chance during that stretch). In 1977, another two teams were added, and the odds shrank to 1 in 26. In 1993, another two teams were added, and, once again, the odds shrank to 1 in 28 (except for 1994, when there was no World Series). Finally, in 1998, the last two expansion teams were added, providing the Cubs with a 1 in 30 chance of winning the World Series from 1998 until 2012.

The odds that the Cubs would not win a title in 1909, for example, was 15 in 16, since only one team can win. By extension, we can calculate the odds that the Cubs would not win a title in 1909, 1910, 1911, and on and on, until we reach 2012. When combining each of those individual odds, we're left with a mere 0.4543 percent chance that the Chicago Cubs would not win a World Series in any of the seasons between 1909 and 2012. That's a 1 in 220 shot.

Heck, even if you consider only the seven times the Cubs have made the World Series after 1908—the most recent appearance, sadly, was 1945—

the odds of not winning a single one of those series is just 1 in 128 (again, assuming a simplistic 1 in 2 chance of winning each series). Of course, even if the Cubs had won, say, the 1929 World Series, you're probably not feeling too much better about your fandom today. Still: 1 in 128.

What are we to make of this seemingly absurd and cosmic bad luck? Do the dice simply hate the Cubs? Maybe so. But here's the thing: that entire calculation was premised on the idea that every team goes into each season with an equal shot of winning it all. As fans, we know that isn't true. Perhaps, rather than having a horrific run of bad luck, the Cubs have had a horrific run of a lot of bad things. Some of which were undoubtedly within the organization's control.

Ultimately, teams lose for many reasons. Bad players, bad management, bad ownership, bad contracts, bad trades, bad drafts, bad timing, bad bounces...

Or the shortstop takes his eye off the ball at the wrong moment.

The idea that the Cubs have lost for so long for myriad reasons is at once comforting (at least it isn't God unleashing His wrath in perpetuity) and depressing (I can't fix this—I just have to watch and hope). But, just as I put away childish things and accepted that I can't actually make the Cubs hit home runs, we all must accept that there are no mystical, magical reasons why the Cubs have not won it all since 1908. There are many real, tangible, analytical, and literal reasons why the Cubs haven't won.

And this book explores those reasons.

~Brett Taylor
April 2013

CONTENTS

PREFACE 1

CHAPTER 1: 8
NEAR MISSES (1910-1945)

CHAPTER 2: 34
NEAR MISSES (1969-2008)

CHAPTER 3: 64
DAFT DRAFTS

CHAPTER 4: 90
ONES THAT GOT AWAY

CHAPTER 5: 124
SPECIAL OPS

CHAPTER 6: 150
ONE-HIT WONDERS

CHAPTER 7: 174
MONEY MATTERS

CHAPTER 8: 210
MANAGING...GENERALLY AND BAD

CHAPTER 9: 246
BLUNDERS (PHILOSOPHICAL, HISTORICAL,
AND JUST PLAIN STUPID

EPILOGUE: 291
YEAR 105?

PREFACE

"I can't believe the Cubs are going to the World Series."

I made this fateful statement on October 14, 2003. I was sitting on my couch, speaking to my wife who was in the kitchen. The Cubs were leading the Florida Marlins 3-1 in the eighth inning of Game 6 in the 2003 National League Championship Series. Two days earlier I had turned thirty-five years old...

...and in about twenty-eight hours, I would finally grow up.

I began to follow the Chicago Cubs closely in 1977 as an eight year old. I was born a Cubs' fan, since that's what my dad was...a fate I *seriously* considered sparing my own son. That was the year I got *hooked*...the team contended for much of the summer, and I became captivated by players such as Bobby Murcer, Ivan DeJesus, Bill Buckner, Rick Rueschel and Bruce Sutter. The '77 Cubs would fade down the stretch (go figure), and the team would finish at 81-81.

The next spring my family vacationed in Arizona coinciding with the Cubs' spring training. In 1978, Scottsdale, Arizona, was not the bustling place I rediscovered upon a return visit in 2010. Like the then-small size of Scottsdale, the Chicago Cubs' spring training was minuscule compared to its current popularity. The games were attended...just not as immensely. The players' accessibility and willingness to sign autographs were at levels that will never be seen again. I can recall watching Billy Williams working with a couple of players in the batting cage (a cage that was under the bleachers, reachable for both players and fans), and just *two* other kids and I were watching...*after* we had gotten Billy's autograph.

It would be the following day that would turn my Cubs' fandom from a passion into an addiction. My family and I were walking into the stadium to attend a Cubs' game against the Cleveland Indians. The crowd was thick and dense, and I remember struggling to weave in and out of the throng of people. I was proudly wearing my Cubs' hat and T-shirt...a clothing choice that was soon to become monumentally advantageous.

As we continued to make our way through the crowd, a man appeared out of nowhere with a question. "Would you like to be the Cubs' batboy today?"

I vividly recall the sense of shock, amazement and dream-like feeling I had...this couldn't actually be happening. Yet after a quick "yes" from me and my parents, I was whisked away through the Cubs' clubhouse and out onto the field. The game was about to start, and I found myself in the surreal position of standing with my heroes for the "Star-Spangled Banner." Dave Radar, the Cubs' catcher, emerged from the clubhouse steps, and apparently realizing he was late, said "Ah...Sh*t!"

I was shocked to realize that Major League Baseball players swore...nine-year-old naiveté at its best.

The game began and my dream-like feeling continued. I was part of *the Cubs*...if only for a day. Many of the memories are hazy, yet there are some embedded in my brain. I recall getting so into the game at one time that I neglected my batboy duties; the umpire was tapping a bat on home plate, a polite reminder to an awestruck kid. Dave Kingman hit a towering home run to left field, and I was there at the end of the line to give him five. When the final out was recorded, the Cubs had won the game. I didn't realize it at the time, but it was probably the emptiest Cubs' victory I ever experienced. I wanted that game to last forever.

Back home I got a little taste of celebrity (I am using that term very loosely). My picture was in the paper with an accompanying article. I had a very cool thing to take for the "All-About-Me" week in Mrs. Samuelson's fourth grade class. I have a very clear memory of the cutest girl in fourth-grade looking at my article, looking at me and giving me a smile. Ah, the perks of a one-time batboy! I had no idea there would be more perks to come.

On my first day of junior high, I was an extremely scared and shy 11-year-old boy. As my teacher, Mrs. Mooney, was falsely telling us what an old witch she was (*a scare tactic...she was awesome*), the school's principal, Mr. Anderson, came walking into our classroom. Mr. Anderson, a former basketball player and coach, stood at least 6'5" and had an intimidating appearance. As he fixedly approached my desk, my face was surely the palest of pales. I knew I had done nothing wrong...but it was the first day, and the principal was bearing down on me.

"Are you Chris Neitzel?" Mr. Anderson asked. I have no recollection at all of responding to him, but I recall what he said next. He told me he was a huge Cubs' fan, and that he knew all about me as batboy for a day. You see, Mr. Anderson's son had been one of my little league coaches during the previous summer. Mr. Anderson went on gushing about how cool he thought being a batboy was, and what a big Cubs' fan he was. We talked long enough that I began to feel embarrassed by the attention I was getting in front of the other kids. Mr. Anderson made it clear: he was my pal. Junior high became a lot less intimidating.

For the next few years it didn't matter how lousy the Cubs were...my addiction was in full force. I inhaled all things Cubs as they became available to me throughout the limited resources of the late 1970s. The late 1970s and early 1980s proved to be a fruitless era for the Chicago Cubs, and Cubs' fans, such as Mr. Anderson and I, had little to cheer about. At least our friendship was beneficial; when I was called into the office for gambling with other students, Mr. Anderson gave me a very stern, "Just don't get caught at school doing this." He also questioned one of my co-conspirators for his betting choices. (I think it had something to do with the Bears...Mr. Anderson came over the PA system *during* school to announce the Bears had drafted Jim McMahon...pretty cool to sports nuts like me and my little buddies.) I walked out of the office unscathed; a couple of dollar bets would not tarnish my record.

My entrance into high school coincided with Dallas Green's hiring by the Chicago Cubs in 1982, and by the end of my sophomore year (spring 1984), Green had built a contending team. Also that spring I met a girl in my health class. I made an instant connection with this sixteen-year-old girl...she loved the Cubs and actually knew all of the players! I was hooked at that point as well...I just wasn't fully aware yet.

That fall was the beginning of my junior year and the Cubs played in the 1984 National League Championship Series against the Padres. I think I lost any chances I had with the cheerleader I was taking to homecoming that fall when she saw the dorky-looking "Cubs Power" button I wore the day the NLCS commenced. I fared no better with her than the Cubs did against the Padres. The homecoming dance took place the same night the Cubs were playing the Padres in Game 4. My "date" spent her time trying to reel in her former boyfriend while I, a couple of my friends, and the girl from my health class kept leaving the gymnasium to get updates on the game. We had to use a pay phone (look it up if you don't know what one is) and call this thing called *Sports Phone*. Sports Phone gave updates every fifteen to twenty minutes…and for only seventy-five cents! The last update we received detailed Steve Garvey's game-winning home run. I am not sure if my "date" even left with me…I cannot recall…the Game 4 loss was all that was on my mind.

***Due to post-traumatic stress, I will not discuss Game 5 at this time… later in the book the event will be addressed.

In the fall of 1986, I attended Illinois State University in Bloomington-Normal. After bickering and battling with White Sox fans my entire life, I was relieved to find so few of them on campus. At ISU, there was no Cubs-Sox rivalry…it was solely Cubs-*Cardinals*. I was thrust into a whole new world… *Central* Illinois did not seem like *Illinois* to me. The abundance of Cardinals' fans at ISU amazed me…and their appearance in the 1987 World Series was tough to handle. But in 1989 we ISU Cubs' fans got our revenge…and my roommate and I shouted "The Cubs are Division Champs!" out of our apartment window for all Cardinals' fans to hear.

As I settled into my new job as a social studies teacher and coach in the early 1990s, the Cubs were busy playing pretty crummy baseball. The team almost lost me for good in 1992 when they elected not to re-sign Greg Maddux. That led me to a semi-boycott of the team…I still followed them…just *bitterly*. The rest of the 1990s were great for me…marriage, kids, house, and a good job. The 1990s for the Chicago Cubs…not as productive. Aside from the 1998 wild-card team that was swept by Greg Maddux and the Atlanta Braves, the 1990s was barren of Chicago Cubs' success.

An influx of talent after the turn of the century saw the team become contenders in the early 2000s. Two dynamic young pitchers, Kerry Wood and Mark Prior, would put the Cubs into a position they were not accustomed to…

five outs away from the World Series. The Cubs' ascension to the World Series finally seemed inevitable, so close that it prompted me to let my guard down.

"I can't believe the Cubs are going to the World Series," I stated with confident surprise to my wife...the girl from my sophomore health class who shared a passion for the Cubs in 1984. By 2003, she had grown up. She still wanted them to win, but she was not having a nervous breakdown after every pitch like I was.

Many Cubs' fans could tell similar tales up to this point; recounting how the Cubs have intertwined with elements of their lives. How the Cubs connect with important people, places and key events. Those same Cubs' fans probably felt the same misery I did as the Cubs lost Game 6...and Game 7 of the 2003 NLCS to the Florida Marlins. A collective agony would once again be felt among millions of fans.

After Game 7, my Cubs' odyssey took a divergent turn. As another devastating loss became reality, I secluded myself in our guest room and got into bed. I didn't wait for the final out; I instructed my wife to get me if the Cubs happened to come back. I knew this would not happen.

I chose the guest room as I knew that it was going to be a sleepless night and I did not want to disturb my wife. Shortly, I heard her turn the TV off and go to bed in the next room. The house became quiet, and I was left to my Cubs' stress-induced insomnia. Tossing...turning...grabbing the pillow...nothing could get the thought of another Cubs' devastation out of my head. Hours and hours seemed to go by...I occasionally drifted for minutes, and my mind would trick me into thinking the game was not over. My own subconscious was not showing any mercy.

Then it happened. The strongest epiphany I have had in my life. The closest thing I have had to a "spiritual" experience. It was as though God (Yahweh, Allah...whatever works for you) slapped me across the face. It was like Vito Corleone slapping Johnny Fontaine in *The Godfather* and saying, "What the hell is the matter with you?" Something cleared my head...probably the closest thing I have ever had to a "vision." A clear and strong thought entered my brain like a bolt of wisdom lightning:

"Why do you allow things to stress you out that you have no control over?"

It may sound insane, but I cannot fully describe the relief that I felt. The stress and anxiety just seemed to lift from my body like an unwanted evil spirit…and it floated away. It was one of the most content feelings that I have encountered…and it felt good. I didn't fall asleep immediately, but I would be within minutes.

That experience changed my life. I am still a passionate sports' fan. I am dogged in my pursuit of knowledge about all things Cubs, Bears and Blackhawks. (The Bulls lost me after Michael Jordan.) As much as I enjoy sporting events, I will never lose a minute of sleep due to a loss. I learned my lesson that evening…and I will never regress to my former self. I can't control it…therefore it will not control me.

This has not lessened my interest in following any teams; to the contrary, it has made it easier. I am no longer obsessed with the end outcome…I now enjoy the means *to* that end. I still soak up all of the information I can get, and I even get just as excited about potential trades and acquisitions…the losses just don't make me angry anymore. Why should they?

Therefore, when the Cubs lost in the play-offs in both 2007 and 2008, there was no tossing or turning at all. I would have preferred they win of course, but I was able to deal with it in a mature and reasonable fashion. I am now able to look at the Cubs in a rational way. In my opinion, this does not make me any less of a fan…I just have an altered perspective.

I am hoping that the sensible reasons I present in this book will help Cubs' fans do the same, to help make sense of what appears illogical. A 104-year title drought presents itself as something more than what it is…and fans begin to accept irrational ideas out of desperation. It is hard to wrap your brain around the concept of such a prolonged stretch of failure, and it becomes easier to invoke silly excuses…even invoking supernatural forces or the wrath of a barnyard animal's owner.

I don't expect all readers to have the same relief from Cubs' angst I have experienced; I wish to alter perspectives a bit and provide some rational answers to questions a lifelong Cubs' fan might have.

I still am and will always be a Cubs' fan; I just know that they aren't cursed and Steve Bartman was not the reason the Cubs lost the 2003 National League Championship Series.

~C.N.
March 2013

CHAPTER 1

REASON 1—THE 1910 WORLD SERIES:
CHIEF BENDER AND JACK COOMBS
It only took two pitchers to defeat the Cubs in the 1910 World Series…
no seriously…only two guys pitched.

REASON 2—THE 1918 WORLD SERIES:
WORLD WAR I AND THE BABE ON THE MOUND
While American soldiers were battling in Europe,
the Cubs were facing the greatest home run hitter of all time…as a pitcher.

REASON 3—THE 1929 WORLD SERIES:
CONNIE MACK AND THE "MACK" ATTACK
The Philadelphia Athletics had Hall of Famer Mack as a manager
and a record-setting rally that still stands eighty-four years later.

REASON 4—THE 1929 WORLD SERIES:
HALL OF FAME SLUGGERS (PART 1)
The Cubs and Athletics had lineups full of sluggers…
but the A's had Jimmie Foxx and Mickey Cochrane.

REASON 5—THE 1930 SEASON:
THE CARDINALS GET HOT… *REALLY HOT!*
Thirty-nine years before an amazing Mets' finish caught the Cubs,
the Cardinals did it better.

REASON 6—THE 1932 WORLD SERIES:
HALL OF FAME SLUGGERS (PART 2): THE BABE & LOU GEHRIG
For some silly reason the Cubs taunted the Babe…
and he may or may not have predicted his epic home run.

REASON 7—THE 1935 WORLD SERIES:
TIGERS' PITCHING, INCLUDING THE GENERAL AND THE SCHOOLBOY
The Cubs lost three one-run games to a Detroit team
that had some interesting nicknames.

REASON 8—THE 1936 AND 1937 SEASONS:
BACK-TO-BACK SECOND PLACES
The Cubs would have won the wild card…
if it wasn't fifty-seven years away from existing.

REASON 9—THE 1938 WORLD SERIES:
IN A NEW YORK BEATING
The Yankees were loaded and the Cubs were getting old.
Any guesses how this one turned out?

REASON 10—THE 1945 WORLD SERIES:
HANK BOROWY RUNS OUT OF GAS
There are no mathematical methods to calculate just how many pitches
Hank Borowy threw in this 4-3 series loss to Detroit.

NEAR MISSES (1910-1945)

It's quite astounding when you study the history of the Chicago Cubs...*how futile* of a franchise this has been. Don't get irritated with that statement, as the evidence doesn't lie. After 2012, the Chicago National League baseball club has competed in 137 seasons. The team has won exactly two World Series' titles, 1907 and 1908. They actually "tied" for a World Series title in 1885, but that's when they were known as the **Chicago White Stockings**. The team then became the **Chicago Colts** (*kinda* cool), then the **Chicago Orphans** (a bit creepy and weird) before eventually becoming the **Chicago Cubs** for good in 1903. After losing 101 games in the 2012 season, it's now been 104 years since the last World Series title. So for the record, that makes it *137 seasons* with exactly two championships.

A more pitiful way to look at it: The Cubs have won a championship in 1.4 percent of their total seasons played. By contrast, the New York Yankees have won a championship in 24 percent of their total seasons. In other words, no one reading this book will be alive to see the Cubs overtake the Yankees in total World Championships. Perhaps the Cubs will dominate the 2100s.

Nevertheless, the history of the Chicago Cubs gets more pathetic upon closer scrutiny. The first category of "reasons" is called **Near Misses**. This first classification will be broken down into two chronological portions: CHAPTER 1: NEAR MISSES (1910-1945) and CHAPTER 2: NEAR MISSES (1969-2008). Before diving into these chapters, I really have to clarify what a Cubs' near miss looks like.

The Cubs have made the play-offs sixteen times in their 137 year history, a whopping 11.7 percent of the time. (The Yankees have made the play-offs fifty-one times in their existence.) Since the Cubs' last title in 1908, the team has only finished higher than third-place *twenty-three* times! Not only are the Cubs incredibly bad at winning championships, they are inept at even *getting into a position* of having a near miss. Thus, Cubs' near misses are reminisced and romanticized because they are few and far between. Consequently, twenty-eight years *after* the fact, I can still recollect a considerable amount of the 1984 season. When the Yankees lose in the American League Championship series, it's barely a blip on the radar screen of their collective history. To really comprehend the type of futility I am talking about here, examine this brief synopsis of the Cubs since 1920:

The Cubs in the 1920s

In the eight-team National League the Cubs finished no higher than fourth until 1928 when they finished third. Then in 1929, they won the National League… of course only to lose to the Philadelphia Athletics in the World Series.

The Cubs in the 1930s

This was a great time to be a Cubs' fan! (…unless you were affected by that Depression thingy that was going on.) The Cubs were contenders *each* year of the decade, were *over .500 every year,* and appeared in three World Series! They did *lose* all three of those World Series, but the 1930s can definitely be classified as the "Golden Age" of the Chicago Cubs.

The Cubs in the 1940s

Aside from their lucky World War II-influenced appearance in 1945, the Cubs were horrible in this decade.

The Cubs from 1948–1966

Historically, truly and factually dreadful! This is just an inexpressibly horrendous period in Cubs' history. Let's just look at this:

1948—8th out of 8	1949—8th out of 8	1950—7th out of 8
1951—8th out of 8	1952—5th out of 8	1953—7th out of 8
1954—7th out of 8	1955—6th out of 8	1956—8th out of 8
1957—7th out of 8	1958—5th out of 8	1959—5th out of 8
1960—7th out of 8	1961—7th out of 8	1962—9th out of 10
1963—7th out of 10	1964—8th out of 10	1965—8th out of 10
1966—10th out of 10		

Wow. Not a chance.

The Cubs from 1967–1972

The Cubs were a contending team in each of these years, with 1969 being *the year* people remember. The Cubs were just as close to winning in '70 and '71; minus the catastrophic September fade. Yet, beggars cannot be choosers, and this time period has to qualify as another of the team's flourishing eras...even with a lack of any play-off seasons.

The Cubs from 1973–1983

The Cubs were particularly mediocre for the rest of the 1970s, with highlights being 1977 (81-81), '78 (79-83) and '79 (80-82). (Yes, I called those years' *highlights*.) In Cubs' terms, these were decent teams that *semi*-competed, and contended early in their respective seasons. **1980-83** were terrible seasons for the Cubs, as they never finished above fifth place.

The Cubs from 1984 to the Present

I realize this is an extended period to lump together, but there has been some consistency (as consistent as this franchise has been!). The Cubs have had six play-off appearances in the last twenty-eight seasons, an average of one play-off appearance every 4.6 years. This might be unacceptable for many franchises, yet for a team with droughts as immense as the Cubs...it qualifies as *pretty good*.

Ponder this thought: If you were born in 1945, you had to wait *thirty-nine years* to see the Cubs make the play-offs. If you were born in 1975, your biggest gap between play-off seasons has been nine years.

I *guess* that's *progress*.

Therefore in these first two chapters, their near misses that would be more accurately titled as "Cubs' Near Misses or Only Near Misses for a team as lousy as the Cubs." There are legitimate near misses: World Series losses in 1910, 1918, 1929, 1932, 1935, 1938, and 1945. A World Series loss would count as a near miss for any organization. However, the Cubs have not even been to a World Series in sixty-seven years! During those sixty-seven years, they have been to the post-season in 1984, 1989, 1998, 2003, 2007, and 2008. Those years all fall under the near miss classification for our Cubs.

The Cub's near miss category includes seasons in which the team missed the play-offs altogether, yet were close. For the Cubs, even the close seasons are sporadic!

Thus, as you read the first two chapters, keep in perspective how near misses have been "Cubs-defined." Similarly, keep in mind that when I write my "THREE REASONS WHY IT'S BEEN THREE YEARS SINCE THE YANKEES HAVE WON A WORLD SERIES" pamphlet, there won't be any Cubs-like near misses at all. The New Yorkers aside, the Cubs' near misses can still be explained with logical and rational reasons.

With a fandom as passionate, loyal, and (some might say) crazy as the Cubs, near misses take on mythic proportions. An understandable reaction when you have millions of fans who have never experienced their team win a championship, and rarely see it come close. I will attempt to show during the course of these first two chapters that there are explanations for the near misses for the 104-year title drought. I will likewise demonstrate that these reasons have nothing to do with curses, barnyard animals, or a fan sitting in a very unfortunate location.

REASON 1

THE 1910 WORLD SERIES: CHIEF BENDER AND JACK COOMBS

The 1910 World Series between the Chicago Cubs and the Philadelphia A's was probably especially tough on one particular group of Cubs' fans...*dead ones*. Would any of us current Cubs' fans feel better about our team if the Cubs' World Series drought was 102 years instead of 104? A majority of Cubs' fans probably have no idea that the Cubs were even in the 1910 World Series. Still, it *has* been 104 years and not 102; therefore, the 1910 World Series is listed as **Reason 1**.

The Athletics won the 1910 World Series four games to one. Philadelphia secured the first three games by resounding scores of 4-1, 9-3 and 12-5. The A's then gave the Cubs a charity 4-3 extra inning victory in Game 4, which left the Athletics up three games to one. The Athletics put the Cubs away... winning 7-2 in the fifth and final game. If you are scoring at home (who scores at home anymore, and why do commentators still ask that?), the composite score of the series was 35-15. The Athletics outscored the Cubs by twenty runs collectively.

A common theme the reader will identify in the first two chapters is that Cubs' fans have to take near misses where they can find them. A year in which the Cubs *made* the World Series definitely constitutes a near miss.

Not surprisingly, 1910 Major League Baseball was played quite differently than today's game. Players were instructed to "chop" at the ball, or to basically swing down at the pitch. Consequently, there was only one home run hit in the entire 1910 World Series, by both teams combined! That home run was hit by the A's Danny Murphy. Ironically, the apparently unaptly named Home Run Baker of the A's did *not* hit any. There was no World Series MVP awarded at this time, and even if there had been, it would not have been Danny "one home run" Murphy.

The most extraordinary numbers from the 1910 World Series are the pitching statistics for the Philadelphia Athletics. Before viewing these numbers, keep in mind the 1910 World Series started on Monday, October 17, and finished on Sunday, October 23. The entire five games of the 1910 World Series were played over six days. Here are the complete pitching statistics for the Philadelphia Athletics in the 1910 World Series:

	GAMES	IP	ER	H	BB	SO	W-L
Jack Coombs	3	27	10	24	14	17	3-0
Chief Bender	2	18.2	4	13	4	14	1-1

If you are looking for names of other pitchers, you won't find any. The Athletics only used *two* pitchers for the entire 1910 World Series. Let's look at it like this:

Monday—Bender pitches 9 innings

Tuesday—Coombs pitches 9 innings

Wednesday—off day

Thursday—Coombs pitches 9 innings

Friday—off day

Saturday—Bender pitches 9.2 innings

Sunday—Coombs pitches 9 innings

Pitching this much was not unusual in 1910 Major League Baseball. Pitch counts were nonexistent at the time and pitchers were *expected* to finish games. We can estimate that Bender and Coombs threw between 115 and 120 pitches per game. With this *conservative* approximation, Coombs threw at least 350 pitches in five days, and Bender threw 250-plus in six days. Each man probably threw more than this amount. *My* arm hurts just thinking about it!

Nonetheless, Bender and Coombs threw all 45.2 innings and were a huge reason the Philadelphia A's were the 1910 World Series Champions, and the Chicago Cubs were not. The Cubs and their fans were two years removed from their 1908 World Series title. Therefore, the team and its followers probably didn't dwell on the loss, thinking the Cubs could win it the *next* year…oh, the irony.

REASON 2

The 1918 World Series: World War I and the Babe on the Mound

The Cubs faced the Boston Red Sox in the 1918 World Series. This 1918 World Series holds the distinction of being the only World Series played entirely in September. In the twenty-first century, the World Series is consistently held in mid to late October, even creeping into November some years. The *1918* Major League Baseball season was shortened due to the United States' involvement in World War I. The 1918 World Series is also unique in that it is *one* of only *three* World Series in which *no* home runs were hit…an ironic fact considering the greatest home run hitter who ever lived was playing in this World Series. One more surprising stat was that the Red Sox won the series while scoring a *total* of *nine* runs…for the *whole* series! The Red Sox had an anemic .186 team batting average for the six games. Simply put, the Red Sox hit .186, scored nine runs in six games…*yet won!* Feel free to plug in your own joke regarding the Cubs being the *only* team that could possibly do this. If you don't feel like making jokes about the Cubs yet, you will have plenty of opportunity throughout our journey to 104.

Not only did WWI shorten the series, it cost the Cubs their best pitcher: Grover Cleveland Alexander. Alexander would go on to win an astounding 377 games throughout his career. In 1917 with the Philadelphia Phillies, Alexander won *thirty* games! The Cubs acquired Alexander via trade following the 1917 season. It was suspected that the Cubs were only able to acquire Alexander because Philadelphia did not want to deal with his upcoming military absence. Prophetically, due to his military draft in 1918, Alexander only won two games for the Cubs.

Regrettably for the Cubs, the Red Sox did not lose *any* of their pitchers to the war effort. The Sox were led by starting pitchers Carl Mays and a young left-hander named Babe Ruth. Most baseball fans are cognizant of the fact that Babe Ruth was a pitcher prior to becoming a legendary hitter, but few fans are aware of just *how good of a pitcher* Ruth was. In Jayson Stark's book *The Stark Truth*, Stark lists the most overrated and underrated players in history at every position; Babe Ruth is his top left-handed starting pitcher. Mays and Ruth each started two games apiece, and were almost equally as dominant. Carl Mays allowed only two earned runs over eighteen innings pitched. Ruth nearly matched Mays, allowing two runs over seventeen innings.

Not only did Ruth win Game 4 on the mound but he also knocked in two of the three runs scored by swatting a double. Ruth's hitting in the 1918 World Series was just a brief glimpse of his offensive force that evolved over the next fifteen seasons. While Babe Ruth *the pitcher* was a reason the Cubs didn't win in 1918, Babe Ruth *the hitter* would keep the Cubs from a title in the 1932 World Series.

The Cubs actually scored ten runs and had five more total hits than the Red Sox in the six games. The Cubs broke the .200 barrier...hitting a whopping .210 for the series.

There have long been rumors that the Cubs actually "threw" this series, one year prior to the infamous 1919 "Black Sox" scandal. The speculation began when White Sox pitcher Eddie Cicotte mentioned that they had gotten the idea from the 1918 Cubs. These rumors have never been substantiated. I think perhaps Cicotte just misinterpreted the Cubs' horrible play in the 1918 Series.

Likely, the 1918 World Series was "on the level," and the Red Sox just beat the Cubs fair and square. Babe Ruth and Carl Mays were just too much for the Cubs. Fortunately for the Red Sox, they were able to scratch across a few more runs in key situations. The Cubs were denied their third World

Series championship. The Chicago Cubs are still looking for that third title...
and looking...*and looking*. After 104 years, that third Cubs' World Series
championship has been *rather* elusive...hasn't it?

REASON 3

THE 1929 WORLD SERIES: CONNIE MACK AND THE "MACK ATTACK"

In 1929 the Cubs won ninety-eight games and faced the Philadelphia Athletics
in the World Series. Both teams boasted strong lineups: the Cubs with Rogers
Hornsby, Hack Wilson and Riggs Stephenson, all of whom had OPS (*on-base
plus slugging percentage*) of above 1.000. (If you are unfamiliar with OPS, 1.000
is really freaking good!) The year 1929 would have been the rare season to have
a bunch of Cubs on your fantasy team...although I doubt anyone was playing
fantasy baseball in 1929. The Philadelphia A's also boasted a lineup full of
offensive prowess led by Hall of Famers Jimmie Foxx (seriously, you should look
at his numbers sometime if you haven't), Mickey Cochrane and Al Simmons.
The A's appeared to have the better pitching with twenty game winners Lefty
Grove and George Earnshaw. Pat Malone's twenty-two wins was tops for the
Cubs. **Reasons 1** and **2** have already given evidence to the fact that teams handled
pitchers differently in this era. However, A's manager Connie Mack's approach
proved to be way, way, *way* ahead of his time...and his philosophy was costly to
the Cubs.

Historically, the Cubs have been a predominantly right-handed hitting
team. The Cubs' lineup was stacked with right-handed hitters in 1929. With
Mack's two top starters (Lefty Grove and Rube Walberg) being left-handed;
Mack made the bold decision of having them pitch relief in the series. Mack
deployed a "righties-only" strategy when it came to the starting pitchers. In
the first game, Mack decided to start thirty-five year old side-arm thrower
Howard Ehmke. Ehmke had only won seven games during the regular season,
yet Mack did not let that deter his strategy. Connie Mack continued to exhibit
more forward thinking by having Ehmke scout the Cubs for the last three
weeks of the regular season.

Starting Howard Ehmke in Game 1 based on his right-handedness was seen as a daring and surprising move…but it worked. The right-handed power hitters of the Cubs were stymied by Ehmke's throwing at them from the third base side; unable to pick up or see Ehmke's pitches coming at them. According to *Baseball Almanac.com*, Mack's foresight proved critical in the A's Game 1 victory (3-1) as Ehmke dominated the Cubs by striking out thirteen.

Game 2 was *all* Athletics, as they won 9-3 with Jimmie Foxx and Al Simmons homering in the romp. On the road and trailing two games to none, the Cubs bounced back behind the solid pitching of Guy Bush for a 3-1 victory in the third game of the contest. The series stood two games to one, with the Cubs having the ability to knot it up in Game 4.

It appeared that the Cubs *would* tie the series as Game 4 saw the Cubs jump out to an 8-0 lead, as Connie Mack's "righties only" strategy backfired and the Cubs pounded forty-five year old Jack Quinn. The Cubs would hold that lead until the seventh inning when what would become known as the "Mack Attack" took place.

The score was 8-0; the Cubs were leading, with only *nine* outs to go. The famed "Mack Attack" then occurred…a *ten-run Athletic outburst* off of Art Nehff, and losing pitcher Sheriff Blake (Sheriff?). The Cubs resorted to bringing in Pat Malone, who was scheduled to start Game 5, just to end the inning. The final tally was 10-8, and the Athletics led the series three games to one. Ninety-three years later, the eight run deficit that the A's overcame is still the largest in play-off history.

Game 5 saw Mack stick with his "righties only" strategy with Game 1 winner Ehmke once again taking the mound. This time, the Cubs were able to get to Ehmke for two runs as they jumped out to a 2-0 lead. The Cubs' lead would hold up all the way until the dreaded bottom of the ninth inning. Cubs' manager Joe McCarthy decided to stick with starter Pat Malone to finish out the game.

As fate would have it, a walk-off double by the Athletics' Bing Miller capped a three run Athletic rally off Malone to win the game *and* the World Series. In back-to-back contests, the Cubs had blown leads, including the *substantial* lead of eight runs in Game 4. The 1929 World Series could have easily been 3-2 in favor of the Cubs, yet after two stunning defeats…it was now over. Another potential World Series title for the Cubs had been put off.

Connie Mack's "righties only" strategy may have only fooled the Cubs in the first game, but it definitely worked in getting the Athletics on the right path to win the 1929 World Series. The "Mack Attack" would doom the Cubs in Game 4 with a record-setting blown lead that stands today...much like the Cubs' title drought that still exists.

REASON 4

The 1929 World Series: Hall of Fame Sluggers (Part 1)

1929 began a stretch in which the Chicago Cubs would boast a fearsome lineup and compete for the National League title for the next decade. A consistent winning team is hard for us modern day Cubs' fans to fathom. After '29, the Cubs would appear in the '32, '35 and 1938 series. They battled for the National League title against the St. Louis Cardinals and New York Giants. Believe it or not, the Cubs appeared in the World Series *four* times over a *nine*-year period. How? Take a look at these offensive numbers from 1929 (Fantasy baseball players, try not to get your drool on the pages!):

PLAYER	SIGNIFICANT 1929 OFFENSIVE STATISTICS
2B Rogers Hornsby	.380 with 39 HRs, 149 RBIs
OF Hack Wilson	.345 with 39 HRs, 159 RBIs
OF Kiki Cuyler	.360, 102 RBIs, League-Leading 43 Stolen Bases
OF Riggs Stephenson	.362, 17 HRs, 110 RBIs in only 136 Games

Wow, and I thought my beloved **1984** Cubs had some impressive offensive stats! These statistics would prove to be typical for these players, allowing the Cubs to be perennial contenders in the 1930s. Unfortunately, the Cubs could not capitalize and win a World Series in this nine-year stretch as other teams were posting absurd offensive numbers too. The Philadelphia Athletics were an offensive powerhouse throughout the decade.

In **Reason 3** we examined Connie Mack's pitching maneuvers and the famous "Mack Attack" ten-run inning in the fifth and final game of the '29 World Series. Considering the 1929 Athletics' lineup, the ten-run inning appears less of a fluke. The Athletics boasted three eventual Hall of Famers; Jimmie Foxx (did you look up his numbers yet?), Al Simmons, and catcher Mickey Cochrane.

Foxx and Simmons each had two home runs as the A's out-homered the Cubs 6-1 collectively in the '29 World Series. The Cubs' lone homer in the series came from Charlie Grimm. In a battle of two "slugging" offenses, the Cubs were extremely out-*slugged*. Connie Mack's "righties only" approach slowed the vaunted Cubs' attack, but it couldn't *completely* stop it. Kiki Cuyler and Riggs Stephenson each hit above .300. Hack Wilson was eight for seventeen (.471) yet apparently had no one to knock in, as he did *159 times* during the regular season. In a World Series that featured two outstanding offenses, the one with the most Hall of Famers in it prevailed:

- Cochrane hit .400 for the series and walked seven times, for an on-base percentage of .591.

- Foxx hit .350 for the series and was the first player ever to homer in the opening two games of a series.

- Non-Hall of Famer Jimmy Dykes hit .421 with four RBIs.

The Athletics had enough offense to outlast the Cubs, and the World Series title drought extended to twenty-one years. Cubs' fans of this period could take solace in the fact that the team would have a great offensive core of players for the next decade. Yet, the American League teams that would be waiting in the World Series were consistently just as talented offensively. Those American League teams would include the same Philadelphia Athletics who bested the Cubs in 1929 and a squad that included the greatest home run hitter of all time. In retrospect, the promise of a World Series title in the 1930s was not as attainable as Cubs' fans of the time probably believed it to be.

REASON 5

THE 1930 SEASON:
THE CARDINALS GET HOT...*REALLY HOT!*

If you played fantasy baseball back in the 1930s, you would have been about fifty years ahead of your time...and you would have *loved* the 1930 Cubs. The offensive promise shown in 1929 was back (minus Hornsby) and the Cubs appeared destined for another World Series appearance. Let's look at some of the 1930 Cubs' numbers that would have made Roto-Geeks scream like 1960s teens at a Beatles' concert. Would you be excited to have any of these guys on your fantasy baseball team?

- Catcher Gaby Hartnett hit .339, with 37 HRs and 122 RBIs

- Hack Wilson hit .356, with 56 homers, oh yeah...and 191 RBIs!

- Kiki Cuyler hit .355, with 134 RBIs and 37 stolen bases

- Infielder Woody English hit .335 and added 14 HRs

- Riggs Stephenson hit .367, leading the team in average

The 1930 Chicago Cubs and their prolific offense were indeed poised to return to a World Series rematch with the Philadelphia Athletics, which had the American League race in hand. In late August of 1930, the National League appeared to be "in hand" as well.

On Saturday, August 30, 1930, the Cubs pounded the Cardinals 16-4. The victory increased the Cubs' lead to 5.5 games over the second place New York Giants. The loss put the Cardinals in fourth place, 7.5 games out of first. Over the next twenty-nine days things would alter greatly, and not unpredictably... poorly for the Chicago Cubs.

So let's take a look at what transpired over those last twenty-nine days of the 1930 season:

NATIONAL LEAGUE STANDINGS ON SUNDAY, SEPTEMBER 1, 1930

1st Place—Chicago Cubs

2nd Place—New York Giants   5.5 games out

3rd Place—St. Louis Cardinals   7.5 games out

Then this happened…

RECORDS FOR THE REST OF THE SEASON

TEAM	W	L	PCG
St. Louis Cardinals	22	4	.846
New York Giants	17	13	.566
Chicago Cubs	13	14	.486

The Cardinals went 22-4 with an astounding .846 winning percentage! The Cubs went 6-0 over the last six games of the season. However, the Cardinals went 5-1 and the Cubs finished two games out of first. Today's Cubs' fans have become accustomed to thinking the collapse of 1969 was the most colossal free-fall to end a season. The slow death march that was the end of the 1930 season was worse than 1969. The Cubs lost a 7.5 game lead in less than a month due to one freakish Cardinals' hot streak.

The 1930 Cubs' fans were lucky in that the Cubs would be in another World Series just two short years later. The 1969 Cubs' fans would have to wait fifteen years for a shot at redemption, albeit another futile one. The 1930 season *should* have been a shot at the World Series title for the Chicago Cubs. Instead it is yet another near miss, and a reason for the Cubs' continued failure.

REASON 6

THE 1932 WORLD SERIES: HALL OF FAME SLUGGERS (PART 2): THE BABE & LOU GEHRIG

One of the most entertaining baseball books I have read is *The Big Bam: The Life and Times of Babe Ruth*, by Leigh Montville. I highly recommend you rush out and buy it…right *after* you have completed reading this book. I have read *The Big Bam* numerous times, and without hijacking too much of Mr. Montville's work, here are some highlights:

- The Babe was like a living deity in the U.S. during the 1920s! The book illustrates just how *incredibly popular* the Babe was in this era.

- The Babe lived his whole life thinking he was *one year older* than he really was.

- Yes…you get all the sordid details of the excesses that the Babe indulged in: hot dogs, beer, and lots and lots of women.

The Big Bam also gives a marvelous account of the 1932 World Series against the Cubs. There is no definitive answer for the debatable "called shot" that has been rehashed for eighty years. The book does give a detailed account of how the Cubs were razzing the Babe prior to this historic at-bat. My question to the 1932 Cubs would be, "Why the hell would you do this? You don't tug on Superman's cape, right? In 1932, why talk smack to the Babe?!" Like the 1932 World Series itself, the strategy of hurling insults and taunts at the Babe did not work out well for the Cubs.

Throughout these first chapters of near misses, I will continue to reiterate that the "near" in near miss has to be used loosely in regards to the Chicago Cubs. In that respect, the Cubs *did appear* in the World Series in 1932. Unfortunately, so did the New York Yankees who won 107 regular season games. After a series against the Philadelphia Athletics with future Hall of Famers Foxx, Simmons, and Cochrane just three seasons prior, the Cubs now went head to head with Lou Gehrig and the Babe. Ruth and Gehrig are historically baseball's greatest offensive 1-2 punch. In 1932 Ruth hit .341, with 41 homers and 137 RBIs; while Gehrig nearly matched him at .349, 34 HRs and 151 RBIs. The Cubs and their fans knew what they were up against. Take a look at how Gehrig and Ruth performed in the Yankees' World Series runs in 1927 and 1928:

Year	Player	Regular Season	World Series Performance
1927	Babe Ruth	.356, 60, 164	6-15, 2 HRs, 7 RBIs
1927	Lou Gehrig	.373, 47, 175	4-13, 2 2Bs, 2 3Bs, 4 RBIs
1928	Babe Ruth	.323, 54, 142	10-16, 3 2Bs, 3 HRs, 4 RBIs
1928	Lou Gehrig	.374, 27, 142	6-11, 4 HRs, 9 RBIs

The Yankees were heavy favorites to defeat the Cubs, and they did not disappoint. The Cubs only held leads twice throughout the four-game sweep. The Yankees put twelve and thirteen runs on the board in Games 1 and 4 respectively. Gehrig was an absolute monster for the series, hitting .529 with three HRs and eight RBIs. The Babe did not dissatisfy…going five for fifteen with two HRs and six RBIs.

One of Ruth's homers is conceivably the most famous of all time. Debate rages still today about the "called shot" that Ruth hit, and the truth may forever be stuck in a haze of false memories and legend. In the HBO *Sports Documentary: Babe Ruth*, a home movie clearly shows Ruth gesture, but *to where* is unclear. The debate is whether Ruth was pointing to the center field bleachers, or he was volleying verbal taunts back at the Cubs' bench. Regardless of *where* the Babe was pointing, the home run added to his unprecedented legendary status.

For the 1932 Cubs, that historic home run would be an exclamation point added to the thrashing they encountered in the 1932 World Series. This Cubs' team would get more chances throughout the 1930s (1935 and 1938), but Ruth and Gehrig made sure that 1932 was not going to be *the* year for the Cubs.

REASON 7

THE 1935 WORLD SERIES: TIGERS' PITCHING, INCLUDING THE GENERAL AND THE SCHOOLBOY

Ripper Collins, Wild Bill Hallahan, Kiddo Davis, Spud Davis, Cookie Lavegetto, Pie Traynor, Babe Phelps, Pretzels Pezzullo, Blondy Ryan, Rabbitt Warstler, Sugar Cain, Bobo Newsom, Babe Dehlgren (come on!…there is only one Babe!), Pinky Higgins, and Sad Sam Jones. These are just a few of the nicknames of some of the Major League players in 1935. Today's MLB could use some names like these, don't you think? How about a *Ripper* Rodriguez, *Slugger* Soriano or *Jumpy* Jeter? Okay…maybe *not*.

The year 1935 saw the Cubs face the Detroit Tigers in the World Series; the Cubs' second World Series of the decade. The Detroit Tigers' staff in the 1935 World Series had two names that could be included in the list above: General Crowder and Schoolboy Rowe. The Cubs' roster could not match the Tigers in creatively odd nicknames. Nor did the Cubs match the Tigers in a World Series the Cubs *could* have won. Surprisingly, the Cubs were actually *favored* to win the 1935 World Series. The 1935 Cubs won one hundred games, ten games better than their American League counterpart. The 1935 Chicago Cubs team also still holds the distinction of *winning* twenty-one games in a row!

The Tigers would win (not surprisingly) the 1935 World Series four games to two; taking all of the games in dramatic fashion. The 1935 Tigers would win three one-run games, an extra-inning game, and get a walk-off bottom of the ninth victory. The 1935 World Series can accurately be classified as a near miss. The opportunity was at hand for the Cubs to win. Had they won, Cubs' fans would be dealing with a seventy-seven year title-drought…and I would have thirty-seven fewer reasons to identify, research and develop.

The Cubs won the first game behind a shut out as Lon Warneke defeated Schoolboy Rowe. (I wonder how that "schoolboy" nickname would go over in 2013.) But the Tigers quickly evened up the World Series at one game apiece with an 8-3 thrashing of the Cubs. Cubs' starting pitcher Charlie Root could not even escape the first inning. The Game 2 triumph was costly for the Tigers; Hank Greenberg (.328, 38 HRs, 170 RBIs) broke his wrist and was out for the remainder of the World Series. Thus the Cubs and Tigers were tied at one game heading back to Chicago for Game 3. In today's sporting universe, the cliché, "We accomplished our goal and stole one at their place," would have been uttered by at least one Cubs' player. With the injury to Greenberg, I suspect Cubs' fans were feeling confident.

As the series did shift to Wrigley, the Tigers and Cubs engaged in some epic battles. Game 3 saw the Cubs score twice in the bottom of the ninth to send the game into extra innings. Schoolboy Rowe, Detroit's Game 1 starter, came on in relief and shut down the Cubs. A key error by third baseman Fred

Lindstrom led to the Tigers grabbing the lead in the top of the eleventh. A tough extra inning loss put the Tigers up two games to one.

Game 4 also went the Tigers' way as the aforementioned General Crowder outpitched Cubs' starter Tex Carleton in a 2-1 game. The Tigers were one game away from the World Series title. Remarkably in Game 5, Lon Warneke outdueled the Schoolboy and the Cubs won 3-1…sending the World Series back to Detroit.

Game 6 pitted Tommy Bridges (Detroit's winning pitcher in Game 2) against Cubs' starter Larry French. Both hurlers lasted until the ninth with the score tied at three. With two outs in the bottom of the ninth, Goose Goslin (a little known Hall of Famer) knocked in Mickey Cochrane (a *well-known* Hall of Famer) and the Tigers won the World Series on a walk-off hit. The Cubs lost 4-3 in the ninth and a rare chance to play in a decisive Game 7 disappeared.

The Cubs lost three one-run games in the 1935 World Series…consequently this really was a near miss! The era of the 1930s Cubs was ending, and the team had lost the '29, '32, and 1935 World Series. The Cubs' 1930s corp of players would get one more chance in 1938.

This kind of World Series participation by the Cubs in the 1930s is unfathomable to present-day Cubs' fans. Can you imagine a stretch like this? I can't either…it's why our modern near miss perspective is distorted. One hundred and four years tends to change various perspectives, and causes a fan base to accept illogical reasons for failure.

In the 1935 World Series the Chicago Cubs lost a *close* one…yet it was still a *loss*.

REASON 8

THE 1936 AND 1937 SEASONS: BACK-TO-BACK SECOND PLACES

Major League Baseball is a sport that has historically attempted to make the regular season of vital importance, meaning the MLB has consistently lagged behind other professional leagues in the number of teams it allows to make the post-season. While the NBA, NHL, and NFL have constantly expanded the number of post-season teams, Major League Baseball has been consistent in resisting that urge.

From 1901 (the inception of the American League) until the 1969 season, only one team from each league made the "play-offs," which basically was the World Series at that point. Starting in 1969, baseball "expanded" the play-offs to include one more team from each league and the leagues were divided into Eastern and Western Divisions. After the 1994 Major League Baseball strike, two wild-card teams were added to each league's play-offs. In 2012, the MLB increased the number of play-off teams with another "wild card" to each league; albeit teams that would compete in a "one-game" *play-in* contest. Let's sum up this information:

YEARS/MAJOR LEAGUE BASEBALL	TOTAL NUMBER OF PLAY-OFF TEAMS
1909-1969	2 out of 16, 2 out of 20 ('61-62)
1969-1993	4 out of 26, 4 out of 28 ('93)
1995-2011	8 out of 28, 8 out of 30
2012	10 out of 30

How can we relate this information to Cubs' futility in actually making the play-offs? In regards to first place finishes, the Cubs have only accomplished that feat ten times since 1908. Another amazing fact about the Cubs' ineptitude: In this same 104-year period, the Cubs have finished in second place only ten times!

Fortunately, in 1998 and 2003 those second place finishes resulted in wild-card play-off berths. Prior to those years, the Cubs' rare second place finishes can be classified as near misses.

One Chicago Cubs' history lesson you have learned so far is that you can be very proud of the Cubs' performance…*in the 1930s*. After appearing in the 1932 and 1935 World Series, the Cubs continued to be vital contenders for another three seasons. In 1936 and 1937, the New York Giants kept the Cubs from appearing in the World Series. The Giants lost to their inner-city rivals, the Yankees, in both '36 and '37…perhaps the Cubs would have fared better against the powerful Yanks. (Insert your own snicker.)

In 1936 the Cubs were atop the league for much of July. The Giants, led by Mel Ott and Carl Hubbell, surpassed the Cubs in late July and held a secure lead for the rest of the season. The 1936 Cubs were no longer the offensive force they had been for the early part of the decade. Only Gaby Hartnett remained in '36, from a lineup that once included Kiki Cuyler, Hack Wilson, and Riggs Stephenson.

In 1937 the Cubs either led or were tied for the National League lead from June 15 until September 1. September would soon become the time that Cubs' fans are conditioned to fear. The Cubs never got closer than one and a half games to the Giants for the rest of the month. Even in a remarkably *good* September, the Cubs could not prevail.

LAST 20 GAMES OF 1937	W	L	WINNING PERCENTAGE
New York Giants	15	5	.750
Chicago Cubs	14	6	.700

LAST 10 GAMES OF 1937	W	L	WINNING PERCENTAGE
Chicago Cubs	8	2	.800
New York Giants	7	3	.700

The 1937 Chicago Cubs accumulated a record of 93-68, a .604 winning percentage…but it wasn't good enough. The '37 Cubs played .700 baseball over their last twenty games, and *.800* over their last ten…and it *still wasn't good enough!*

As Cubs' fans, we are trained to automatically look for scapegoats, bad luck and other fabricated excuses for failure. It's much easier for Cubs' fans to say the team folded, faded or blew it, rather than acknowledge the obvious: there are times when the Cubs are beaten by a better team. In 1937, the New York Giants were *just enough* better to win the National League and earn the right to lose to the Yankees. The 1930s version of the Cubs would get one more shot at a World Series in 1938. Unless you did not notice the title of the book, you'll realize the Cubs did not fare any better in 1938.

REASON 9

THE 1938 WORLD SERIES: IN A NEW YORK BEATING

The 1938 season was the last gasp of the successful 1930s Cubs' teams. The Cubs had played in three World Series and contended for the National League crown in every season. The 1938 Cubs won the National League by two games over the Pirates. The stage was set for *another* matchup against the New York Yankees. Unfortunately for the Cubs, and the entire National League, it put in motion *another* predictable conclusion. Regardless of the eventual outcome, there were positives for the Cubs in 1938; evidence that there were no curses or September-fades in this particular Cubs' season.

In 1938 the Cubs took over first place on September 28, five days before the season's end. The Cubs rattled off a ten-game winning streak that vaulted them past the Pirates and Giants. The Cubs would hoist the National League pennant; something they would only do one more time in the next seventy-four years, (good thing fans didn't know that then!) and the afore-mentioned Yankees were waiting.

The Babe was no longer there, but the Yankees had grown beyond the Babe. The Yankees' lineup now consisted of:

PLAYER	AVG	HR	RBIS
Joe DiMaggio	.324	32	149
Lou Gehrig	.295	29	114
Bill Dickey	.313	27	115
Tom Henrich	.270	22	91
Joe Gordon	.255	25	97

The '38 Cubs' leading hitters were Frank Demaree with a .320 batting average and Ripper Collins who had thirteen home runs. The Cubs were just a *bit* overmatched offensively going into the 1938 World Series. The Cubs matched up better on the mound; nevertheless, the Yankees had the pitching advantage. The Yankees had two future Hall of Famers in Red Ruffing 21-7,

3.32, and Lefty Gomez 18-12, 3.35. The Cubs countered with Bill Lee, whose twenty-two victories led the National League, and hard-throwing nineteen-game winner Clay Bryant who led the NL in strikeouts.

The Yankees were a team *loaded* with future Hall of Famers. The Cubs were at the end of the team's most consistent period of competitiveness. The 1938 World Series played out as expected, with a couple surprises.

- The Yankees swept the Cubs in four games (not a surprise).

- Hall of Famer Ruffing threw two complete game victories (not a surprise).

- 2B Joe Gordon led the Yankees offensively with 6 RBIs and a .400 batting average (a *surprise* on a team with Gehrig and DiMaggio).

- Gehrig was held without a home run or an RBI while DiMaggio went deep just once (surprise).

- The composite score of the four games was 22-9 (surprise...it could have been worse).

The 1938 World Series was *closer* than it might have been. Had Gehrig or DiMaggio performed as they had in the regular season, these games would have been consequently more lopsided. A beating that *wasn't that bad* of a thrashing...the kind of *positive* you have to take in the sad history of the Chicago Cubs.

The 1938 loss to the Yankees closed the most successful run in Cubs' history, albeit without the "success" of a World Series title. The Cubs would return to the World Series seven years later, with an entirely different team and in a new era. If you happen to be a Cubs' fans that has time-traveling ability, I would suggest the 1930s as a great period to visit and watch some Cubs' baseball! You won't see them win a World Series, but the team will *appear in* the World Series quite frequently. If you do go back, buy some Babe Ruth baseball cards and keep them in mint condition...and try to avoid that "Depression" thing that will be going on.

REASON 10

T HE 1945 WORLD SERIES: HANK BOROWY RUNS OUT OF GAS

Are you old enough to remember the 1984 Chicago Cubs? Do you know much about the 1984 season? One of the major reasons for the Cubs' success in '84 was the acquisition of Rick Sutcliffe. Sutcliffe would go 16-1 for the Cubs, establishing himself as the team's ace. Thirty-nine years earlier, the Cubs made a similar move that vaulted them into post-season play. In 1945 the Cubs' acquisition was pitcher Hank Borowy. Borowy went 10-5 for the Yankees for the first half of 1945; he was subsequently purchased by the Chicago Cubs on July 27, 1945, for $97,000.

For the second half of 1945, Hank Borowy went 11-2 with a 2.13 ERA as the Cubs held off the Stan Musial-*less* (military service) Cardinals and won the National League pennant by three games. The Cubs were set to face the Detroit Tigers in the 1945 World Series. The Tigers were propelled by twenty-five game winner and future Hall of Famer Hal Newhouser. The Tigers were getting slugger (and HOF) Hank Greenberg *back* from his WWII military service, giving the team an enormous offensive boost. Much of the league's talent had been drained due to World War II and neither team was accorded respect by baseball experts at the time. The first three games of the '45 World Series were played in Detroit due to Major League Baseball's World War II travel restrictions; the teams only traveled once over the course of the series.

It was indeed the aforementioned Hank Borowy who pitched for the Cubs in Game 1, and they trounced the Tigers 9-0 on October 3, 1945. The Tigers would tie the series behind the pitching of Virgil Trucks. The teams would split Games 3 and 4; the Game 3 winner for the Cubs was Claude Passeau and Dizzie Trout (yes…Steve's dad) was the victor for the Tigers in Game 4.

As the series stood at two games apiece, Hank Borowy was set to pitch Game 5 on three days' rest. The plan backfired as Bowory could not pitch past the fifth inning and the Tigers outscored the Cubs 8-4. The next day, the Tigers were on the verge of winning the World Series with the score tied at seven going into the ninth inning. The Cubs brought in (Da…dada…da!) *Hank Borowy* to pitch relief. Hank threw four scoreless innings, the Cubs pushed across a run in the bottom of the twelfth, and the 1945 World Series came down to a deciding Game 7!

The teams had the day off on Tuesday, October 9, before Wednesday's decisive Game 7. There was much speculation as to whom the Cubs would start in Game 7, and Cubs' manager Charlie Grimm's choice was (Da...dada... da!)...you guessed it...Hank Borowy! Before looking at the results of Game 7, let's examine Hank Borowy's week in early October 1945.

- Wednesday, October 3—Borowy starts the game and throws nine innings.

- Sunday, October 7—Borowy starts again and throws five plus innings.

- Monday, October 8—On the very next day, Borowy throws four innings of relief.

On Wednesday, October 10, Hank Borowy started Game 7 and could not get through the first inning. The Tigers scored five times in the first en route to a 9-3 romp. The Tigers won the World Series four games to three and the Cubs' drought extended on.

Fun fact: this is the *only* World Series' Game 7 in Chicago Cubs' history. Cubs' manager Charlie Grimm made the fateful decision to start Borowy; after Borowy had thrown an already extraordinary amount during the week. When we examine managerial decisions in later **Reasons,** you will learn that Grimm's decision was questioned even in 1945.

Had the Cubs won in '45, the satisfaction of the victory may have been tainted. Their appearance in the Series itself has long been attributed to the weakness of the league due to the military absence of many stars of the National League. Regardless, it would have ended the Cubs' World Series title drought at thirty-seven years.

Therefore, Hank Borowy and his lack of a bionic arm is **Reason 10.**

CHAPTER 2

REASON 11—TOM SEAVER
The 1969 Mets were amazing, but Tom "Terrific" was incredibly amazing!

REASON 12—THE 1969 SEASON:
SORRY, THE METS WERE BETTER…WHEN IT MATTERED
*The Cubs' 36-16 start to the 1969 season was almost
as good as the Mets' finish…almost.*

REASON 13—THE 1970 SEASON:
BET YOU DIDN'T KNOW
*If the 1969 and 1970 seasons were siblings, 1970 would be Jan Brady, Jim Belushi,
Tommie Aaron or any member of the Jackson 5 other than Michael.*

REASON 14—THE 1984 NLCS:
THE PERFORMANCE OF THE PADRES' BULLPEN
…STARRING FORMER CUB CRAIG LEFFERTS
*In the 1984 NLCS the Cubs pounded San Diego's starters…
the Pads' bullpen was a different story.*

REASON 15—THE 1984 NLCS:
THE PADRES' 1970S ALL-STARS OUTPERFORM THE CUBS' 1970S ALL-STARS
*The Cubs' and Padres' rosters were full of all-stars from baseball's grooviest decade…
the Padres were just groovier.*

REASON 16—THE 1984 NLCS:
THE CUBS' HORRIBLE PITCHING IN SAN DIEGO
*Apparently the Cubs' pitchers forgot to pack their abilities
on this disastrous trip to southern California.*

REASON 17—THE 1989 NLCS:
WILL NUSCHLER CLARK
*He may have an odd middle name, but Will Clark demolished
the Chicago Cubs in the 1989 NLCS.*

REASON 18—THE 1989 NLCS:
STEVE BEDROSIAN
The man known as "Bed-Rock" had saves in three of the Giants' four victories.

REASON 19—THE 2003 NLCS:
AN ERROR BY ALEX GONZALEZ
A key error by the Cubs' shortstop opens the flood gates…
yet is overshadowed by the unluckiest fan to ever attend a Cubs' game.

REASON 20—THE 2003 NLCS:
KERRY WOOD IS PRETTY MUCH TOAST BY NLCS TIME
Wood dominated the regular season, he dominated the Atlanta Braves…
yet he struggled mightily against the Florida Marlins. Why?

REASON 21—THE 2003 NLCS:
IVAN RODRIGUEZ SIGNS WITH THE MARLINS…NOT THE CUBS
Prior to the 2003 season, Ivan "Pudge" Rodriguez was a free agent looking for a team.
In October, Rodriguez was the MVP of the 2003 NLCS against the Chicago Cubs.

REASON 22—THE 2003 NLCS:
JACK MCKEON
The Marlins fired Jeff Torborg after the team got off to a 16-22 start; the team hired
seventy-two-year-old Jack McKeon…and the Marlins began a remarkable run that
commenced with the defeat of the Chicago Cubs.

REASON 23—THE 2004 NLCS:
ANOTHER LATE SEASON COLLAPSE
With Greg Maddux, Derek Lee, and Nomar Garciaparra, the Cubs were poised
for a long play-off run…they just didn't get there.

REASON 24—THE 2007 NLDS:
SWEET LOU GETS US CLOSE…NOT REALLY
In just his first season with the Cubs, Lou Piniella got the Cubs into the post-season…
where they were thoroughly destroyed by the Diamondbacks.

REASON 25—THE 2008 NLDS:
NOT REALLY CLOSE…AGAIN
In just his second season with the Cubs, Lou Piniella
got the Cubs into the post-season…
where they were thoroughly destroyed by the Dodgers.

NEAR MISSES (1969-2008)

REASON 11

TOM SEAVER

With *104 Reasons Why It's Been 104 Years*, you had to figure that 1969 would account for at least *one* reason. The year 1969 has long been seen as one of the biggest Cubs' failures of all time. I grew up hearing tales of black cats, Ron Santos' heel-clicking and day game fatigue. Those are not the types of rationalizations I will accept in this book. There are rational, logical and factual reasons why the Cubs failed to make the post-season in 1969. One gigantic reason: George Thomas Seaver.

Tom "Terrific" Seaver was the driving force behind the 1969 Mets and the chief cause for their astonishing record down the stretch. Tom Seaver went *25-7* with a 2.21 ERA in 1969. Tom Seaver's *twenty-five* wins is a *remarkable* number. Tom Seaver's 2.21 ERA is an *incredible* number. Yet, as *remarkable* and *incredible* as Seaver's 1969 statistics are, they pale in comparison to some particulars *inside* these numbers.

How about this: In Tom Seaver's last eight starts of 1969, Seaver went *8-0*, with *eight* complete games…three of those shut outs! In Seaver's five victories in which he did *not* shut out his opponent, he allowed eight earned runs… total! For the absolute and pure beauty of Seaver's work, look at it like this:

SEAVER FROM AUGUST 26, 1969 (LAST EIGHT STARTS)

	IP	HITs	ER	SO	W/L
Tom "Terrific" Seaver	9	4	3	6	W
	9	7	0	11	W
	9	5	1	7	W
	9	5	1	5	W
	9	6	2	4	W
	9	8	0	9	W
	9	4	1	4	W
	9	3	0	4	W

Let's total those numbers up.

GAMES	W	L	IP	HITS	RUNS	ER	BB	SO	ERA
8	8	0	72	39	9	8	16	50	1.00

Wow. I am struggling to decide which of these numbers is the most amazing!

- Eight earned runs over 72 innings?
- 4.8 hits per game?
- 1.9 walks per game?

When the 1969 season gets brought up, how often do you hear Tom Seaver *even mentioned?* I bet the narrative you most often hear is "how the Cubs choked," or one of the ridiculous excuses I mentioned earlier. I highly doubt you have heard anyone say, "Seaver just pitched his ass off and the Mets beat us." Cubs' fans have been trained to look for ghosts, goblins, curses, and whatever else our fractured psyches demand…a dominating pitcher is not enough.

The 1969 New York Mets had the best pitcher in baseball and the team won the World Series. The Mets (as all teams did in 1969) were using a four-man rotation. Having a guaranteed victory every fourth game momentously attributed to the Mets' phenomenal stretch-run.

The pitching of Tom Seaver is a simple and rational reason why the Cubs did *not* win in 1969, and Mr. Seaver is quite worthy of being **Reason 11**.

REASON 12

THE 1969 SEASON:
SORRY. THE METS WERE BETTER…WHEN IT MATTERED

The 1969 season has always been viewed as one of the Cubs' utmost near misses. I always had the impression that 1969 was a "fluke" or that the Mets came out of nowhere and stole the National League's Eastern division title. Actually, the '69 race between the Mets and Cubs wasn't *that* close. The Mets won the division by eight games. The final margin was not *one* game, or two, but *eight!* The 1969 Western Division race saw four teams within eight games of the first place Atlanta Braves. Have Giants', Reds' and Dodgers' fans been lamenting this season for the last forty-four years? Those three teams were all as close (or closer!) to winning as the 1969 Chicago Cubs.

If you were invested in the 1969 Cubs, the sensation that season gave you was different; it was special. You like to believe that the Mets' record of 37-11 over the last forty-eight games was an absolute statistical anomaly…a simple fluke. The Mets were just on a lucky streak and the Cubs were laboring (20-28 over the last forty-eight games) to the finish. The Mets' winning percentage of .771 over the last forty-eight games was astounding; yet over a 162 game season there are many statistical "anomalies." Here is an example:

The 1969 Cubs started out 36-16 (.692) over the first fifty-two games while the Mets were 29-23. (The Mets did win ten games in a row to get to 29-23!) Thus the Mets "miraculous" finish was just a touch better than the Cubs' start to the season. Over a 162 game schedule, there are many stretches that can be cherry-picked as useful data. The Mets' 1969 finish was improbable, but it was not the only reason they finished eight games better than the Chicago Cubs.

Looking at the teams objectively, the only area in which the Cubs were superior was overall team power; the Cubs had four players with twenty-plus home runs. Only hitters Tommie Agee (26 home runs) and Cleon Jones (.340 batting average) look special when perusing the Mets' offensive stats; the rest of the offensive numbers are ordinary. On the mound, Fergie Jenkins (21-15, 3.21) was the Cubs' ace, but Jenkins did not match Seaver's dominance. The Cubs' had solid starters in Bill Hands (20-14, 2.49) and Ken Holtzman (17-13 3.59), but the Mets had a plethora of quality pitching arms. Take a look:

1969 METS PITCHER	1969 SIGNIFICANT STATS
Jerry Koosman	17 wins, 180 strikeouts, 2.28 ERA
Tug McGraw	9-3, 12 saves, 92 strikeouts, 2.25 ERA
Ron Taylor	9-4, 13 saves, 2.72 ERA
Nolan Ryan	92 strikeouts in 89 innings
Jim McAndrew	4 saves, 90 strikeouts in 135 innings

The Mets' "power arms" in the bullpen were ahead of their time. The depth of the Mets' pitching was superior to the Cubs. With the type of pitching the Mets received in 1969, winning streaks and "hot" stretches are not surprising. After overtaking the Cubs, the Mets defeated a powerhouse Baltimore Orioles team that won 109 games. The 1969 New York Mets were much-deserved World Series champions, better than the '69 Chicago Cubs anyway. (*Sorry.*)

I apologize to my dad and his generation of Cubs' fans, Ron Santo, Jack Brickhouse, the original bleacher bums and anyone else who has been hanging on to 1969…but it's time to let it go! *Get over it!* The Mets were better when it mattered most, and they won the division by *eight* games.

The year 1969 was preceded by twenty-two pitiful seasons; the most atrocious stretch in the 137 year history of the Chicago Cubs. Therefore it's easy to understand why 1969 seemed so special; the Cubs were closer than they had been in a very long time.

Imagine if you hadn't eaten for a few days. Then somebody brought you a pizza, let you smell it, touch it, yet you weren't allowed to eat it. How would you feel? Would you remember that experience? I bet you would have a hard time forgetting it…just like 1969.

REASON 13

THE 1970 SEASON: BET YOU DIDN'T KNOW

Would you like to win some money? Of course you would! I have a fairly easy bar bet to win. If you don't frequent bars, it can be an *at home* or an *at work* bet. If it makes you uncomfortable to win a bet by "hustle" or "conning" your opponent, then maybe this isn't for you. Somehow you need to innocently bring up the Cubs' notorious history of fading in September to your potential betting partner. You may frame the queries differently, but you could ask any of the following:

- In what season between 1960 and 1984 did the Cubs finish closest to first place?

- Fill in the blank. On September 24, _____, the Cubs trailed the division leader by 2.5 games.

- In what season were the Cubs in first place from mid-April to mid-June, and never more than two games out of first from September 2 to September 24?

Most likely, your betting partner confidently answers, "**1969!**" before you even finish asking. He has probably listened to the same 1969 "lobbyists" and "apologists" referenced in **Reason 12**. The correct answer is…**1970**! Yes, this Cubs' team that you probably never heard about actually finished closer to the first place Pirates (five games) than the legendary 1969 Cubs did to the Mets (eight games). The 1970 Cubs may have been a better team. Blasphemy, I know! Take a look at comparative seasons by some of the key players:

1969 SEASON	AVG	HR	RBI	1970 SEASON	AVG	HR	RBI
Billy Williams	.293	21	95		.322	42	129
Jim Hickman	.237	21	54		.315	32	115
Ron Santo	.289	29	123		.267	26	114
Don Young	.239	6	27				
Johnny Callison					.264	19	68

At age thirty-nine, Ernie Banks' production was relatively similar, yet he played in fewer games in 1970. Middle infielders Glenn Beckert and Don Kessinger had almost identical numbers in 1969 and 1970. The overall production of the pitching staff was comparable as well:

1969	W-L	ERA	1970	W-L	ERA
Fergie Jenkins	21-15	3.21		22-16	3.39
Bill Hands	20-14	2.49		18-15	3.70
Ken Hohltzman	17-13	3.59		17-11	3.35
Dick Selma	10-8	3.62			
Milt Pappas				10-8	2.67

The 1970 Chicago Cubs were closer to first place than the 1969 Cubs and had eerily equivalent statistics produced by key players. The 1970 team was good, and it had an excellent chance of making the play-offs. The 1970 Cubs' season was more of a near miss than the 1969 squad endured…and I bet you didn't know it. I bet your friend and his twenty dollars won't know either.

Oddly, Cubs' fans don't bemoan the 1970 Pirates and the slugging of Willie Stargell and Bob Robertson. Cubs' fans don't whine about Pirate pitchers Doc Ellis and Luke Walker. The 1970 Pittsburgh Pirates are nowhere near as infamous as the '69 Mets in the collective consciousness of Cubs' fans. Yet the 1970 Pirates are just as valid of a *Reason* for keeping the Cubs title-less…and I bet you never knew it.

REASON 14

THE 1984 NLCS:
THE PERFORMANCE OF THE PADRES' BULLPEN…STARRING FORMER CUB CRAIG LEFFERTS

The year 1984 was a magical summer for the Cubs. Dallas Green joined the Cubs as general manager prior to the 1982 season, and in two short seasons the Cubs found themselves one game from the 1984 World Series. For those of us who grew up in the 1970s and 1980s, this is our 1969. Unfortunately, this was *much, much* closer.

The Cubs won the first game of the 1984 NLCS 13-0 behind Rick Sutcliffe and an offensive barrage. After a 4-2 victory in Game 2, the Cubs only had to take *one of three* games in San Diego. Classic Cubs' horror followed; the Padres swept the final three games in San Diego preventing the Cubs from going to the World Series. As a sixteen year old who fought back tears after the final out, let me ask, "How in the world did this happen?"

Maybe you have heard some of the stories, rumors and excuses:

- Sutcliffe couldn't sleep the night before Game 5 and therefore wasn't rested.

- Leon Durham spilled a Gatorade/Coke on Ryne Sandberg's glove (or maybe it's the other way around).

- Las Vegas was set to lose big money since millions of Cubs' fans placed wagers on the long-shot Cubs prior to the season; thus, the *fix* was in.

Don't believe a word of it!

A major reason for the Padres' five game series victory over the Cubs was the work of their bullpen. Aside from the mop-up work done by Greg Harris in the Cubs' 13-0 Game 1 rout, the Padres' bullpen pitched outstandingly in Games 2-5. Take a look:

PLAYER	GAMES	WL	IP	H	ER	Ks	ERA	SAVES
Dave Dravecky	3	0-0	6	2	0	5	0.00	0
Craig Lefferts	3	2-0	4	1	0	1	0.00	0
Andy Hawkins	3	0-0	3.2	0	0	1	0.00	0
Rich Gossage	3	0-0	4	5	2	5	4.50	1
Greg Booker	1	0-0	2	2	0	2	0.00	0
Totals		**2-0**	**19.2**	**10**	**2**	**14**	**0.92**	**1**

In a short five-game series, this kind of relief pitching made a remarkable difference. The innings listed above account for 45 percent of the innings pitched for all Padres' pitchers. Of the Padres' starting pitchers, only Game 3 winner Ed Whitson lasted more than *four* innings. The Cubs flat-out *pounded* the Padres' starters. Regrettably, when the Cubs knocked the starters out, they did virtually nothing against the Padres' bullpen.

Dallas Green was the architect of the 1984 Cubs, primarily through a series of trades. In my opinion, Green's tenure with the Cubs was as successful as any executive in team history. However, one of Green's deals did come back to bite the Cubs in this series. In characteristic Cubs' fashion, Craig Lefferts was a Cubs' draft pick who was traded the previous winter in the three-team deal that brought the Cubs Scott Sanderson. Lefferts would earn wins in two of the three Padres' victories, allowing only one hit over three appearances.

Lefferts was not the only Padres' reliever who dominated the Cubs; Dave Dravecky threw six scoreless innings, while striking out five. Andy Hawkins and Greg Booker combined to throw five scoreless frames. Here is a simple, yet telling way to look at the dominance of the Padres' bullpen over the Cubs' hitters:

COMPOSITE SCORE BY INNINGS 6-9 FOR THE 1984 NLCS

	6	7	8	9	Total
Cubs	2	0	2	0	4
Padres	7	6	0	2	15

In the entire five games series, three starting pitchers lasted longer than six innings: Rick Sutcliffe and Steve Trout of the Cubs, and Ed Whitson of the Padres. The scoring numbers listed above show a basic and accurate portrayal of the importance of the relief pitching in the '84 NLCS. The numbers also illustrate a huge reason the San Diego Padres won the 1984 National League pennant.

1984 was a *true* near miss. It was an extremely bitter end to what was a magical year for the Chicago Cubs and their fans. Those of us who experienced it may never be able to rid the displeasure from our collective brains. Twenty-nine years later it continues to haunt Cubs' fans still searching for reasons. Here is one conclusion *this* Cubs' fan can make:

The Padres' bullpen was a vital reason in ending the Cubs' first post-season in thirty-nine years.

REASON 15

THE 1984 NLCS:
THE PADRES' 1970S ALL-STARS OUTPERFORM THE CUBS' 1970S ALL-STARS

I began following baseball in the 1970s. Steve Garvey and Ron Cey were perennial National League All-Stars who led the Los Angeles Dodgers to multiple play-offs and World Series appearances. Larry Bowa was an All-Star shortstop for the Philadelphia Phillies who helped them to four play-off appearances and a World Series title in 1980. I would have been in Cubs' Heaven if any of these guys played on the North Side in the 1970s.

Sports' fans can relate to this scenario: Your team acquires a player five years too late, past what would be considered his "prime." The initial reaction of joy, when the team you root for acquires the player, quickly fades as you realize he is *not* the player he once was. As the 1984 Chicago Cubs and San Diego Padres battled to go to the World Series, both squads employed players who had been All-Stars in the previous decade. Each team had players past their prime.

The **Padres** had:

1B—Steve Garvey	National League All-Star 1974-81
3B—Graig Nettles	American League All-Star 1975, 77-80
RP—Rich "Goose" Gossage	American League All-Star 1975-78
SS—Gary Templeton	National League All-Star 1977 and 1979

The **Cubs** had:

3B—Ron Cey	National League All-Star 1974-79
SS—Larry Bowa	National League All-Star 1974-76, 78-79
LF—Gary Matthews	National League All-Star 1979
IF—Davey Lopes	National League All-Star 1978-79
SP—Dennis Eckersley	American League All-Star 1977

If you haven't repressed the memories of these games, you know Steve Garvey was the Most Valuable Player of the 1984 National League Championship series.

Steve Garvey nearly signed with the Cubs as a free agent the previous winter. (Ironic, don't you think?) Here is a look at how each team's "All-Stars" performed in the **1984 NLCS**:

FORMER ALL-STAR HITTERS	AB	R	H	2B	3B	HR	RBI	AVG
Padres' All-Stars	49	4	15	2	0	1	11	.306
Cubs' All-Stars	50	8	9	3	0	3	8	.180

Dennis Eckersley was knocked out early in his start for the Cubs in Game 3. The numbers above illustrate the meager production of the Cubs' hitters. The offensive numbers look more pathetic if you take out Gary Matthews' two home runs and five RBIs in the Game 1 blowout. Ron Cey's lone home run came in the Cubs' 13-0 romp as well. Larry Bowa went 3-15 with one RBI throughout the five games. Other than Game 1 at Wrigley Field, these former All-Stars were terrible for the Cubs.

For the victorious Padres (saying that *still* stings!), shortstop Gary Templeton hit .333 and Rich "Goose" Gossage pitched in all three Padres' victories. Steve Garvey hit .400 over the five games with seven RBIs. Garvey performed remarkably in the clutch, hitting a home run off of Lee Smith to win Game 4. Steve Garvey was the standout of all the former All-Stars appearing in Chicago and San Diego.

No matter what sport it is, it's hard *not* to get excited when your team acquires former All-Stars. In the 1984 National League Championship Series, fortunately for the Padres, their "wash-ups" were less washed up than the Cubs'. The Padres' *ex*-All-Stars got the job done, while the Cubs' did not.

My fondness for Gary "The Sarge" Matthews and Ron "The Penguin" Cey made this a tough *Reason* to write. (Bowa...*not so much*) Steve Garvey, Rich Gossage, and Gary Templeton were vital contributors...thus their performance is **Reason 15**.

REASON 16

THE 1984 NLCS:
THE CUBS' HORRIBLE PITCHING IN SAN DIEGO

The human brain has a marvelous ability to rationalize. This capability is enhanced in Cubs' fans to a superior level. It's been almost thirty years since the Cubs' historic loss to the Padres, yet it still pains us to recollect it. As years have passed, the Leon Durham error in Game 7 and the failure of Lee Smith are two of the rationalizations Cubs' fans have come to accept. Upon closer scrutiny, there are simple reasons that get disregarded or conveniently forgotten, but the reasons *are* there.

Statistically, the Cubs and Padres were relatively equal offensive teams going into the 1984 NLCS. The Cubs had *some* statistical advantages:

1984 TEAM STATISTICS	RUNS/GAME	HOME RUNS	OPS
Cubs	4.7	136	.727
Padres	4.2	109	.686

Therefore, the Cubs were a slightly better offensive team heading into the NLCS. The numbers above also indicate that the Padres were *not* a great offensive team. Yet the Padres scored **7, 7,** and **6** runs in the final three games of the NLCS. A Padres' offense that averaged just four runs a game during the 1984 regular season mustered up 6.6 over the fateful last three games.

How? Let's look at the Cubs' pitching statistics in San Diego:

	IP	H	ER	BB	SO	ERA
Eckersley	5.1	9	5	-	-	8.44
Sanderson	4.2	6	3	1	2	5.78
Sutcliffe	6.1	7	5	3	2	7.10
Frazier	1.2	2	2	0	1	10.78
Stoddard	2	1	1	2	2	4.50
Brusstar	2.1	2	0	0	1	0.00
Smith	1.33	3	2	0	2	13.53
TOTALS	**23.2**	**30**	**18**	**6**	**10**	**6.84**

Starting pitchers that the Cubs counted on, Eckersley, Sanderson, and Sutcliffe, were pounded in their combined starts in San Diego. Eckersley gave up five runs and nine hits in five plus innings. Sanderson could not make it into the fifth inning, allowing six hits and three runs. After going 17-1 (including his Game 1 victory) for the Cubs, even Sutcliffe was roughed up for seven hits and five runs. The three starters collectively struck out four Padres in 15.1 innings pitched in San Diego. Not *one* of them pitched well enough to win a play-off game.

The majority of the relievers were as bad as the starters. Lee Smith allowed Steve Garvey's game-winning home run in Game 4. George Frazier and Tim Stoddard both allowed damage to be done in their brief appearances. Only reliever Warren Brusstar's (2.1 innings) performance was respectable.

The Cubs were one win away from their first World Series in thirty-nine years, and not one of their pitchers came through in Games 3, 4, and 5.

In the title of **Reason 16,** I describe the Cubs' pitching in San Diego as *horrible.* Upon further examination, I firmly stand by that assessment. Perhaps you might prefer awful, terrible, atrocious, astonishingly bad, ghastly or hideous. However you describe it, the Cubs' pitching in San Diego during the 1984 NLCS is a strong reason the Cubs did not advance to their first World Series since the end of World War II.

REASON 17

THE 1989 NLCS: WILL NUSCHLER CLARK

The Cubs made it to their second NLCS in five years in 1989 and proceeded to lose to the San Francisco Giants four games to one. I will reiterate once again, for many franchises, losing four games to one would not be considered a near miss. As we have established, Cubs' fans have to take near misses where we can find them.

I must admit upon researching, I was surprised to see that this series was a bit closer than I had recalled. The individual games were much tighter than I remembered. Perhaps after the mental scarring I took from 1984, my psyche decided it best just to chalk this one up as a Giants' butt-kicking. Upon further review, the Cubs did have a chance in this 1989 NLCS. That chance was negated mostly by one man: Will Clark of the Giants.

Clark's overall stats for the series are ridiculously good. Just take a look:

1989 NLCS	AB	R	H	2B	3B	HR	RBI	AVG	OBP	OPS
Will Clark	20	8	13	3	1	2	8	.650	.682	1.882

Wow. For those still not versed in modern statistics like OPS (*on-base plus slugging*), *1.882* is freaking awesome. For fans who aren't interested in "new" stats, how does a *.650 batting average* sound? Are you impressed with Clark's *eight* RBIs and *eight* runs scored? Will Clark put up Hall of Fame caliber numbers in early October 1989.

Clark's implausible stats for the entire NLCS only tell part of the story. Clark single-handedly won Game 1 for the Giants. He drove in the first run of the game, scored the second, and then his grand-slam in the fourth inning opened up what was a close game. In Game 5, the Cubs led 1-0 until the seventh when Clark tripled and then scored on a sacrifice fly by Kevin Mitchell. In the eighth inning with the score tied at one, Clark's two RBI single put the Cubs out of their collective misery. For the series, Clark scored or knocked in sixteen of the thirty runs scored. Simply put, Will Clark was a *monster* in the '89 NLCS.

If you did not know much about this series or are too young to remember, you may have some questions. The little baseball manager inside your head may ask, Why did the Cubs *even pitch to* Will Clark? Why didn't they pitch around him? I was not on the bench for those games, but I would imagine it would have something to do with the guy batting behind Clark...Kevin Mitchell. In the 1989 regular season Kevin Mitchell hit *.291* with *forty-seven* home runs and *125* RBIs...numbers good enough to be the 1989 National League MVP. Mitchell behind Clark forced the Cubs to pick their poison, and with runners on in front of him, pitching around Clark was not an option.

The 1989 Eastern Division title was a surprise for Cubs' fans; many of us were happy "just to be there." In reality the Cubs matched up well and had chances in many of the games. Perhaps like me, you had conveniently forgotten much about the 1989 National League Championship Series. I *do* remember

Clark crushing the ball all over the place, and wanting to cry "uncle" after his last hit in Game 5. As of this writing, Will Clark is *not* a Hall of Famer and most likely never will be. Unfortunately for the Cubs, he did a very fine imitation of a Hall of Famer over the course of the 1989 NLCS. Had Clark come close to having a career comparable to this series, he would have been a very worthy Hall member.

Regardless, Will Clark is worthy of being **Reason 17**.

REASON 18

T HE 1989 NLCS: STEVE BEDROSIAN

In **Reason 17,** I confessed I was startled to recall that three games in the 1989 NLCS were close. For twenty-four years I chalked this Cubs' series failure up by saying, "They were just lucky to be there" or "The Giants were just better." Perhaps I only recollected Game 1, an 11-3 Giants' romp and suppressed the other four games deep into my subconscious.

The Cubs bounced back and won Game 2 at Wrigley 9-5. With the NLCS tied at one, the Cubs needed to win one of the three games in San Francisco to ensure a Game 6 at Wrigley Field. Having the 1989 NLCS return to Chicago for Game 6 nearly happened.

The Cubs lost Game 3 by the score of 5-4 as the Giants scored two in the eighth inning. The Cubs dropped Game 4 to the Giants 6-4. In Game 5, with the Cubs facing elimination, they lost 3-2. Collectively, the Cubs lost games 3, 4, and 5 by four runs total. Losing two one-run games was not exactly the beating I remembered the Cubs taking from the Giants. The Cubs held a lead in *all three* of the games in San Francisco.

As **Reason 17** so eloquently pointed out, Will Clark's amazing performance contributed to the Cubs' 1989 loss to the Giants. Clark's offensive production garnered him the MVP of the 1989 NLCS. If a *second* MVP was awarded for the series, that man would be Steve Bedrosian. Bedrosian saved *all three games* in San Francisco for the Giants. For the series Bedrosian had four appearances, allowing only one run.

1989 NLCS	GAMES	IP	HITS	ER	BBs	SOs	SAVES
Steve Bedrosian	4	3.1	4	1	2	2	3

Bedrosian did *not* lead the Giants in saves during the regular season. Ironically, that distinction went to Craig Lefferts; the same Craig Lefferts who won two games in the 1984 NLCS for the Padres. In the 1989 NLCS, the Giants wouldn't need Lefferts to repeat his heroic '84 performance. Bedrosian's performance was enough to vanquish the Cubs from *another* Cubs' post-season. Mind you, the use of the words "another" and "Cubs' post-season" rarely appear in the same sentence. The years 1984 and 1989 being extremely rare occasions (the 1930s, the 2000s) in which the Cubs were in the post season *twice* in a decade. (Wow…twice in a decade, a Cubs' accomplishment that *did not* happen in the 20s, 40s, 50s, 60s, 70s, or 90s. Yikes!)

The 1989 NLCS was not the blow-out I remembered. The Cubs had opportunities to win the 1989 NLCS. Had the Cubs figured out a way to have Clark and Bedrosian *miss* these games, they probably would have advanced to the 1989 World Series. Consequently, the Giants would be swept in the World Series by their cross-town rivals, the Oakland A's. The 1989 World Series was interrupted by an earthquake that delayed the games for ten days. Had the Cubs defeated the Giants, Game 3 of the World Series would have been played in Chicago, thus avoiding the earthquake…unless an earthquake hit Chicago—an event more likely than the occurrence of a Cubs' World Series in the city.

REASON 19

THE 2003 NLCS:
AN ERROR BY ALEX GONZALEZ

I began this book by discussing how the Cubs' loss in 2003 ultimately altered my thinking of my beloved Cubs. When the time came to research the 2003 NLCS, it was still tough not to feel a bit of post-traumatic stress. The Cubs were five outs away from the World Series. I remember the Cubs losing in 2003, but I have worked hard to repress it for ten years. The mind has a tremendous ability to protect itself from pain…and Game 5 of the 2003 National League Championship series…was *painful.*

The name most commonly associated with the fateful eighth inning, and the loss, is poor Steve Bartman. However, Mr. Bartman did not make an error on a groundball that would have allowed the Cubs to retain the lead; that would be Alex S. Gonzalez. In fairness, Mr. Gonzalez should be paying Mr. Bartman a yearly sum, thanking him for taking blame that should have been more accurately directed at him.

If you are versed in baseball history, and even those of you who aren't, you are probably familiar with the error made by Bill Buckner in the 1986 World Series. Bill Buckner was instantly vilified (not by me, I loved him too much from his Cubs' days) and was the scourge of Boston Red Sox fans for many years. Today, the Boston faithful have apparently forgiven Buckner. The Red Sox fans were much more willing to forgive Buckner almost twenty years later…after they broke their own "curse" and won a World Series in 2004.

The blame that Bill Buckner received always bothered me. The Mets had already *tied* Game 6 of the 1986 World Series prior to Buckner's error. Bill Buckner's error was merely the *last part* of the collapse. Why has ex-Red Sox reliever Bob Stanley, who threw the wild-pitch that tied the game, been spared a similar fate as Buckner? Why has Calvin Schiraldi, who was unable to get the third and final out…when there were already two outs and nobody on base… been spared? How about manager John McNamara who replaced Buckner late in games during the regular season? These people were all shielded from the wrath that Bill Buckner received. (I realize I have gotten on a bit of a tangent; I just wanted to defend ex-Cub Billy Buck a bit.)

Let's get back to Alex (*thank God for the Bartman-incident*) Gonzalez. At the time of Miguel Cabrera's groundball to Gonzalez, the score was Cubs 3, Marlins 1. If Gonzalez fields the grounder, the Cubs likely turn the double-play. If the Cubs *had* turned the double-play, the team goes to the ninth inning leading *at least* 3-1. After batting in the bottom of the eighth inning, the Cubs would have been three outs away from going to the World Series. Gonzalez's error was a *much costlier error* than the one committed by Bill Buckner in the 1986 World Series. It is certainly more costly than the Bartman play, which is not even debatable in its importance. When Moises Alou tracked that fateful foul to the seats, did he really have a chance to catch that ball? Was Alou's subsequent temper tantrum just to show the world he was interfered with? There were many fans attempting to catch the ball; why were *they* spared the fate of Steve Bartman? Cubs' fans will never know all of the facts surrounding the "Steve Bartman play." It is a fact that Mark Prior had the opportunity to get that hitter out, and the Gonzalez play later that inning would have ended the rally.

(Baseball cliché alert!!!) Baseball is a team game, and it's unfortunate when *any player* bears the brunt of an outcome that has many variables and permutations. I am not asking Cubs' fans to grab their torches and pitchforks and head out looking for Alex Gonzalez. I am merely trying to point out that in attempting to expose multiple (*like 104 multiple)* reasons for the Cubs' continued futilities, Alex Gonzalez is much more deserving than Steve Bartman. All Cubs' players on the field in Game 6 had more influence on the outcome of Game 6 than the unfortunate Steve Bartman.

Wherever you are, Mr. Bartman, please know that this is one Cubs' fan who *never* held you responsible. I am sure there are many Cubs' fans that hold the same viewpoint...sort of like a silent majority. I also do not hold Alex Gonzalez *solely* responsible for the Cubs not advancing to the 2003 World Series. Nevertheless, the error by Alex Gonzalez is worthy of being **Reason 19**...*not* Steve Bartman.

REASON 20

THE 2003 NLCS:
KERRY WOOD IS PRETTY MUCH TOAST BY NLCS TIME

I have always liked Dusty Baker. Perhaps it's because he held my son when he was only a few months old and posed for a picture with him. But I always felt bad that the Cubs' faithful went from "In Dusty We Trusty" to wanting him gone in just a couple short seasons. Dusty always had two big impressions working against him: **1)** Dusty didn't like playing young players, and **2)** Dusty abused his pitchers. On the first count, I find him innocent (or a *no contest plea*) because the Cubs had no young prospects for Dusty to play. Regrettably on the second count, there is some pretty damning evidence. Enough evidence, anyway, to warrant another *Reason* later in the book. In regards to 2003, let's look at some facts.

Kerry Wood was dominant in the 2003 NLDS against the Braves prior to facing the Marlins in the NLCS. Wood was 2-0 against the Braves, allowing only seven hits in fifteen innings, striking out eighteen, and compiling an ERA of 1.76. Then in the 2003 NLCS against the Marlins, Kerry Wood allowed ten earned runs in 12.3 innings. Wood allowed fourteen hits and struck out thirteen. Wood's pitching was superior against the Braves (an excellent hitting team) to his performance against the Marlins (a weaker hitting team). Kerry Wood's regular season numbers: a 3.20 ERA, only 152 hits allowed in 211 innings, and 266 strikeouts. Look at it this way:

	HITS PER 9	KS PER 9	ERA
2003 Regular Season Kerry Wood	6.5	11.3	3.20
2003 NLDS Kerry Wood	4.2	10.8	1.76
2003 NLCS Kerry Wood	10.2	9.4	7.30

So what happened? Kerry Wood dominated the National League for most of the 2003 season, and then followed it up by dominating the National League's best offense (5.4 runs per game, 235 HRs) in the 2003 NLDS. Next, while facing a *far* inferior Marlins' offense (4.6 RPG, 157 HRs), Wood gets hit...*hard*. The only logical reason is Kerry was not the same pitcher by the time the 2003 National League Championship Series started. Why might that be?

Here is a good place to start...Kerry Wood's pitch counts for his last six starts of the 2003 regular season: **125, 120, 122, 114, 125,** and **122.** That's an average of **121** pitches per start. In a year when pitchers throughout the league threw 125 pitches or more only *seventy times*...Wood was close to *averaging* that number over his last six starts. Wood threw **124** and **117** pitches against the Braves in the National League Divisional Series. Adding those totals, Wood *threw 969 pitches over eight starts.* Over a period of thirty-nine days Kerry Wood threw 969 pitches or 124 pitches on every fifth day.

Are these high pitch counts and totals solely to blame for Kerry's poor outings against the Marlins? Before placing ALL blame on Dusty Baker, remember Kerry was prone to high pitch counts (high strikeouts, lots of walks) throughout his career. Nevertheless, it is a fact that Kerry Wood was not the same pitcher against the Marlins that he was during the regular season or in the NLDS. Did Kerry's skills briefly erode? Perhaps Kerry had a mental lapse against the Marlins? Was the pressure of the NLCS too much? I find it highly probable that Kerry's high pitch totals cost him velocity and his "stuff."

Ask yourself this question: If the same Kerry Wood who pitched against the Braves pitched in Games 2 and 7 of the NLCS, do the Cubs go to the 2003 World Series? *My* answer would be yes. Depending on which Kerry Wood then faced the Yankees, the World Series title drought possibly ends… and I am not writing this book.

I will examine Dusty Baker's use of the 2003 Cubs' pitching staff in a later section. Perhaps the Cubs don't make the 2003 play-offs or defeat Atlanta… if Kerry Wood *did not* throw as many pitches. Regardless of the explanations why, Kerry Wood *did* throw too many pitches over a short period in 2003… and his sub-par performances after those countless throws is **Reason 20**.

REASON 21

THE 2003 NLCS:
Ivan Rodriguez Signs with the Marlins…Not the Cubs

Part of the torment of being a Cubs' fan is there really isn't an off-season. As Cubs' fans, there probably isn't *one* day of the 365 day calendar year where at least one Cubs' thought doesn't cross our collective minds. In the off-season, it is most intense from mid-November through January, when baseball's winter meetings and free agency take place. The Cubs are invariably coming off another bad season and we fans are waiting and hoping to see some improvements to the roster.

For me, it's almost like Charlie Brown trying to kick the football while Lucy Van Pelt holds it. I fall for it *every* year! I get excited for the winter meetings and follow the proceedings almost stalker-like. There is usually one big move I am hoping for from my Cubs. Some years, there is one particular player heading my wish list (I am looking at you, Brian Roberts!). Habitually, the Cubs leave the winter meetings without the "big move" or my desired player. I then get suckered into thinking there is plenty of off-season time left, and there *will* be moves. More years than not, the moves are not made, and the Cubs' off-season is as disappointing as the preceding year *on the field*. This does not stop me the next winter from rehashing the entire cycle...again. Because that's what we do as Cubs' fans...wait and hope.

During the winter of 2002-2003, my Cubs' wish list was headed by catcher Ivan Rodriguez. The Cubs were linked as a possible landing spot for Rodriguez, who some in baseball (apparently the Texas Rangers) felt was washed up. After years of not getting much offensively out of the catching position, I set my measly hopes on the Cubs getting Ivan "Pudge" Rodriguez. I wasn't as enthusiastic as I would later be about the prospect of acquiring Brian Roberts (him again!) or Nomar Garciaparra, but I was hoping for Rodriguez just the same.

Rodriguez eventually signed with the Florida Marlins on January 28, 2003, for one year at $10 million. I recall rationalizing the $10 million price tag in my head as probably a good reason the Cubs did not land Rodriguez. After almost ten years and much hindsight, my perspective has altered.

Ivan "Pudge" Rodriguez was the MVP of the 2003 National League Championship Series. He hit .321, with two home runs and a team-leading ten RBIs. Pudge also played stellar defense and handled the Marlins' staff that out-pitched the Cubs. Pudge was an enormous reason the Marlins won the 2003 NLCS.

I don't remember much discussion about the fact that Rodriguez could have become a Cub during or after the 2003 season. Perhaps the rumors I had read of "mutual interest" between Rodriguez and the Cubs were overstated during the off-season. We can *ponder...*what if the Cubs had signed Rodriguez instead of the Marlins? Even if Rodriguez had signed with a team *other* than the Marlins, it would have had impacted the Cubs' post-season success. Can you imagine if the Cubs were in on Rodriguez until the end of his free agency, and a couple million stop their pursuit? Let's say the Cubs were willing to go $8.5 million on a one-year deal, *then* six months later Rodriguez is the guy preventing them from going to the World Series. That scenario would be tough to swallow for any team and its followers, let alone a fandom as starved as the Chicago Cubs.

Unfortunately, Ivan "Pudge" Rodriguez *did* sign with Marlins. If Rodriguez did not sign with Florida, there is no guarantee he would have signed with the Cubs. There is also no guarantee that Rodriguez's presence on the Cubs would have *guaranteed* a World Series appearance or title. I *can* guarantee this: the Marlins would not have beaten the Cubs in the 2003 NLCS without Ivan (**Reason 21**) Rodriguez.

REASON 22

THE 2003 NLCS: JACK MCKEON

On May 22, 2003, the Florida Marlins' record stood at 19-29. The team had just gone 3-7 in their first ten games under manager Jack McKeon who replaced Jeff Torborg (16-22). The hiring of the seventy-two-year-old McKeon was viewed as a curious choice. Jack McKeon is known as "Trader Jack" for his willingness to deal frequently as general manager of the San Diego Padres. McKeon made one regrettable move during his tenure there (1980-1990); trading away Ozzie Smith, yet he was the architect of the 1984 National League Champion San Diego Padres. Yes, *those* Padres that crushed our collective Cubs' spirits in the 1984 NLCS.

In the first ten games under McKeon, the Marlins were not looking like a team that could eventually make the play-offs and win a World Series. Can you imagine the Cubs making the play-offs after a start such as this? Neither can I. From May 23 until the end of the season, the Marlins would go 72-42 to finish 91-71. Even with that amazing stretch of baseball, the Marlins were not able to climb into second place for good until September 8. They finished ten games behind the Atlanta Braves, but the 91-71 record was good enough to make the play-offs as a wild card. The Marlins' eventual victory over the Cubs in the NLCS was surprising, yet perhaps not as astounding as the Florida Marlins *just making the play-offs* in 2003.

Was Jack McKeon responsible for this remarkable Marlins' turnaround in 2003? An old baseball cliché is, "The manager gets too much credit when a team wins and too much blame when a team loses." Nonetheless, with a turnaround this drastic, one would have to believe that McKeon was responsible for the Marlins' resurgence. Directly or indirectly, McKeon made a massive impact on the 2003 season for the Marlins. The managerial change alone may have been the catalyst for the Marlins' sudden inspired play...the fact that McKeon was *not* Jeff Torborg. Likewise, McKeon may have been the driving force behind the Marlins' miraculous recovery. Either scenario qualifies Jack McKeon as a *Reason* the Cubs were kept out of the 2003 World Series.

When Jack McKeon's name appeared among the **104 Reasons,** you probably surmised it was because he out-managed Dusty Baker. McKeon did use his starting pitchers out of the bullpen, something Baker *did not do*. Aside from that difference, after meticulous examination of the 2003 NLCS box scores, I found that McKeon and Baker made similar moves. McKeon's relief pitchers performed much better than Baker's did when making comparable moves. If Alex Gonzalez fields a ground ball in the eighth inning and the Cubs go to the World Series, Dusty ends up looking like a genius. The Cubs would have gone to the World Series and Baker is a Chicago icon for the rest of his life.

Unfortunately, there was no scenario that allowed the Cubs to advance past the Marlins, and McKeon was viewed as the better manager in most people's perception. Regardless of McKeon's 2003 NLCS managerial performance, getting the Marlins into that position was an astonishing feat. And Jack McKeon was rewarded as the 2003 National League Manager of the Year.

To put it simply: as a *good* manager, a *great* manager, or just as a seventy-two-year-old guy sitting in a dugout...Jack McKeon was a *Reason* the Cubs did not go to the World Series. McKeon took a team that was floundering (really... no pun intended) under Jeff Torborg and the Marlins made an improbable run that ended with the 2003 World Series championship. Jack McKeon is **Reason 22** because *his* Marlins knocked the Chicago Cubs from the 2003 NLCS (...in case you had forgotten).

REASON 23

THE 2004 SEASON: ANOTHER LATE SEASON COLLAPSE

Perhaps some Cubs' fans have not recovered from the collective hangover that was the 2003 NLCS. Game 6 and 7 of the 2003 NLCS were the "**nearest misses**" that most Cubs' fans have dealt with. The wound is deep… on par or greater than 1984.

A Cubs' fan gets used to living in a world full of clichés: "Wait 'til next year," "This *is* the year," or "Hope springs eternal." Hope did spring again on March 23, 2004, as the long-rumored return of Greg Maddux became official. Greg Maddux's departure had been a "1969" in itself for Cubs' fans, and his return was met with a great amount of joy. Maddux's return was the cure for *my* personal 2003 hangover; adding Maddux to an already strong Cubs' pitching staff helped ease the pain of the previous October. General manager Jim Hendry made giant offensive upgrades in Derek Lee, Michael Barrett, and Todd Walker. Next, on July 31, the Cubs acquired shortstop Nomar Garciaparra from the Boston Red Sox. I was so thrilled about the Garciaparra acquisition, I told my daughters that day was to be renamed *Nomar Day*! (Turns out, Nomar Day was only celebrated once.) The 2004 Cubs appeared to be loaded and the plan was to make 2003 a distant memory. Unfortunately, "Cubs" and "plan" cannot coexist in the same sentence…let alone in reality.

Kerry Wood and Mark Prior battled injuries throughout the entire 2004 season, a sad prelude to their futures. The two combined to go 14-13 and neither consistently displayed the dominance flashed in 2003. The Cubs' injuries, coupled with the dynamo that was the 2004 St. Louis Cardinals (105-57), quickly relegated the Cubs to wild card contenders.

Ah, but strong wild card contenders they were! Greg Maddux went from a luxury to a necessity, winning sixteen games. Carlos Zambrano picked up the Wood/Prior slack, winning sixteen and showing the dominance that Wood/ Prior had the previous season. The offense was very solid with four players topping thirty homers in Derek Lee, Sammy Sosa, Moises Alou, and Aramis Ramirez. There were also solid offensive seasons from Corey Patterson,

Michael Barrett, and Todd Walker. The Garciaparra addition seemed to be the *final* offensive piece. Who cared if the Cardinals were running away with the division? The Cards led the second place Cubs by fifteen games by mid-August. The reality of the wild card era in Major League Baseball is "all you have to do is get in." (See Marlins, Florida 2003...*sigh*). On September 24, the Cubs beat the Mets 2-1 for their fourth win in a row. The Cubs led the wild card race by a game over the San Francisco Giants and were two games ahead of the Houston Astros. Regrettably, the season did not end on that day.

The Cubs proceeded to go **2-8** over the remaining ten games, five of the eight losses being of the "bullpen-blowing, one-run" variety. Reliever LaTroy Hawkins gets a disproportionate amount of the responsibility for the collapse. The *entire* Cubs' bullpen warrants blame...*four different* relievers earned defeats during the latest Cubs' fade. The Astros were able to overtake the Cubs for good on September 28, four days after the Cubs had led the Astros by two games. It would be the Giants and Astros fighting for wild card over the final days of the 2004 season; the Cubs permanently excused themselves from the race.

Could the 2004 Chicago Cubs have succeeded in the play-offs? I will put this delicately....*hell, yes*! Carlos Zambrano was pitching well, and combined with Maddux, it's easy to speculate that the Cubs had an outstanding chance in a play-off series. Mark Prior also seemed to be healthy as he struck out sixteen Reds on the final day of the season. The fateful 2-8 stretch with the total bullpen flop cost that play-off chance.

The harsh reality of 2004 is it was the beginning of the end for these Cubs, the closing of the window of this team's World Series hopes. The conclusion of one of the most capable and talented versions of the Cubs ever assembled. 2004 was also the prologue of the end for one wrist-band wearing, toothpick chewing manager.

2004 is not associated with 1969, 1984, or 2003, yet it deserves to be placed with these other hallowed failures. In this book, *2004* gets the infamy it deserves, and it also gets to be **Reason 23**.

REASON 24

THE 2007 NLDS: SWEET LOU GETS US CLOSE…NOT REALLY

Dusty Baker went from hero/savior to run-out-of-town/horrible manager in a matter of two short seasons. By the end of 2006, the carnage that was 2003 and 2004 coupled with two bad seasons had the Cubs searching for a new manager. General manager Jim Hendry got his man in Lou Piniella. Piniella's no-nonsense approach was the answer to player-friendly Dusty. (Did you ever notice that this cycle repeats itself in all sports with franchises that can't find the right coach? The team goes from players' coach to hard ass to players' coach…etc.) Surprisingly, as Baker had done before him, "Sweet" Lou got the Cubs into the 2007 play-offs in his initial season with the club.

The near miss title of this chapter will once again get a loose interpretation. The Cubs *did* make the National League play-offs and faced the Arizona Diamondbacks…yet, it was not close. How *not close*? Consider:

- The Diamondbacks swept the Cubs three games to zero.

- The Diamondbacks outscored the Cubs 16-6 in the three games.

- The Cubs *never* had a lead after the completion of a full inning; they briefly led Game 2 2-0 after scoring two in the top half of the second, only to have the D-Backs answer with four runs in the bottom of that same inning.

- The Diamondbacks hit .266 with six home runs and 16 RBIs; the Cubs hit .194 with one home run and six RBIs.

- Of the Cubs' three starting pitchers, only Carlos Zambrano in Game 1 made it past the *fourth inning*.

- The Cubs had four extra base hits over the entire three games, three doubles and a homer. Pitifully, one of the doubles was by Zambrano and another by pinch-hitter Daryl Ward.

Calling the 2007 NLDS close would be an insult to the word "close" and all of its synonyms. The closest game was Game 1 (a 3-1 D-Backs win) in which the game was tied after six innings. Starter Carlos Zambrano was removed after six innings, and in typical "we need *someone* or *something* to blame" Cubs' fan tradition, this move was annoyingly second-guessed. Considering that the Cubs did not score again, perhaps the removal of Zambrano's bat from the lineup could be rationally questioned. However, the idea that Piniella's removal of Zambrano cost the Cubs a chance at winning the series is preposterous. As with most Cubs' near (and in this case *not near at all*) misses, the Chicago faithful need an excuse of some kind, which is many times neither rational nor logical. This unique part of a Cubs' fan's psyche is what we are examining and disputing in this book. Why must Cubs' fans always look beyond the obvious results on the playing field to explain the team's misfortunes? Why does this continue when there is sensible evidence?

The logic of **Reason 24** is pretty simple. The Diamondbacks thoroughly out-played the Cubs in the 2007 National League Divisional Series. There was not one "turning" point in the series that can be second-guessed, questioned, analyzed, or even discussed in a serious baseball conversation. The 2007 Cubs qualify as near miss merely because the franchise rarely gets near enough *to* miss.

REASON 25

THE 2008 NLDS: NOT *REALLY* CLOSE...AGAIN

The year 2008 seemed to bring a weird sense of entitlement to Cubs' fans. It was as though the one hundredth anniversary of the 1908 Cubs' World Series set up some kind of automatic Cubs' championship in 2008. The number 100 does have significance, and apparently it seemed more likely that the Cubs would win in year 100, rather than...I don't know...say, the previous **99**! However, for much of 2008, the events on the field seemed to give credence that the one hundredth year was *finally* going to be it.

There were eight Cubs on the All-Star team. Eight, I say! This tied a National League record. As a kid, I was happy when the Cubs would just get one! The 2008 Cubs won ninety-seven games during the regular season and finished seven games ahead of the Brewers. The oft-injured, yet dominant when healthy, Rich Harden was added via trade to a strong pitching staff that had two seventeen game winners in Ryan Dempster and Ted Lilly. Carlos Zambrano (fourteen wins) was still a vital part of the rotation and the Cubs had an incredibly dominant 1-2 punch with Kerry Wood and Carlos Marmol in the bullpen. The offense had five players hit twenty home runs: Derek Lee, Alfonso Soriano, Aramis Ramirez, Geovany Soto, and Mark DeRosa.

There were some warning signs for those who hadn't already purchased their 2008 World Series Championship gear. The batting order featured only one left-handed hitter in Jim Edmonds (another mid-season pick-up), and Derek Lee was the only better-than-average defensive player. The pitching was solid, but only a healthy Harden could be considered "dominant." The team lacked a pitcher to nail down a post-season game; as Kerry Wood and Mark Prior did to the Braves in 2003.

Yet, most fans and baseball prognosticators forecasted the Cubs defeating the Los Angeles Dodgers in the NLDS. I was not one of them; the Dodgers' right-handed starters concerned me against the Cubs' right-handed hitters. Even so, the most cynical naysayers like me could not have predicted the slaughter to come. The 2008 NLDS closely resembled the whipping the Cubs took from the Diamondbacks just one year prior. The beating may have been even worse. Take a look:

- The Cubs scored six runs, in the *whole* series.

- The Cubs held the lead for only two and a half innings.

- The Cubs hit one home run during the series.

- Once again Zambrano was the only starter to last into the fifth inning, and he allowed three earned runs over six innings; because of poor Cubs' defense, the team trailed 6-0 in Zambrano's start.

- Cubs' pitchers had an ERA of 5.19 compared to the Dodgers' 2.00.

- The Cubs made six errors (four in one game); the Dodgers made one error...for the entire series.

- Four of the Cubs' regulars had two hits or less for the entire three game sweep (Ramirez 2, Soto 2, Soriano 1, and Kosuke Fukudome 1)

- Cumulative score: Dodgers 20, Cubs 6

After the second NLDS thrashing in two years, Cubs' fans were left with numerous questions. There were no goats, no curses, not even a poor fan with headphones sitting next to the bullpen to blame. The above facts should show that the 2008 NLDS was never close. But Cubs' post-season appearances are so rare, the typical Cubs' fan can't say, "Well, they sure were a hell of a lot better than us."

The Cubs were *in* the 2008 play-offs, thus it ranks as a near miss. Only a team with such limited post-season appearances would consider 2008 close to a championship, yet it still qualifies as **Reason 25**.

When I began this project, I didn't think the near miss chapters would contain twenty-five reasons. When a team is rarely close, the near misses are remembered. The book will now be focusing on reasons *why* the Cubs rarely *get close*. It takes many failures, poor decisions, and blunders to have a history as awful as the Chicago Cubs. Luckily, I still have seventy-nine more spots to fill.

CHAPTER 3

REASON 26—FIRST ROUND FIRST
Analyzing just the first round picks of the Chicago Cubs…
not surprisingly there has been little success.

REASON 27—FIRST ROUND PITCHER FAILURES
When contrasting the Cubs' selection of first round pitchers to the rest of
the National League, clear evidence emerges…the Los Angeles Dodgers
are much better than the Chicago Cubs…so is most of the National League.

REASON 28—THE 1965 DRAFT:
THE FIRST DRAFT EVER
Perhaps most teams didn't know what they were doing in the first ever draft;
it is evident that the Chicago Cubs didn't.

REASON 29—THE 1966 AND 1967 DRAFTS:
TWO COMPLETE WHIFFS
Over the course of these two drafts, the Cubs made almost seventy selections…
none of them good.

REASON 30—THE 1968-1972 DRAFTS:
5 CUBS' DRAFTS VS. THE NATIONAL LEAGUE EAST
A look at Cubs' drafts compared to their direct competition at the time
and how it affected the rest of the decade.

REASON 31—SCOT THOMPSON AND 1979
Scot Thompson's 1979 season was "decent" for a Cubs' rookie;
compared to players drafted in the same year, "decent" turns to "not so good."

REASON 32—THE 1975 AND 1976 DRAFTS:
WAR—WHAT IS IT GOOD FOR?

*Wins Above Replacement player is a respected new baseball statistic;
it is also really good at demonstrating how poorly the Cubs
drafted in 1975 and 1976.*

REASON 33—THE 1977-1980 DRAFTS:
I DON'T EVEN NEED TO USE STATS

*You will recognize the names of many players
the Cubs passed on during these two drafts…
and it may get you angry.*

REASON 34—THE 1988-1998 DRAFTS:
ONE BAD ALL-CUBS' DRAFT TEAM

*I made up a team using players the Cubs drafted during these years.
(Hint…it's not very good)*

REASON 35—TY GRIFFIN VS. ROBIN VENTURA

*The Cubs had a choice to make in the 1988 MLB draft…
they made the wrong one.*

REASON 36—THE 1999 DRAFT:
KARMA?

*The Chicago Cubs were willing to make a
controversial pick in Ben Christensen…
any guesses on how that turned out?*

DAFT DRAFTS

If you are a fan of *any* professional sport, you appreciate the significance of that sport's amateur draft. General managers (in all sports) repeat the identical mantra of building teams through the draft. Organizations that thrive in the draft process have sustained success, while those that struggle drafting rarely prosper. A team's draft results are not simple to evaluate; it often takes years to gauge how a franchise has done. Several teams' draft histories are easy to criticize with the advantage of hindsight.

If you follow the NBA, you know that the Portland Trail Blazers selected Sam Bowie over Michael Jordan (thank bleeping God!). You may remember that twelve teams passed on Kobe Bryant (yikes!). If you are a Bulls fan, you might recall that a coin flip cost the Bulls the chance to draft Magic Johnson; which left them with David Greenwood.

Like the NBA, the history of the NFL draft is bursting with examples of *hits* and *misses*. Who can forget the debate over who was the *better* quarterback prospect: Peyton Manning or...Ryan Leaf? The Oakland Raiders selected JaMarcus Russell (complete bust) over potential Hall of Famers Adrian Peterson and Calvin Johnson. The Chicago Bears lost a coin flip that cost them the chance to draft Terry Bradshaw. (Hey...wait a minute.)

Traditionally, the Major League Baseball draft does not merit the coverage or exposure that the NBA and the NFL drafts receive. Draft picks in other major sports make a quicker impact; therefore, a more tangible sense of gratification is achieved by the fans *and* the team. Patience is required by baseball fans to follow their teams' drafts; in Major League Baseball it takes years to examine the results of a draft. The lack of historic attention and coverage (with the advent of the MLB network, the draft gets covered now) does not lessen Major League Baseball amateur draft's significance. Simply put, MLB draft picks become prospects that rarely make it to the major leagues. They are often traded from organization to organization. A Major League Baseball team's draft *does* represent a team's future success on the field, its financial success, and the team's long-term competitiveness. It should not be shocking to discover the Cubs have been categorically and historically bad at drafting.

The first baseball draft took place in 1965. Prior to 1965, teams just signed amateur players to contracts. This meant that teams with the most money were able to sign the preeminent players. (*I am looking at you, Yankees!*) Initially, the MLB had three different drafts in January, June and August. The June draft has always been the most prominent. The August draft was eliminated after only two years; while the January draft lasted until 1986. After June of 2012, there have now been forty-seven years of Major League Baseball drafts.

In this chapter we will look at some particular years in which the Cubs' poor draft will be counted among our **104 Reasons**. There are too many variables that go into making draft selections for teams to *never* make errors. All teams (in all sports) have a few gigantic busts on their ledgers. The Chicago Cubs are not the only professional sports franchise with a problematic draft history. (*See Bears, Chicago.*)

In typical Cubs' manner, the team's draft history is poor enough to warrant *many* of our reasons. A year-by-year assessment of Cubs' drafts reveals that there are rare years that would *not* be considered reasons for the team's epic one-hundred-year failures. Therefore this author had to get creative in analyzing and categorizing these drafts. I could have gone year by year; 1965, 1966, 1967... etc., but that would have been quite tedious for the author and the reader.

That method would have taken up most of the book.

Therefore I will examine a few years individually, years in pairs, five-year periods, a decade or two and a couple of interesting stand alone selections. The Cubs have so much failure in their sorry history it's easy to label, categorize and package. There are plenty of *Daft Drafts* to help fill **104 Reasons**.

REASON 26

FIRST ROUND FIRST

A draft is a crapshoot...at least that's the expression I have often heard. The point being...there is an element of uncertainty and luck in any draft process. First round picks, in any sport, should be a team's best chance at success. Using that logic, we will examine just the Cubs' first round selections.

From 1965 until 2012, the Cubs selected sixty players in the first round. With the addition of supplemental picks, there are drafts when teams have more than one first round pick. Technically the Cubs had three first round picks in the June 2012 draft. Of the sixty first round picks that the Cubs selected since 1965, thirty-one were pitchers and twenty-nine were position players (*eerily* equal).

First, some facts about the thirty-one pitchers selected the first round by the Chicago Cubs since 1965:

- *None* of the selections are Hall of Famers.
- *None* of the pitchers drafted ever won twenty games in the majors...(gulp)
- *One* of the pitchers won 100 Major League games...Jon Garland (132).
- Only one pitcher other than Garland won *at least* fifty games in the Major Leagues...Kerry Wood (86).
- Only *four* other pitchers won over ten games in their entire Major League careers...Mark Prior (42), Mike Harkey (36), Randy Martz (17), and Don Schulze (15).
- Consequently, only *six* of the thirty-one pitchers the Cubs have selected in the first round won more than ten games in the Major Leagues (19 percent).
- Twelve of those first-round pitchers *never* even made it to the Major Leagues.

Okay, the Cubs' record of selecting first round pitchers is a bit...dicey (*at best*).

How have the Cubs fared with the first round hitters they have selected? I bet you could make a good guess:

- The Cubs have drafted one hitter who has had "Hall of Fame Numbers"...Rafael Palmeiro. Palmeiro may have a difficult time getting in to the Hall, though. (No comment.)
- Other than Rafael Palmeiro, only four players have had 1,000 Major League at-bats: Joe Carter, Shawon Dunston, Doug Glanville, and Corey Patterson.

- Joe Carter was a very good Major League Baseball player. Shawon Dunston had a solid (not spectacular) career. Corey Patterson and Doug Glanville had sustained Major League careers.
- Only Shawon Dunston appeared in an All-Star game (as a Cub).
- Of the hitters who had more than 1,000 at-bats, only Rafael Palmeiro hit above .277 for his career.
- Palmeiro, Carter, Patterson and Dunston are also the only first round picks to hit more than sixty career home runs.

Considering that Palmeiro, Carter and Glanville played the majority of their careers with other teams, Shawon Dunston is the only first round "Cubs" hitter of any consequence. Shawon Dunston was the number one overall pick in 1982; thus I judge his career with a bit more scrutiny.

When making first round selections, the Cubs have proven to be inept at picking both hitters and pitchers. With sixty selections, the Cubs should have had a few more "hits" than those listed above…consequently, their lack of first round success is **Reason 26**.

REASON 27

FIRST ROUND *PITCHER* FAILURES

In **Reason 26,** I examined the Cubs' lack of success in the first round of the draft. Since the inception of the draft in 1965, the Cubs have drafted thirty-one pitchers in the first round. Of those pitchers selected, Jon Garland has the most Major League wins with 132. Most of Garland's wins were with the…*ahem*… Chicago White Sox. After Garland, Kerry Wood, Mark Prior, and Mike Harkey have the most wins by first round pitchers, and only Wood has more than fifty (eighty-six)! After discovery of this data, I pondered if the numbers posted by the Cubs' picks were typical of most Major League teams. Conceivably, many teams could have similar totals if I compared wins accumulated by their first round picks. I decided to add up *total Major League wins* by pitchers drafted in the first round by *all* National League teams since 1965. I excluded expansion teams: the Colorado Rockies, Florida/Miami Marlins, and Arizona Diamondbacks.

I also only included *continuous* National League franchises from 1965. (Sorry, Milwaukee Brewers.) Here is the cumulative data:

FRANCHISE	WINS BY FIRST RD PICKS	DIFF.	NL PENNANTS	WORLD CHAMPS
1. Los Angeles Dodgers	792	—	7	3
2. New York Mets	741	51	4	2
3. San Francisco Giants	626	166	4	2
4. Houston Astros	607	185	1	0
5. Philadelphia Phillies	566	226	5	2
6. St. Louis Cardinals	556	236	7	4
7. Atlanta Braves	550	242	5	1
8. San Diego Padres	541	251	2	0
9. Cincinnati Reds	482	310	5	3
10. Montreal/Wash	445	347	0	0
11. Chicago Cubs	346	446	0	0
12. Pittsburgh Pirates	187	605	2	2

Yeah! We beat the Pirates! I am not a statistician, but I think some correlations can be drawn. The numbers are conclusive: ***Successful first round pitchers lead to winning Major League Baseball teams.*** Consider these facts:

- The Dodgers have been excellent at drafting first round pitchers… and have the successes to show for it.

- The Dodgers have had an astonishing 446 more wins out of their first round pitchers than the Cubs (792 to 346). That is *one-hundred* more wins than the Cubs' total!

- 72 percent of the teams that have had at least 550 wins from first round starters have won at least one World Series.

- The dreaded Cardinals come in sixth in the standings, yet still have a significant 210 more wins than the Cubs.

- The nominal differences between the other teams on the list (for example, the Phillies at 566 and the Braves at 550) are insignificant compared to the difference between the successful teams and the Cubs/Pirates.

With our beloved Cubs finishing eleventh out of twelve in this category and with the parallels listed above, I can confidently conclude that the Cubs have been particularly awful at selecting first round pitchers. The Dodgers, Giants, and Cardinals have significantly more first round wins than the Cubs, and those teams have eighteen World Series appearances and eight championships combined.

The Cubs have *zero* in both categories.

The first round is only the commencement of every draft. Consequently, a first round pick is not necessarily a harbinger for a team's success in subsequent rounds. Perhaps as I continue to examine Cubs' drafts from different perspectives, the results will not be as disappointing. Maybe the Cubs have succeeded in every round but the first. (Insert your own snicker, giggle, or scoff.)

Reason 27 denotes the Cubs' failure in drafting first round pitchers. Unfortunately as a Cubs' fan, you already have a good idea of how the Cubs will rank aside from *just* first round selections and regrettably in positions other than pitcher. Failure for the Chicago Cubs is not limited to rank, classification, category, class, grouping, type or any other appropriate synonym.

REASON 28

THE 1965 DRAFT:
THE FIRST DRAFT EVER

Rick James. Have you ever heard of him? No, not the much-lampooned late funk master of the 80s…*the baseball player.* C'mon, you know him; the former Cubs' pitcher! The player the Cubs drafted sixth overall in 1965. (Okay, so that is a bit of sarcasm.) You would have to be an older Cubs' fan, with freakish recall, to dredge up the Cubs' career of one Rick James…*the pitcher.* Let's look at some of the career highlights of Rick, not the *Super Freak*, James:

- Mr. Rick James appeared in three Major League games.
- Mr. Rick James had a career Major League record of 0-1.
- Mr. Rick James had a career ERA of 13.50.

Perhaps the *funky Rick James* could have pitched as well as Cubs' draft pick Rick James. Former-Cub Rick James may be a really nice guy (I have never met him), but I think it's safe to say he could be classified a bust of a first round pick. How did the Chicago Cubs do in the rest of the 1965 draft? They made one great pick in the fourth round; Ken Holtzman. Holtzman went on to win three World Series...with the Oakland A's. Out of the twenty-eight names the Cubs selected other than James and Holtzman, only two are recognizable: Darrell Evans and Tom House.

Darrell Evans, who the Cubs drafted but did not sign, went on to have a fine career with the Braves, Giants, and Tigers. Tom House is most notable for catching Hank Aaron's 715th home run in the Atlanta Braves' bullpen. Mr. House is also famous for the *towel drill* used as a training technique for pitchers. Therefore, of the thirty players selected by the Chicago Cubs in the inaugural draft of 1965, only Holtzman contributed to any Cubs' success. The Cubs then traded Holtzman so he could have mega-success with the A's. Regardless of that fact, let's examine other players drafted in '65, and where they were selected:

PLAYER	ROUND	PICK #	COMMENTS
Johnny Bench	2	36	Best catcher ever!
Larry Hisle	2	38	A solid OF, .273 BA 166 HRs
Andy Messersmith	3	58	130-99, 2.86 ERA for career
Graig Nettles	4	74	Perennial Gold Glove 3B, 390 HRs
Amos Otis	5	95	Gold Glove CF for Royals, 193 HRs
Sal Bando	6	119	Three- time World Series 3B
Nolan Ryan	12	295	Other than Bench, 293 worse picks
Gene Tenace	20	340	Three- time World Series C/1B

Considering that all Major League teams drafted 293 players *before* the Mets selected a hard throwing right-handed pitcher out of a Texas High School, I can't blame the Cubs alone for not drafting Nolan Ryan. Considering Johnny Bench and Ryan are two preeminent Hall of Famers, I am amazed they were in the same draft! Bench was the type of pick who completely altered the Reds' franchise, and it was demonstrated in their 1970s dominance.

The other players listed above were solid contributors throughout the 1970s and 1980s. All teams miss in the draft, but as future lists will prove, the Cubs tend to miss *a lot*. The Holtzman pick was the only worthy pick in '65, actually UN-Cubs-like in its goodness. (Did I mention they traded him?) Regrettably, the Cubs' draft of 1965 was not as worthless as some of their future drafts would prove to be, and they were one for thirty!

Let's just dream and imagine if the Cubs *had* selected Bench or Ryan. Can you picture a world where Johnny Bench breaks in with the Cubs' teams of the early 1970s? How about Nolan Ryan coming up with the 1969 Cubs as opposed to the '69 Mets? Wait, my imagination is not that good...it's too unrealistic. The Cubs *did* get Rick James in the **first draft ever** (our **Reason 28**); he just wasn't the funky one.

REASON 29

T HE 1966 AND 1967 DRAFTS: TWO COMPLETE WHIFFS

When I decided to include a chapter devoted to Cubs' draft failures, I realized I could not devote a *Reason* for *every* year of the draft. Other than being quite tedious for the reader, including all draft years individually would take up almost half of the 104 reasons. Therefore I will be condensing and combining many of the drafts. I begin this process by combining the Cubs' drafts of 1966 and 1967. It is a rather easy pairing...they are almost identical in their awfulness.

First let's look at **1966**, the second year of the MLB amateur draft:

- The Cubs' first pick pitcher Dean Burk (fifth overall) never even made it to the Major Leagues.

- In fact, NONE of their first thirteen picks made it to the Majors.

- Of the thirty-eight picks the Cubs selected, only three players (all pitchers) made it to the Major Leagues.

Three for bleeping thirty-eight…and three that just *made it* to the big leagues; here are the career numbers for the Cubs' entire 1966 draft:

PLAYER	GAMES	W	L	ERA
LHP Rich Nye	113	26	31	3.71
RHP Bill Stoneman	245	54	85	4.08
RHP Archie Reynolds	36	0	8	5.73

Thirty-eight picks and the players above are all the Cubs had to show for it? Surely the Cubs couldn't do worse the next year…could they?

Here are a couple of **1967** Cubs' draft facts:

- The Cubs had the second overall pick in the draft and used it on SS Terry Hughes. (What? You've never heard of him?)

- Hughes was one of only *three* players who made it to the Major Leagues from the Cubs' entire 1967 draft.

Amazingly the Cubs had only three players make it to the highest level… for the second straight year! In 1967 the Cubs had thirty picks, so their success rate (three for thirty) was actually *higher* than in 1966 (three for thirty-eight). However, the 1967 draftees were a bit more insignificant than the draft class of 1966…which is hard to believe.

PLAYER	GAMES	THEY'RE WORSE THAN THE '66 STATS
SS Terry Hughes	54	86 career at bats, 1 HR, .209 AVG
OF Jimmy McMath	6	14 at bats, 2 career hits (Yikes!)
RHP Gary Lance	1	2 IP, 1 ER, 2 hits, 2 walks and 1 loss

Looking at 1966 and 1967 in their totality:

- The Cubs had sixty-eight total draft picks in the June 1966-1967 drafts and only *six* players made it to the Major Leagues.

- Of those six, only Rich Nye and Bill Stoneman had careers that lasted more than one year.

The Cubs could have skipped these drafts entirely and the impact on the franchise would have been the same. Did the Cubs even scout the players they drafted? Were the Cubs intentionally *not* trying...just turning up their noses at the draft process? So it seems.

Let's examine if the Cubs missed out on any players that they could have drafted but chose differently. In order to save my favorite team some embarrassment, I've decided to be selective in choosing players from the 1966 and 1967 drafts:

PLAYER	YEAR	ROUND	CAREER COMMENTS
Steve Garvey	1966	3rd	Borderline HOF, .294 BA, 272 HRs
Dave Cash	1966	5th	Starting 2B for '71 W.S. Champ Pirates, .283 BA
Charlie Hough	1966	8th	216 career wins, 216 career losses
Ken Forsch	1966	9th	521 career games, 114-113 3.37
Bill Russell	1966	9th	Three-time All-Star, Dodger SS for 15 years
Jim Barr	1966	9th	101 career wins, 3.56 ERA
Jon Matlack	1967	1st	Lefty starter, 125 wins, 3.18 ERA
John Mayberry	1967	1st	Long time Royals' 1B/DH hit 255 HRs
Ted Simmons	1967	1st	248 HRs, a solid switch-hitting catcher
Bobby Grich	1967	1st	Power hitting 2B, 224 HRs
Vida Blue	1967	2nd	209 wins, lefty starter for three-time champ A's
Dave Kingman	1967	2nd	442 HRs, oft-traded slugger, eventual Cub
Jerry Reuss	1967	2nd	Solid lefty starter
Don Baylor	1967	2nd	Hit 338 HRs
Steve Yeager	1967	4th	Starting Dodger catcher for 3 World Series teams
Johnnie B. Baker	1967	26th	You know him as Dusty, .278 with 242 HRs

There were not any Hall of Famers drafted in 1966 or 1967, yet there were All-Stars, solid Major Leaguers, and eventual World Series' champions selected. Had the Cubs drafted one or two of these players, the next decade would have been altered dramatically. With sixty-eight chances, the Cubs should have gotten at least one significant player.

The Chicago Cubs received virtually nothing out of the 1966 and 1967 Major League amateur drafts and therefore merits **Reason 29**. Missing entirely for these two drafts cost them in future seasons. Regrettably, '66 and '67 were not isolated Cubs' draft performances…the years were the beginnings of a continuing trend.

REASON 30

THE 1968-1972 DRAFTS: 5 CUBS' DRAFTS VS. THE NATIONAL LEAGUE EAST

Unless you enjoy the sound of a broken record (which I realize is an analogy that may be lost on some of the younger set), you will be happy to hear that I will *not* examine *each* of the forty-seven MLB draft years. If I examined each year, the 1968 results are identical to '65-'67. For the reader's sanity we will take unique and different approaches in our analysis. The next five drafts, 1968-72, will be examined collectively and compared to the Cubs' competition at the time of the drafts.

From 1969-1992, the Cubs competed in the National League's Eastern Division. The National League was composed of twelve teams, with six in each division. The National League East was comprised of the Cubs, Philadelphia Phillies, Pittsburgh Pirates, Montreal Expos, New York Mets, and the St. Louis Cardinals. The Cubs were able to win this division only twice; 1984 and 1989.

I wanted to examine how the Cubs drafted in comparison to the teams in the "old" National League East. Perhaps the draft was new and difficult for **all** Major League teams during the initial years of selecting amateur players. Comparing the Cubs with their division mates' early drafting will indicate if the Cubs were poor at drafting, or close to the status quo.

In the five drafts from 1968-1972, the Cubs selected **169** total players. Of those 169 players, *three* contributed to the Cubs…*at all*. Rick Reuschel (drafted in 1970) was the staff ace for much of the decade. Dennis Lamp (1971 draft) and Ray Burris (1972 draft) were both part of the rotation at times during the mid-to-late 1970s. Both of their career numbers would be comparable to a fourth or fifth starter; Burris was 108-134 with a 4.17 ERA; Lamp went 96-96 with a 3.93 ERA. From 1968-1972, the Cubs accumulated one solid starting pitcher and two *somewhat* successful starting pitchers. Here are brief synopses of how the rest of the National League East drafted from 1968-1972:

St. Louis Cardinals

The Cardinals drafted two future members of their rotation in Bob Forsch ('68) and John Denny ('71). In 1971 the Cards also drafted starting OF Jerry Mumphrey and Keith Hernandez. (You young kids in your late thirties may only know him from his appearance on *Seinfeld!*)

Montreal Expos

In the 1968 draft, the expansion Expos were not allowed to pick at all in the *first three rounds!* For the proceeding rounds, the expansion teams selected at the bottom. (Wow…very *fair,* MLB owners.) The Expo drafts were awful until 1972 when they drafted (BOOM!) catcher Gary Carter (324 HRS) and Ellis Valentine. The late Carter (who died from a brain tumor in 2012) was a Hall of Fame catcher and perennial All-Star. Valentine was a staple in the Montreal outfield with a cannon of an arm during the late 70s. It was during the late 70s and early 80s when the Expos began passing the Cubs in the standings.

Pittsburgh Pirates

The Pirates '68 draft produced Bruce Kison who was a part of the rotation throughout the 1970s and went 13-7 with a 3.19 for the 1979 World Champions. Dave Parker was drafted by the Pirates in 1970. Parker was one of the most dominant players in the Major Leagues from the mid-70s to early 80s. Parker was also instrumental in the Pirates '79 World Series title. The Pirates made another great pick, John Candeleria ('72), who was the staff ace for most of the decade, winning 177 games in the Major Leagues.

New York Mets

The Mets' draft picks during this period illustrate how the Cubs finished ahead of them for most of the decade. Shortstop Tim Foli ('68), OF John Milner ('68) and pitcher Craig Swann ('72) were the only players the Mets had to show from the drafts from 1968-1972…and none of them were above-average MLB players. Coincidently (or not), the Mets finished last three times from 1977-80, losing ninety-five or more games each year.

Philadelphia Phillies

The Phillies had a stellar five-year drafting stretch, selecting power-hitting outfielder Greg Luzinski ('68, 307 HRs), starting catcher Bob Boone ('69), Hall of Famer and generally regarded "best third baseman ever" Mike Schmidt ('71), and starting pitcher Larry Christensen ('73). All four of these players contributed to the three straight division titles the Phillies won from 1976-78 and their World Series title in 1980.

What can we learn from the analysis of all of these teams from the five-year period? Three of the teams would win World Series titles in the ten years following these drafts: the '79 Pirates, '80 Phillies and '82 Cardinals. Consequently in comparing these drafts, *all three* are placed ahead of the Cubs. I would also give the Expos the nod over the Cubs, as Hall of Famer Carter (along with Valentine) led the Expos into eventual contention. The Cubs' five-year haul of Rick Reuschel, Dennis Lamp, and Ray Burris *does* trump the Mets' cumulative drafts from '68-'72. Hence, the Cubs finish fifth out of sixth in draft performance.

This data also demonstrates that even the good teams don't draft players of significance every year. Successful organizations have at least a few "*hits*" in the draft from year to year. Using the Phillies as a model, when they "hit" with Luzinski and unquestionably with Schmidt, they hit *big*. The Pirates did the same in drafting a star in Parker and two rotation pieces in Kison and Candeleria. The Expos hit it "big" with Carter, and the Cardinals connected with a batting champion in Hernandez. This research illustrates that *all* teams make picks that never amount to anything, yet the good teams consistently acquire valuable pieces. The Cubs missed more than they hit from 1968-1972, and their hits were minor compared to their competition.

From a selfish standpoint, I wish I would have been privy to this information long ago. The late 70s Cubs' teams were the first that I followed closely. I watched Dennis Lamp pitch as a rookie. I watched Rick Reuschel pitch numerous times. I also watched the other players listed above play in All-Star Games, win major awards and win World Series championships. Had I been privy to **Reason 30,** the rest of the NL East drafting better than my Cubs, I may have not wasted my time watching the predictable outcomes.

Nah…of course I would have watched, I am a Cubs' fan.

REASON 31

SCOT THOMPSON AND 1979

Scot Thompson was selected seventh overall in the 1974 MLB amateur draft by the Chicago Cubs. Four years later, Thompson debuted for the Cubs over the final nineteen games of the 1978 season and hit a robust .417 in thirty-six at bats. Thompson was positioned to get a shot with the Cubs in 1979, at the tender age of twenty-three. Cubs' fans of a certain age (i.e. *old*, at least forty-plus) may remember Thompson's performance in 1979. I recall it well, as this era was one of unbridled Cubs' bliss for me. I followed every game with great hope and enthusiasm. I was yet to have my psyche bashed into a blue Cubby mess.

Scot Thompson finished the season with a .289 batting average in 128 games, and finished third in the 1979 National League Rookie of the Year voting. Power eluded Thompson, as he only slugged at a .373 percentage. To demonstrate Thompson's lack of power quite simply: of his 100 hits, he had thirteen doubles, five triples and two home runs. Eighty percent of Thompson's hits were singles. Thompson also had a meager RBI total of twenty-nine for the entire 1979 season. As a corner outfielder, the hope was that Thompson's power would develop as he got older. Nevertheless, the Cubs and their fans (including me) felt Thompson had a bright future.

The 1980 season saw Thompson, perhaps feeling the pressure to hit with power, struggle mightily in 257 at bats. Thompson hit just .213 with two home runs and thirteen RBIs. The 1981 season was even worse for Thompson as he hit .165 in a mere 115 at bats. Thompson never got another shot with the Cubs and after brief stints with the Expos and Giants, was out of baseball by age twenty-nine. *If only Thompson had sustained the promise of 1979*, at least that's what I thought at the time. Cubs' fans are conditioned to think like this.

Upon further review, Thompson's performance in 1979 was not special *at all*. Here are players drafted *after* Thompson in 1974, and *their* 1979 performances:

PLAYER	1979 BETTER THAN SCOT THOMPSON'S PERFORMANCE
Bump Wills 2B	.273, 5 HRs, 46 RBIs, and 35 SBs for the Rangers
Gary Templeton SS	.314, 9 HRs, 62 RBIs, 26 SBs and *19 3Bs* for the Cards
Pete Vuckovich P	Cardinals' pitcher was 15-10 with a 3.59 ERA
Butch Wynegar C	Twins' catcher hit .270 with 7 HRs and 57 RBIs
Ed Whitson P	Padres' starter was 5-8 with a 3.56 ERA
Mike LaCoss P	14 wins, 8 losses and a 3.50 ERA for the Reds
Rich Dauer 2B	9 HRs, 61 RBIs, solid defender for AL Champ Orioles
Lance Parrish C	.276, 19 HRs, 65 RBIs, 6 SBs, dominant Tigers' catcher
Scott Sanderson P	9-8 with a 3.43 ERA in limited time with the Expos
Willie Wilson OF	.315, 6HRs, 49 RBIs and 89 SBs (Yes...*eighty-nine*!)
Rick Sutcliffe P	another future '84 Cub! 17-10, 3.46, ROY for Dodgers

Nothing personal against Mr. Thompson, but look at the production of *these* players! Where to begin? The solid pitchers listed above? How about the wealth of players with huge stolen base totals? Perhaps you noticed players at atypical offensive positions (middle infield) who had superior power numbers than Scot Thompson? Each player above contributed more to his respective club in 1979. The year 1979 aside, these players would go on to have Major League careers more significant than Scot Thompson.

I couldn't do what Scot Thompson did for the Cubs in 1979. Perhaps that's one of the reasons why I was impressed at the time. A more likely **reason** is that as a Cubs' fan, I am so starved for success I find it wherever I can...even when it's not there.

***Scot Thompson, if you are out there and have read this, I apologize. You were one of my favorite players; in fact imitating your swing and Bill Buckners' enabled me to switch hit. I am truly sorry. This book is meant to be an indictment of the Cubs, not you. However, you are still **Reason 31**.*

REASON 32

THE 1975 AND 1976 DRAFTS: WAR—WHAT IS IT GOOD FOR?

Many of us *older* types were raised on simple baseball statistics: batting average, home runs, runs batted in and errors. These were the statistics I focused on when I was a kid. In my little brain, I set under .250 as being a "bad" batting average. I felt .280 was "good" and obviously .300 was "really good." I had no idea how many walks a player had, and I really didn't care. Coaches always say, "A walk is as good as a hit," but it's certainly not as sexy.

Twenty-five years later, most teams place a higher value on OBP (on-base percentage) than batting average. Like anything different, some people are frightened by these statistical changes. Many "old school" baseball fans are skeptical of "new" statistics. The recent focus on OBP is one example of how baseball talent evaluators look for new metrics to measure a player's value.

One of the most popular new baseball metrics is **WAR**, **W**ins **A**bove **R**eplacement player. WAR measures how many wins a player would add to his team as opposed to the average AAA player. Typically, all starters should be a two or better. A player that has a four or five WAR is seen as All-Star quality, while eight or more usually merits a player MVP conversation. For a Cubs' example, Ryne Sandberg's WAR was 8.4 when he won the MVP in 1984. In contrast, if a player has a negative WAR, he should be replaced.

Why am I introducing WAR into our Cubs' analysis? For a new and fresh approach to illustrate poor Cubs' drafts! This will offer us a unique way to examine the cumulative 1975 and 1976 Cubs' drafts. Using WAR might quantify differences in abilities more...and bore the reader less.

The Chicago Cubs selected a total of fifty-nine players in the 1975 and 1976 drafts, of which only one had a positive career WAR: Lee Smith with 27.6. Smith was a very nice closer for the Cubs and was the all-time saves leader in Major League Baseball for a period. Using Smith, I will give an example of how WAR represents an accurate depiction of a player's value. Here are the WAR numbers from Cubs' closers from 1987-89:

1987: Lee Smith 2.7

1988: Rich Gossage -.02

1989: Mitch Williams 2.4

In 1987 Lee Smith was *pretty good*, almost three wins better than average. The Cubs traded him and replaced him with Rich Gossage. (He didn't deserve the "Goose" at this point.) In 1988 Rich Gossage was *horrible*, evidenced by his *negative* WAR. This forced the Cubs to make a trade the following winter for Mitch Williams. Williams' WAR demonstrates that in 1989, he was a comparable relief pitcher to Smith.

Back to the Cubs' drafts of 1975 and 1976…Lee Smith was a good pick, but here are other players drafted in '75-'76 and their *career* WAR numbers:

PLAYER	POS	TEAM	CAREER WAR
Alan Trammell	SS	Tigers	67.1
Lou Whitaker	2B	Tigers	71.4
Jack Morris	P	Tigers	39.3
Jason Thompson	1B	Tigers	22.1
Rickey Henderson	OF	A's	106.8
Wade Boggs	3B	Red Sox	88.3
Bruce Hurst	P	Red Sox	31.7
Andre Dawson	OF	Expos	60.6
Carney Lansford	3B	Angels	37.4

Wow. Is it any wonder the Tigers were perennial contenders throughout the '80s and won a title in 1984? On this list of nine players, there are three Hall of Famers, and three (Whitaker, Trammel, and Morris) who were outstanding players…*borderline* Hall of Famers. Every team on this list made the play-offs with one of these players on its roster.

Lee Smith was a good closer for the Cubs and pitched on one play-off team in 1984. Conversely, for the Cubs to *only* have Smith to show for these two particular drafts foretold their lack of success in later years. As we did previously with Johnny Bench and Nolan Ryan…*imagine*:

- Alan Trammell playing with Ryne Sandberg
- Jack Morris in the Cubs' 1984 rotation
- Wade Boggs batting third for the Chicago Cubs
- Rickey Henderson batting lead-off and stealing over 100 bases for the Cubs in the early 1980s

It's really hard for me to imagine *any* of these scenarios…but just one would have made the Cubs an entirely different team. The career WAR numbers of these players reflect their team's success…and how much they contributed. Any of these players would have enhanced the Chicago Cubs' probabilities of making a World Series.

…and the Chicago Cubs missing on these great players in the 1975 and 1976 Major League Baseball amateur drafts is **Reason 32.**

REASON 33

THE 1977-1980 DRAFTS: I DON'T EVEN NEED TO USE STATS

We have established that the Cubs' draft history is pretty pathetic. I have also recognized that coming up with creative and interesting ways to compare and contrast shameful drafts has become a challenge. Let's try this…I am *not even going to use stats*! I am not going to use old stats or new for **Reason 33.** I am going to examine four consecutive drafts, 1977-1980, just using name recognition. The only players drafted by the Chicago Cubs during these four years of any significance are outfielder Mel Hall and pitcher Craig Lefferts. Hall was packaged with Joe Carter in the Rick Sutcliffe trade and had moderate success as a Major Leaguer. Lefferts went on to have an effective career as a reliever for the Padres and Giants. Therefore from 1977-1980 (four complete drafts!), the Cubs drafted *two* players that you *may* have heard of…Mel Hall and Craig Lefferts! Listed below are other players selected from 1977-1980; they just weren't selected by the Cubs.

Players Who Everyone Has Heard Of

Hall of Famer Cal Ripken, Hall of Famer Ryne Sandberg, Hall of Famer Ozzie Smith, Hall of Famer Paul Molitor, may *still become* a Hall of Famer Tim Raines, Yankee Great Don Mattingly, and the most dominant pitcher of the late 1980s Orel Hershiser.

Players Who Baseball Fans Have Heard Of

All-Star and World Series winning "ace" pitchers Bob Welch, Jimmy Key, Frank Viola, and Dave Stieb...as well as All-Stars and solid contributing hitters Harold Baines, Eric Davis, Mookie Wilson, and Chilli Davis.

Players Who 'Old' Baseball Fans Have Heard Of

Rick Aguilera (closer), Jesse Barfield (cannon arm from RF), Steve Bedrosian (closer), Kent Hrbek (two-time World Series winner for Twins), Kevin McReynolds (power hitting OF), Glenn Davis (lots of power...even in Astrodome), Bud Black (solid lefty starter), Brett Butler (lead-off hitter), Tom Brunansky (power hitting OF, another Twin World Series champ), Rob Deer (lots of homers, lots of whiffs), Mike Witt (solid starter), Von Hayes (Phillies traded five guys for him), Doug Drabek (one of best starters of the 80s and early 90s), Terry Steinbach (A's catcher, won World Series), Darren Daulton (power hitting lefty catcher), and Bill Doran (switch-hitting lead-off 2B).

Players Who "Old" Baseball Geeks Have Heard Of

Dave Henderson, Tony Phillips, Eric Show, Alvin Davis, Dave Dravecky, Charlie Leibrandt, Johnny Ray, Bill Gullickson, and Mike Boddicker.

Go back and look at the first list of players again...**HOLY CRAP!** Ripken, Ozzie, Molitor, Ryno, Mattingly, Hershiser, and Raines...all just waiting to be drafted!

The players listed above had far superior careers than the entire '77-'80 Cubs' draft classes. There are All-Stars, four Hall-Of-Famers, and numerous World Series champions. Various teams acquired multiple players on this list, positioning them for 80s success. In the 1980s, Cubs' fans would have gladly taken *any* of these players on the Chicago Cubs.

With such a strong group of Major League regulars selected during this period, it's inconceivable how the Cubs could not draft *any* significant players. The Cubs eventually were able to land a Hall of Famer from these drafts when Dallas Green acquired Ryne Sandberg in 1982. (Green also accounts for a "break" in the Cubs dreadful drafting.) The 1977-1980 drafts were regrettably poor, almost indescribably dreadful. The most accurate way to describe the drafts of 1977-1980 is **Reason 33** as to why the Chicago Cubs have not won a World Series for 104 years.

REASON 34

THE 1988-1998 DRAFTS: ONE BAD ALL-CUBS' DRAFT TEAM

Let me introduce you to a team that I have developed. It is not a *real* team; this *new* Cubs' team only exists on paper. If it were a real team, it would struggle to win games. This team has an ace, and two *reasonably* successful outfielders. The players selected for this team were all Cubs' draft picks from 1988-1998. One caveat; they had to *play* for the Cubs. Jon Garland and Kyle Lohse, selected by the Cubs during this time, are *not* included on this team. Even if we included Garland and Lohse, this team would struggle to win games. So henceforth, here is the batting order, starting rotation and bullpen for the **1988-1998 All-Cubs' Draft Team!** The player's best statistical year is listed, with "best" used rather loosely this case.

BATTING ORDER	POSITION	FINEST MLB SEASON
1. Doug Glanville	CF	.300 4 HR, 35 RBIs and 19 SBs
2. Chad Meyers	2B	.232 with 4 HRs in 142 at bats
3. Corey Patterson	RF	.266, 24 HRs, 72 RBIs and 32 SBs
4. Brant Brown	1B	.291 14 HRs, 48 RBIs
5. Ozzie Timmons	LF	8 HRs, 23 RBIs in 171 at bats
6. Kevin Orie	3B	.275, 8 HRs, 44 RBIs
7. Mike Hubbard	C	64 ABs, 1 HR, 2 RBIs, .203 AVG
8. Jason Smith	SS	0-1 as a Cub, did hit .212 for his career
9. Kerry Wood	P	14-11 3.20 266 Ks in 211 IP

REST OF ROTATION

Steve Trachsel—13-9, 3.03
Lance Dickson—three starts 0-3 with a 7.24
Dave Schwartzbaugh—0-2 6.38 in five career starts
Kyle Farnsworth—could be used as a starter since he started
   prior to relieving...but that's probably *not* a good idea.
   (Look up his stats as a starter.)

There are just a *few* holes in the batting order. (Where is the icon on this keyboard to denote sarcasm?) This is the finest homegrown lineup of players the Cubs' drafted over a ten-year period. A rather pathetic assortment, don't you agree?

This team will need a Kerry Woods' twenty strikeout performance every time he pitches. Of the position players, only Patterson and Glanville had prolonged Major League careers, primarily as fourth outfielders. The Cubs did produce some decent relief pitchers during this time in Farnsworth, Will Ohman, Michael Wuertz, and Terry Adams, which is pretty insignificant if you aren't able to develop any other positions. Now let's summarize this ten-year fiasco:

- There were two quality starting pitchers taken over this period, one who was phenomenal, yet usually hurt.
- Two solid fourth outfielders
- Three decent RH relief pitchers and one lefty reliever
- A shortstop prospect in Jason Smith that could be included in the Fred McGriff trade
- Brant Brown, without whom we would not have Ron Santo's famous "Oh No!" call when Brown dropped a key fly ball during the 1998 wild card race.
- Just a boat load of really bad picks...look at the position players we had to settle for in our fake lineup...pathetic!

This constructed Cubs' lineup may be an imaginary team, but the faux squad makes a very good point. The gaps in this fake lineup were *real* gaps that the *non-pretend* Cubs would have to fill. Thus, the Cubs consistently had to spend money or use other resources to fill these spots, unable to fill them from within.

Ten years of drafts should at least supply a team with more than just a couple pitchers and position "fillers." When teams endure stretches of picks this terrible, it causes long stretches of losing seasons. These ten years definitely helped the Cubs' title-less streak extend into the twenty-first century, and into the millennium's second decade. This fictional All-Bad Draft team deserves to be included as **Reason 34**. Now...let us *never* speak again of this team! (At least until we have the 2008-2018 draft team to compare it to!)

REASON 35

Ty Griffin vs. Robin Ventura

In 1981 the Cubs hired Dallas Green away from the Philadelphia Phillies to be their general manager and executive vice president. Mr. Green came in with his "Building a New Tradition" slogan and brought many of his top people from Philadelphia. Coincidently (or not), with Green's people in scouting and development, the Cubs' drafts from 1981-1987 were pretty good. They were better than the first sixteen years of previous Cubs' drafts...**combined**. There *were* some busts (Drew Hall, Vance Lovelace), but consider the players drafted between 81-87: Joe Carter, Shawon Dunston, Greg Maddux, Jamie Moyer, Joe Girardi, Rafael Palmeiro, Mark Grace and many key contributors like Dwight Smith, Jerome Walton and Damon Berryhill.

Green departed the Cubs in 1987, and coincidently (*or not*) the poor drafts resumed. In 1988 the Chicago Cubs selected Georgia Tech 2B Ty Griffin with the ninth overall pick. Just *one* pick later, the Chicago White Sox selected Robin Ventura from Oklahoma State. The selection of Ty Griffin over Robin Ventura warrants its own discussion. Bad drafting has long been a Cubs' habit, but in **Reason 35** we will look at this one *really* bad choice. Let's first compare the two players by using some statistics.

CATEGORY	ROBIN VENTURA	TY GRIFFIN
Batting average above .280	6 times	1 time...in the minor leagues
Seasons over 20 HRs	9 times	Never...not even in minors
90 RBIs or more	8 times	Nope
MLB All-Star games	4 times	Take a wild guess
Gold Glove winner	6 times	Never made it to majors

I could include more categories, but I would be just piling on Mr. Griffin. Ty Griffin was a terrible pick compared to the guy taken just *one* pick after him. Griffin only made it as far as AA, where he never hit above .237. Ventura finished his Major League career with 294 HRs, a .267 AVG and was a solid defender throughout his sixteen years.

How much different might the Cubs' fortunes have been in the 1990s with Ventura in the lineup? How different would the Cubs' infield have been with Ventura and Grace at the corners? (Yikes! Two lefties in the same Cubs' lineup?!) Ventura, known as an impeccable clubhouse leader, could have been a positive influence on the North Side. Ventura's foray into managing in 2012 proved to be successful and further cemented his image as a solid baseball man. In any organization you never have enough quality people; the 90s Cubs could have used Robin Ventura. The Cubs' fortunes in the 90s could have been radically different with Robin Ventura playing third base at Wrigley Field.

A blunder such as taking Ty Griffin over Robin Ventura, **Reason 35**, is an example of why the Cubs are *the Cubs*. Ty Griffin did not make it to Wrigley Field as a player. Perhaps he visited, but he played as many games there as you and I. Dreadful decisions like these can doom a franchise and can extend historical losing streaks...*for longer than a century!*

REASON 36

T HE **1999** D RAFT:
K ARMA?

In 1999 people (not me) were fretting about the upcoming Y2K. That would be the year 2000 if you have forgotten. As the year progressed, many went as far as buying survival packs and stocking up on bottled water. (You know what I always wonder in these end of the world scenarios? What about time zones? Will the Eastern part of the United States die first?) For Cubs' fans, the end of the century brought a certain amount of doom as well. The team would finish the twentieth century without the elusive World Series, prompting many "Any team can have a bad century" jokes.

In April of 1999, college baseball may have seen its darkest moment. Wichita State pitcher Ben Christensen hit Evansville lead-off hitter Anthony Molina in the face with a thrown baseball...while Molina was warming up. As the story goes, Molina was twenty-four feet away from Christensen, attempting to "time" Christensen's warm-up pitches. Baseball is full of unwritten rules and codes, and Evansville pitching coach Brent Kemnitz viewed Molina's actions as a violation. Christensen hit Molina with a warm-up pitch, square in Molina's left eye, permanently altering his vision. Christensen and his pitching coach were suspended for the season; Anthony Molina's baseball career ended that day.

Christensen, a power right-hander who was 21-1 during the college season, saw his draft status slide following the incident. Many Major League teams wanted nothing to do with Christensen and the media scrutiny that would follow such a selection. Christensen fell to twenty-sixth in the first round of the 1999 draft where he was taken by…the Chicago Cubs.

The pick was not without controversy. Many baseball pundits slammed the Cubs for taking Christensen. Christensen and his supporters maintained that the severe beaning was an accident and Christensen was just trying to throw *near* Molina. Despite all of the controversy, the Cubs saw the upside of getting a top talent at a spot lower than what his abilities should have dictated. The Cubs drafted Christensen and gave him a million dollar signing bonus. (Although never confirmed, it is rumored that Molina received a $400,000 settlement from Christensen.)

All the baggage aside, Christensen was now one of the Cubs' top pitching prospects. In an impressive debut season in 2000, Christensen went 7-3 with 105 strikeouts in 106 innings with a 2.36 ERA between A and AA. Ben Christensen was even ranked as high as the thirty-seventh best prospect in all of Major League Baseball after his initial minor league season. This is when Molina and his supporters would believe the baseball gods stepped in. Beginning in 2001, Christensen suffered a litany of elbow and shoulder injuries and was released by the Cubs just three years later. The once-dominating prospect was now another Cubs' wash-out.

Players drafted within the next two rounds in 1999 included Brian Roberts, Carl Crawford, John Lackey and Justin Morneau. In hindsight it is easy to state that the Cubs should have avoided all of the headaches Christensen brought. Then the Cubs may have ended up with one of the four players listed above. (The Cubs apparently tried to acquire Roberts via trade.)

Were Christensen's injuries fate? Was it karma or the baseball gods? Perhaps neither…it's probably just another example of an unfortunate decision and an illustration of the Cubs' consistent failures. It's also **Reason 36** among our 104.

CHAPTER 4

REASON 37—LOU BROCK
Yep. I bet you have heard about this trade before, but was it really that bad?

REASON 38—MOE DRABOWSKY
The former Cubs' starting pitcher became one of the first closer-type relief pitchers...
for two World Series Champions.

REASON 39—BRUCE SUTTER
The Hall of Fame closer dominated for the Cubs in the late 1970s
before winning a World Series in 1982 with the...Cardinals.

REASON 40—KEN HOLTZMAN
Young dominant left-handed starter...
perfect for a World Series staff...
like that of the '72-'74 Oakland A's.

REASON 41—BILL MADLOCK
Who needs twenty-five-year-old two-time batting champions playing 3B?

REASON 42—FRED NORMAN (KEN HOLTZMAN PART 2)
Not as GOOD as Holtzman, yet good enough to win
two World Series titles with the Reds.

REASON 43—WILLIE HERNANDEZ
The 1984 MVP and Cy Young winner for the
World Series winning Detroit Tigers...
was once on the same Cubs' staff as Sutter.

REASON 44—BILL NORTH
He was fast, he could play center field and he helped
the Oakland A's win two of their World Series titles.

REASON 45—MANNY TRILLO
He was a Gold Glove-winning All-Star second baseman
for the 1980 World Series Champions…the Philadelphia Phillies.

REASON 46—JOE CARTER
I will never second-guess trading him for Rick Sutcliffe;
yet it's still fun to look at "what might have been."

REASON 47—DENNIS ECKERSLEY
Hmmm. Hall of Fame closer? Check. Ex-Cub? Check.
World Series championship upon leaving the Cubs? Take a guess.

REASON 48—JAMIE MOYER
Moyer became a very solid starting pitcher in his thirties and forties…
the Cubs traded him in his early twenties.

REASON 48—JON GARLAND
He developed into a very solid starting pitcher for a
Chicago World Series champion…just not the Cubs.

REASON 50—JOE GIRARDI
With the New York Yankees all he seemed to do was win…
World Series titles.

REASON 51—LUIS GONZALEZ
Yes, he played in an era when all of the numbers were inflated…
but his were REALLY inflated…and could have helped the Cubs.

REASON 52—GREG MADDUX (AAAAAAAAAAHHHHH!)
Perhaps the greatest pitcher of all time…
and he came up with the Cubs.

ONES THAT GOT AWAY

I wonder how many times during my life I have heard mention of the infamous Lou Brock for Ernie Broglio trade. I am guessing the number would be in the thousands. Lou Brock turned into an outstanding player upon leaving the Cubs, and he will be featured in this chapter. Brock had a Hall of Fame career for the St. Louis Cardinals. Yet, Brock for Broglio looked like a fair deal at the time... but obviously did not turn out that way. I also wonder why I rarely hear someone mention the Cubs' fleecing of the Phillies for Ryne Sandberg or the thievery of Sammy Sosa for George Bell from the White Sox. Brock for Broglio has stuck as the Cubs' albatross of a deal for almost fifty years. As the cliché goes, "hindsight is 20/20", and *hindsight* says Brock for Broglio *was* a horrendous move.

In CHAPTER 3, I assessed Cubs' draft history and identified specific examples that contributed to the historic lack of Cubs' success. As I analyzed the drafts, I attempted not to focus on *one* bad choice. I tried to focus on sustained *periods* of bad choices that were rational reasons. This process also involved *hindsight*, which will be prevalent in CHAPTER 4 as well.

In CHAPTER 4 we will be looking at players who succeeded after leaving the Cubs via trade, free agency, or outright release. The focus will be on the player's post Cubs' career...*not* the trade. In CHAPTER 8: MANAGING...GENERALLY AND BAD, I will be examining transaction histories of certain Cubs' general managers. In *that* chapter I will second-guess deals...not in this chapter.

I am not going to question these deals (yet), or compare what was given for what was received. I am just going to explore the careers of these players after they left the Cubs. Thus, their future successes as All-Stars, MVPs, Hall of Famers and World Series Champions will be counted among the 104 reasons. Is that second-guessing? Perhaps...but here is a bit of foreshadowing to help explain:

*In June of 1984, the Cubs traded a package of players including OF prospect Joe Carter to the Cleveland Indians for Rick Sutcliffe. Over the last twenty-eight years I have **never** second-guessed the trade. Sutcliffe was part of the 1984 and 1989 division* *title teams for the Cubs while Carter hit a walk-off home run for the Toronto Blue Jays to win the 1993 World Series. This deal was a win-win for both teams.*

Sutcliffe for Carter was a good deal for both teams, but in this chapter I am still going to examine what might have happened had Carter stayed a Cub. I am going to ask the reader to think along the lines of the *Back to The Future* film series. Had these players' successful careers been with the Cubs, would the team's World Series chances increased? I will do this by using my CAFPR rating system.

CAFPR (Cubs' Alternate Future Past Rating) will assign a value to the possibility of the Cubs winning a World Series had the player remained a Cub. There is no exact formula; these ratings are my speculation based on odds... with 100 percent meaning I would guarantee a World Series title had the player remained a Cub. (SPOILER ALERT...there will NOT be any 100 percents.) CAFPR numbers are highly debatable, and hopefully they will cause you and your friends to argue about them. If you don't have any friends (who own the book...not friends), take this as a sign to encourage someone to go out and buy it.

Since I was a young kid, trades have been one of my favorite parts about following baseball, and later I will be addressing the decisions made in particular deals. However in CHAPTER 4: ONES THAT GOT AWAY, just sit back and imagine that these *ex-Cubs* remained *Cubs*. Would Cubs' history be different? Precisely, would the Cubs have won a World Series with these players?

My contentious CAFPR percentages will enlighten you on what could have been.

REASON 37

L OU BROCK
June 15, 1964: Traded by the Chicago Cubs with Jack Spring and Paul Toth to the St. Louis Cardinals for Ernie Broglio, Doug Clemens, and Bobby Shantz.

WORLD SERIES CHAMPIONSHIPS
Two (1964 and 1968)

PENNANTS
Three (1964,1967, and 1968)

POST-CUB CAREER ACCOMPLISHMENTS
Lou Brock is a Hall of Famer with 3,000 career hits. Brock led the National League in stolen bases eight times, stealing *118* in 1974! Brock ended his career with 938 stolen bases, which ranks second all time. Brock was a six-time National League All-Star.

OVERALL CAREER IMPACT
Lou Brock was hitting .251 after fifty-two games with the Chicago Cubs in 1964. Upon being traded to the St. Louis Cardinals, Brock exploded. Brock hit .348, with twelve home runs and thirty-three stolen bases over the last 103 games. Brock's effect was prodigious enough to help the Cardinals win the 1964 World Series title. The Cardinals most likely would *not* have won the '64 series (or even the pennant) without Brock.

The Cards were in the series again in 1967 and 1968, led by pitcher Bob Gibson. Lou Brock finished in the top ten in MVP voting in both '67 and '68. The Cardinals never appeared in the post-season again with Lou Brock, yet he continued to put together successful seasons before retiring in 1979.

CAFPR—60
With Brock, the '69 Cubs may have held off the Mets and captured the Eastern Division Title. The 1969 lineup with Brock at the top of the order may have been good enough for the Cubs to run away with the '69 division title. The 1970 Cubs would have had a better chance of making the play-offs as well.

The rest of the '70s is difficult to project in a *Cubs with Lou Brock* CAFPR. The Cubs were contenders in the early part of the decade, but rarely competitive for the second half of the 1970s. Having a lead-off hitter like Lou Brock might have made the Cubs contenders on a yearly basis.

More justification for Brock's high CAFPR number is the sheer fact that the Cubs traded him to the *Cardinals*. The Cubs assisted in making their greatest rival considerably stronger for fifteen seasons! How would the Cubs have fared against St. Louis in regular season matchups had Brock been with them, instead of against them?

Brock's 60 CAFPR is high, and justifiably so. In my opinion, the Cubs would have had a slightly better than 50 percent chance of a World Series title with Lou Brock. My CAFPR ratings are highly debatable and are based on *my* projections. I hope this book sparks debates like, "How good might the Cubs have been had Lou Brock stayed?" The departure of Lou Brock prohibited the Cubs from consistent contention. I have confidence that the trade of Lou Brock prevented the Chicago Cubs from winning a World Series title.

This Hall of Famer who "got away" is worthy of **Reason 37**.

REASON 38

MOE DRABOWSKY
March 31, 1961: Traded by the Chicago Cubs with Seth Morehead to the Milwaukee Braves for Daryl Robertson and Andre Rodgers.

WORLD SERIES CHAMPIONSHIPS
Two (1966 and 1970)

PENNANTS
Two (1966 and 1970)

POST-CUB CAREER ACCOMPLISHMENTS
Moe Drabowsky was a two-time World Series champion with the Baltimore Orioles. He set a World Series' record as a reliever with eleven strikeouts in one game, including six in a row.

OVERALL CAREER IMPACT
Moe Drabowsky was a hard-throwing starter for the Cubs in the late 1950s. Drabowsky began to struggle for the Cubs as he appeared to lose

his fastball. Upon being traded, Drabowsky was converted into a reliever and had a tremendous season for the Orioles in 1966. In Drabowsky's first season as a reliever, he went 6-0, with a 2.81 ERA and ninety-eight strikeouts in ninety-six innings. Drabowsky was dominant in '66, including his Game 1 performance in the World Series. Drabowsky entered the game in the third inning and proceeded to strike out eleven, allow only one hit and two walks. Drabowsky allowed no earned runs and picked up the win for the Os. The next three games would be shut outs as the Os swept the Dodgers in four.

Drabowsky was still pitching relief in 1970 when the Orioles won their *second* World Series in four years. Drabowsky was pitching as a "closer" before the position had been developed. Starting pitchers were expected to finish the games in the 1960s and early 1970s; thus Draboswky's save totals (12, 11) do not compare to the modern era.

CAFPR—25

The 1969 Cubs needed an arm like Moe Drabowsky pitching out of the bullpen. The Cubs did not just fade in 1969, the Mets played remarkably. The Mets' triumph was aided by their superior pitching…particularly *relief* pitching. Moe Drabowsky would have allotted the Cubs one more quality arm to match the Mets. The CAFPR requires some imagination on the part of the reader. The CAFPR is projecting a historic change with many different derivatives and outcomes. (Once again, *Back to the Future* fans rejoice!) Therefore, a potential Drabowsky influence on the 1970 Cubs (when the Cubs finished five games back) needs to be considered. Drabowsky's direct impact on either of these two Cubs' teams would have given the Cubs a 25 percent enhanced chance of winning a World Series title in my CAFPR.

Moe Drabowsky (**Reason 38**) was considered a bit of a free spirit, whose jokes and pranks were legendary among his teammates. It is not a joke that Drabowsky won **two** World Series titles on the Baltimore Orioles. That's **two** more World Series titles than the Chicago Cubs have had since 1908.

REASON 39

BRUCE **S**UTTER
December 9, 1980: Traded along with Ty Waller to the St. Louis Cardinals for 3B Ken Reitz and OF/1B Leon Durham.

WORLD SERIES CHAMPIONSHIPS
One (1982)

PENNANTS
One (1982)

POST-CUB CAREER ACCOMPLISHMENTS

Bruce Sutter is a Hall of Famer and led the National League in saves three times. Sutter finished in the top five in the voting for the 1982 Cy Young *and* MVP. Sutter had two saves and a win in the 1982 World Series for the St. Louis Cardinals. Sutter tied the record for most saves in a season with forty-five in 1984 and had two more All-Star appearances in his post-Cubs' career.

OVERALL CAREER IMPACT

Bruce Sutter was the most dominant reliever in the game for three of his six post-Cubs' seasons. Sutter's career ended after his shoulder and elbow gave out from throwing his wicked split-fingered fastball (and one heckuva lot of innings!). Sutter's influence on the Cardinals winning the 1982 World Series is indisputable. Sutter had a win and two saves against the Brewers; Sutter pitched scoreless eighth and ninth innings of Game 7, and his 1982 World Series performance was worthy of MVP consideration.

Sutter's inning totals over such a short period are astounding. He threw over eighty innings in ten different seasons, exceeding *one-hundred innings pitched* five times! Consider that Mariano Rivera, whom some may feel is the *greatest* reliever of all time, has only thrown more than eighty innings once in his entire career. By modern day standards, Sutter was throwing a year and a half each season he pitched.

CAFPR—50

If everything would have broken right (using CAFPR projections), Sutter would have made one *hell of an impact!* Assuming Dallas Green constructs the 1984 Cubs in virtually the same manner, Sutter in the bullpen vaults the Cubs over the Padres in the 1984 NLCS. That year would have most likely been the only year that Sutter could have made a difference since he was out of the game by 1989.

Sutter's impact on a *CAFPR 1984* cannot be questioned. If Sutter was a Cub in '84, Lee Smith is then used as a set-up man. Can you imagine Smith and Sutter in the same bullpen? I believe that CAFPR combo gives the Cubs a 50 percent better chance of a World Series title. Does Steve Garvey hit a game winning home run off of Bruce Sutter instead of Lee Smith? Perhaps the Cubs would have pushed more to *sign* Steve Garvey if they did not acquire Durham for Sutter? The CAFPR of Bruce Sutter offers many possibilities; consequently, the probability of the Cubs winning a championship *with* Sutter rather than *without* him is vastly greater.

Bruce Sutter **(Reason 39)** was the most dominating reliever to pitch for the Chicago Cubs…unfortunately, Sutter never had a chance to pitch when it mattered most.

REASON 40

K EN HOLTZMAN
November 28, 1971: Traded Ken Holtzman to the Oakland Athletics for outfielder Rick Monday. (Monday was my *first* favorite Cubs' player…so I can't complain *too* much about this one.)

WORLD SERIES CHAMPIONSHIPS
Three (1972-1974)

PENNANTS
Three (1972-1974)

POST-CUB CAREER ACCOMPLISHMENTS

Ken Holtzman had two American League All-Star appearances with the A's. Holtzman was a twenty-game winner for the A's in 1973. Holtzman earned at least one win in **all three** straight World Series victories for the Oakland A's from 1972-1974.

OVERALL CAREER IMPACT

Upon arriving in Oakland, Ken Holtzman rattled off four straight seasons with at least eighteen victories: **1972** 19-11 2.51, **1973** 21-13 2.97, **1974** 19-17 3.07, **1975** 18-14 3.14. Those numbers are pretty, pretty good for a left-handed starter.

Beginning in 1972, the Oakland A's made the play-offs in four consecutive seasons. Oakland won the World Series from '72-'74. In 1975, they were dethroned in the American League play-offs by the Boston Red Sox.

Holtzman earned **two** victories against the Mets in the 1973 World Series and won a game each year against the Reds and Dodgers in '72 and '74. Holtzman was the A's number two starter behind Vida Blue. When A's owner Charles Finley decided he didn't want to pay his players anymore, he sent Holtzman and Reggie Jackson to the Orioles.

Holtzman then went to the New York Yankees before returning to the Cubs in late 1978. Holtzman was done pitching in the Major Leagues by 1979.

CAFPR—30

A left-handed twenty-game winner would give *any* team a better chance to win. Consequently, Holtzman could have at least helped the Cubs in '72 and '73. In 1972 the Cubs finished second to the Pirates, and in '73 they ended the season only five games behind the Mets (although in fifth place). Ken Holtzman may have made a significant difference in '72 or '73. The Cubs dealt Holtzman after he turned twenty-five, thus his 1972-74 seasons occurred in his baseball "prime"…which he demonstrated with the A's.

Unlike Lou Brock, Moe Drabowsky, and Bruce Sutter, Holtzman was able to win multiple championship rings in his post-Cubs' career. Ken Holtzman won three World Series rings with the Oakland A's. If I ever write a book about the Oakland A's (not going to happen), I can ponder if the A's would have won those titles without Holtzman.

Ken Holtzman (**Reason 40**) was an outstanding left-handed starting pitcher for the Oakland A's. There is not a single team in the history of Major League Baseball that could not have benefited from having Ken Holtzman (circa 1972-74) on their team. The Cubs **rarely** (I can't emphasize the "rare" enough) have a pitcher like '72-'74 Holtzman...*left-handed or right-handed.* The Cubs may have not had a World Series team in 1972-74...but I like their chances much better with Holtzman on the staff.

REASON 41

B ILL MADLOCK
February 11, 1977: Traded by the Chicago Cubs with Rob Sperring to the San Francisco Giants for Andy Muhlstock (minors), Bobby Murcer, and Steve Ontiveros.

WORLD SERIES CHAMPIONSHIPS
One (1979)

PENNANTS
One (1979)

POST-CUB CAREER ACCOMPLISHMENTS
Bill Madlock won *four* batting titles; two with the Cubs and two with the Pittsburgh Pirates. Madlock collected a World Series ring with the Pirates in 1979 and played in the post-season with the Dodgers and Tigers. Bill Madlock made two All-Star appearances after his stint with the Cubs, and hit .305 for his career.

OVERALL CAREER IMPACT
The point of CHAPTER 4 is not to second-guess these moves. Consequently, I am not debating if it was smart for the Chicago Cubs to trade a twenty-five-year-old two-time batting champion that played third base (...gulp).

This chapter is to analyze if Madlock may have helped the Cubs win a World Series had he remained. Madlock was a driving force for the Pirates in their '79 World Series run after being acquired from the Giants on June 28. Madlock hit .298 overall (.328 for the Pirates) and hit fourteen home runs and knocked in eighty-five runs. Bill Madlock also stole thirty-two bases in 1979. Madlock was a factor in the 1979 World Series as he hit .375 over the seven games. While he was never a candidate for a Gold Glove, he managed to play third base in the National League until 1987.

In his only season with the Detroit Tigers, Madlock again helped a team into the post-season, splitting time between 1B and DH.

CAFPR—25

I score Madlock a CAFPR 25 because the Cubs were not close to winning in the late '70s. Had Madlock been on the team in a CAFPR 1984, his batting average would have been an upgrade over Ron Cey. The 1984 Cubs were primarily a power team, and Madlock would have been the best "average" hitter on the team.

I can't accurately state that any of the *Ones That Got Away* would have destined the Cubs to win a World Series…however, all five of our *Ones That Got Away* netted a World Series upon leaving the Cubs. CAFPRs must consider the *cumulative* effects of what *could* have been. What if Madlock was on the 1977 Cubs' team when Bruce Sutter broke out? How might have a late 70s Cubs' team with Lou Brock leading off and Madlock batting third looked? There are many variables, but a constant does remain: These players won titles with other teams, while the Cubs remain without a ring.

Bill Madlock (**Reason 41**) was a former batting champion who hit an impressive .305 over his *entire* Major League career. Madlock played a position in third base that has been a Cubs' black hole for most of the Cubs' post-Santo history. If Madlock had remained a career Cub, he would have assisted the Cubs in their quest for success. Madlock may actually have been able to assist the Cubs in winning a World Series title…*like he did with the Pirates*.

REASON 42

Fred Norman:
(Ken Holtzman Part 2)

April 26, 1967: Traded by the Chicago Cubs to the Los Angeles Dodgers for Dick Calmus.

WORLD SERIES CHAMPIONSHIPS
Two (1975 and 1976)

PENNANTS
Two (1975 and 1976)

POST-CUB CAREER ACCOMPLISHMENTS

Fred Norman was a member of the rotation for the back-to-back World Series Champion Cincinnati Reds in 1975 and 1976. Fred Norman won 104 Major League games, none of them as a member of the Cubs.

OVERALL CAREER IMPACT

Upon joining the Reds, Norman began a solid seven-year stretch as a member of the starting rotation from 1973 through 1979. Norman did benefit from one of the best lineups in Major League history...the "Big Red Machine." As a kid, I specifically remember asking my dad how the Reds' team (Johnny Bench, Pete Rose, Tony Perez, Joe Morgan, George Foster, Ken Griffey, and Dave Concepcion) was fair. Pitching for the Reds may have been an advantage for Norman, yet he did average twelve wins a season with an ERA never above 3.70. Fred Norman was a sufficient pitcher for one of baseball's greatest teams for seven seasons.

CAFPR—20

From 1972-1976, five World Series champions in a row (A's and Reds) featured a former Cubs' pitcher in a prominent rotation role. Ken Holtzman and Fred Norman were *left-handed* starters on World Championship teams. Did the Cubs have an organizational philosophy to get rid of promising young lefties?

In this CAFPR, Cubs' fans may have seen Holtzman and Norman as two solid lefties for the Cubs. With four-man rotations still the norm in the 1970s, two of the four Cubs' starters would have been lefties. With the emergence of Rick Rueschel by the middle of the decade, the Cubs' rotation could have been formidable. Instead those two holes in the Cubs' rotation were filled by numerous pitchers; none of whom ever won World Series rings.

As with all of our CAFPR projections, I cannot guarantee that Fred Norman would have succeeded with the Chicago Cubs. Irrespective of any kind of assurance, I can question why the Cubs did not see the potential in keeping Fred Norman. Left-handed pitching has forever been a scarce baseball resource. Apparently, the Chicago Cubs in the late 1960s and early 1970s did not value that resource appropriately.

Simply keeping Fred Norman (**Reason 42**) would not have won the Cubs a World Series title. Yet Norman is another example of a player who was a valuable piece to another team's success. The CAFPR for Norman is based on the alternative…that the Cubs decided to keep some of these players. Fred Norman and Holtzman both won World Series titles in the same era…an era when the Cubs were giving away "valuable pieces."

REASON 43

WILLIE HERNANDEZ
May 22, 1983: Traded Willie Hernandez to the Philadelphia Phillies for Dick Ruthven and Bill Johnson.

WORLD SERIES CHAMPIONSHIPS
One (1984)

PENNANTS
Two (1983 and 1984)

POST-CUB CAREER ACCOMPLISHMENTS

Willie Hernandez won the 1984 Cy Young **and** the 1984 MVP in the American League. He was an American League All-Star from 1984-86. Hernandez's astounding 1984 season helped the Detroit Tigers become World Series Champions.

OVERALL CAREER IMPACT

Willie Hernandez accomplished the rare feat of winning *both* the Cy Young and MVP awards in the 1984 season. He pitched an amazing *140* innings, had a 9-3 record and saved thirty-two games. Hernandez also had a sparkling 1.92 ERA in 1984. Hernandez saved two of the four victories in the 1984 World Series.

Like Sutter, Hernandez was probably a victim of throwing a lot of innings, and was out of the game by 1989. He did help Detroit into the 1987 ALCS, making his third post-season appearance.

CAFPR—50

Once again, Cubs' CAFPRs create numerous factors and variables to contemplate. If you just plop Willie Hernandez on the 1984 Cubs, he would have made an *enormous* difference. A dominant lefty to bring in against Tony Gwynn and the Padres may alter the results of the 1984 NLCS.

Imagine if the Cubs had *both* Sutter and Hernandez in the '84 season. This left/right combo would have given the Cubs the most dominant bullpen in all of baseball. Ponder that Lee Smith could have been part of that bullpen as well. Would you rather have Smith, Sutter and Hernandez or Smith, Warren Brusstar, George Frazier, and Tim Stoddard? Detroit is not waiting for the Cubs in the 1984 World Series without Willie Hernandez.

It's difficult to fathom Sutter, Hernandez and Smith all in the same Cubs' bullpen. Hernandez was one year removed from the Cubs when he was embarking on his MVP and Cy Young season. Removing Sutter out of the CAFPR would still have left the Cubs with Hernandez *and* Smith…a formidable duo capable of revising Cubs' history.

Willie Hernandez (**Reason 43**) is yet another ex-Cub who obtained a World Series ring upon leaving Chicago. After seven *Ones That Got Away* our total of post-Cubs' World Series titles stands at twelve...with all seven winning at least one.

I may see a pattern developing.

REASON 44

BILL NORTH
November 21, 1972: Traded Bill North to the Oakland Athletics for pitcher Bob Locker.

WORLD SERIES CHAMPIONSHIPS
Two (1972-1973)

PENNANTS
Three (1972-1973, 1978)

POST-CUB CAREER ACCOMPLISHMENTS
Bill North led the American League in stolen bases twice and won two World Series titles with the Oakland Athletics.

OVERALL CAREER IMPACT
Bill North is probably not a name most Cubs' fans would expect to see on this list, yet helping the A's ascend to *two* World Series qualifies him. North batted lead-off for most of the '73 season for the A's. A badly sprained ankle forced him to miss the last twenty games and the play-offs. He did manage to swipe fifty-three bases before the injury, and hit .285 with an on base percentage of .376. North may have missed the fall classic, but he was a big part of Oakland making the play-offs in 1973.

In the '74 season, North's average dropped to .260, yet he maintained a .347 OBP. North stole fifty-four bases in '74 as they won their third straight title. Bill North's career ended after brief stints with the Giants and the Dodgers in the late 1970s. North did appear in the '78 series for the Dodgers. North's forte was helping teams *get* to the series, for once he got there, North...*struggled.* In fifty-nine World Series at bats Bill North could only muster three hits...a minuscule .051 average. North did at least *get* there, and he has the rings to prove it.

CAFPR—15

It's rather doubtful Bill North by himself helps the Chicago Cubs win a World Series; hence his low CAFPR. Nonetheless, I wonder why a team that historically has lacked speed was willing to deal it in an era when speed was so coveted. North twice led all outfielders in total chances, meaning he covered a lot of ground. In Wrigley's relatively small outfield, North may have been a Gold Glove center fielder. ***Foreshadowing/Spoiler Alert*** In CHAPTER 9 we will look at the Cubs' historic lack of Gold Glove outfielders and how correlative Gold Glove outfielders are to winning. (*More hints and spoilers...* the Cubs rarely have outfielders such as these.)

Bill North (**Reason 44**) is definitely the most insignificant of the players we have included so far in our *Ones That Got Away* chapter. North does add two more titles to the total won by this particular group of *ex*-Cubs. North is also the second player so far to win said titles with the Oakland A's. The A's saw value in North and Ken Holtzman that the Cubs apparently did not.

Fast center fielders and good starting left-handers must have been *plentiful* in the Cubs' system in the early 1970s.

REASON 45

MANNY TRILLO
February 23, 1979: Traded by the Chicago Cubs with Greg Gross and Dave Rader to the Philadelphia Phillies for Henry Mack (minors), Derek Botelho, Barry Foote, Jerry Martin, and Ted Sizemore.

WORLD SERIES CHAMPIONSHIPS
One (1980)

PENNANTS
Two (1980 and 1983)

POST-CUB CAREER ACCOMPLISHMENTS
Manny Trillo won three Gold Gloves, made three All-Star appearances and won two Silver Slugger awards. Trillo won a World Series title with the Philadelphia Phillies in 1980.

OVERALL CAREER IMPACT
When playing for the Cubs, Manny Trillo did this little thing where he would field a grounder, quickly glance down and appear to read the ball, and then sling it over to first. My little buddies and I mimicked this many times in the backyard. Naively, when Trillo was traded to the Phillies in 1979, I assumed he wasn't a good player anymore. My little ten-year-old brain presumed the Cubs would only deal a player if they felt the trade would help them win. The Trillo deal may have had *something* to do with the fact that in his last year with the Cubs he was making $50,000 and just *two* years later in Philadelphia he was making $375,000. Manny was about to get costly, and the Cubs *knew it*. *(Another spoiler alert...*I will later examine the Cubs' *uncanny* ability to deal players right *before* they became expensive!)

In Manny Trillo's post-Cubs' years he played in three All-Star games, won three Gold Gloves and two Silver Slugger awards. Manny won a World Series Championship with the Phillies. (Wow...when I started writing this chapter, I knew there would be several post-Cubs' titles...but this is outrageous!)

After his stint in Philadelphia, Trillo played for the Indians, Expos and Giants before (as they all seem to do rejoining) the Cubs. This is a strange phenomenon with many ex-Cubs...reappearing with the club to show off their championship rings they won playing elsewhere.

CAFPR—20
The odds of Trillo himself being the difference in bringing a World Series title to the North Side seem remote. His CAFPR rating is based strictly on the idea that he could have been an integral part in tandem with other CAFPR

events occurring. The nucleus of the 1977 team including Trillo, Bruce Sutter and Willie Hernandez may have had great success had they stayed together as Cubs. Manny might not have won the Cubs a World Series, but permitting a player like Trillo to leave makes for another compelling reason why they haven't.

Manny Trillo (**Reason 45**) *does* have a championship ring from the 1980 Philadelphia Phillies, something every Cubs' second baseman since 1908 has not been able to attain while playing for the Cubs.

REASON 46

JOE CARTER
June 13, 1984: Traded by the Chicago Cubs with Darryl Banks (minors), Mel Hall and Don Schulze to the Cleveland Indians for George Frazier, Ron Hassey, and Rick Sutcliffe.

WORLD SERIES CHAMPIONSHIPS
Two (1992-1993)

PENNANTS
Two (1992-1993)

POST-CUB CAREER ACCOMPLISHMENTS
Joe Carter was a five-time American League All-Star. Carter had twelve seasons of *at least* twenty home runs and ten seasons of *at least* 100 RBIs. Carter had six 20-20 seasons (HRs and SBs). Carter hit a walk-off World Series winning home run for Toronto and hit 396 career home runs.

OVERALL CAREER IMPACT
Joe Carter, quite simply, is one of the greatest players the Cubs' system has produced. The pure power and speed numbers are something Cubs' fans typically do not see in their homegrown players. Remember, I am not second-guessing the trade of Carter, just looking at a hypothetical situation in which he stays with the Cubs.

Joe Carter was an enormous reason the Blue Jays won back-to-back titles in 1992 and 1993. In hitting the '93 walk-off, Carter joined Bill Mazerowski as the only players in Major League history to accomplish the feat.

Carter was briefly the Cubs' color commentator in 2001-2002, during which time he asked former Bear's QB Jim McMahon if he had spoken recently with former (and deceased) NFL commissioner Pete Rozelle. Oops.

CAFPR—50

This takes some serious Cubs' *Back to the Future* CAFPR imagination, but Carter winning a title with/for the Cubs is at least a 50/50 proposition. Dallas Green's success with the Cubs (full disclosure…I am a fan of Green's Cubs' resume) wasn't supposed to happen quite as fast as it did. Green and his team were doing great things with the farm system, yet the Cubs found themselves in the unlikely position of contending in 1984. The Sutcliffe for Carter trade *had* to be made. Imagine (CAFPR-style) if Carter had remained a Cub and subsequent drafts remained the same. Ryne Sandberg and Carter would have played together with each player in his "prime." Add Mark Grace, Rafael Palmeiro, Jamie Moyer, and Greg Maddux and the Cubs' have a phenomenal late 1980s nucleus…capable of winning a World Series. This type of speculation (imagine a 2-3-4-5 of Sandberg, Grace, Carter, and Palmeiro) would require many CAFPR events to occur simultaneously:

- Dallas Green remains with the Cubs, not resigning in 1987.

- Green does not trade Palmeiro and Moyer as Jim Frey did.

- Green would make alternative subsequent moves to bolster the alternative Cubs.

Okay, okay…I realize I am messing with that whole "space-time continuum" thing from *Back to the Future*. There are many "ifs" and "buts" that I am making assumptions on, yet I stick to my premise that Joe Carter gives the Cubs a 50 percent chance of winning a World Series.

Back to reality, and Joe Carter (**Reason 46**) is just another ex-Cub that won a World Series. Actually…make that *two* World Series' Joe Carter won.

REASON 47

D ENNIS ECKERSLEY
April 3, 1987: Traded by the Chicago Cubs with Dan Rohn to the Oakland Athletics for Brian Guinn (*WHO?*), Dave Wilder *(WHAT?)*, and Mark Leonette (*WHERE?*).

WORLD SERIES CHAMPIONSHIPS
One (1989)

PENNANTS
Three (1988-1990)

POST-CUB CAREER ACCOMPLISHMENTS
Dennis Eckersley is a member of the Hall of Fame. Eckersley won the American League MVP *and* Cy Young in 1992 for the Oakland Athletics. He was a four-time All-Star and had eight seasons of at least thirty saves…and Eckersley won the 1989 World Series with the Oakland A's.

OVERALL CAREER IMPACT
The Cubs were justified in trading Eckersley in 1986, in regards to where his career was at the time. Nonetheless, it's still fun to speculate. With Eckersley winning the Cy Young *and* MVP in 1992, it places him in the unique company of…Willie Hernandez. Do you think any other team has traded away *two* players who went on to accomplish such a rare feat?

Eckersley was one of the most dominant closers the game has ever seen. Eckersley's accomplishments as a closer came after making the transition from starter to reliever at age thirty-two. He helped lead the A's to three straight

World Series appearances, 1988-1990. (What is it with the Cubs historically helping the A's? Holtzman, North, Eck?) Tony LaRussa's specialized use of Dennis Eckersley altered the way bullpens would be constructed over the next twenty-plus years.

How about these numbers "Eck" posted:

- 51 saves in 1992

- 0.61 ERA in 1989

- Seven walks over 130 innings in 1989-90 (Seven walks! That's two Carlos Marmol innings.)

- 114 appearances with allowing only those seven walks

- *Averaged* forty saves or more from 1988-1992

Dennis Eckersley is a Hall of Famer who wore numerous caps throughout his career, including the Cubs…it's just not the one he's wearing on his plaque.

CAFPR—20

Eckersley is another tough one to predict, one that requires imagination. There are so many CAFPR variables. Would Eckersley have become a closer for the Cubs? If he had and the 1989 Cubs remain constant, "Eck" makes a gigantic difference. Place *closer* Dennis Eckersley on a Cubs' team with Greg Maddux, Andre Dawson, Ryne Sandberg, and Mark Grace…and the early 1990s look pretty good.

Unfortunately, Dennis Eckersley (**Reason 47**) did leave the Cubs in 1986. Like many players*** before him, Dennis Eckersley won his World Series ring while playing for a team other than the Cubs.

***Every flipping player we have examined so far!

REASON 48

JAMIE MOYER

December 5, 1988: Traded by the Chicago Cubs with Drew Hall and Rafael Palmeiro to the Texas Rangers for Luis Benitez (minors), Pablo Delgado (minors), Paul Kilgus, Curt Wilkerson, Mitch Williams, and Steve Wilson.

WORLD SERIES CHAMPIONSHIPS
One (2008)

PENNANTS
One (2008)

POST-CUB CAREER ACCOMPLISHMENTS

Jamie Moyer has 269 career wins (twenty-eight with the Cubs). As a forty year old, Moyer went 21-7 and was an All-Star in 2000 with the Seattle Mariners. Moyer has three top ten finishes in Cy Young voting...*after* age thirty-seven. Moyer won a World Series with the Phillies at age forty-five after going 16-7 during the regular season.

OVERALL CAREER IMPACT

As of this writing, Jamie Moyer has yet to officially retire and is still attempting to pitch in the majors. He went 2-5 for the Rockies in early 2012, before being released at age *forty-nine.* Moyer's baseball numbers have long defied age. Two hundred twelve of his 269 career victories have come after he turned thirty-three years old. If Moyer had more success and fewer injuries in his twenties and early thirties, he would have been a lock for 300 wins and the Hall of Fame. Regardless of his early career struggles, consider:

- Jamie Moyer won twenty-one wins at age forty.

- Moyer averaged fourteen wins a season at ages forty-four, forty-five, and forty-six.

- From the age thirty-three to forty-six, Moyer had double-digit wins in thirteen of fourteen seasons...a streak that ended as he went 9-9 at age forty-seven.

Is Jamie Moyer a Hall of Famer? Regrettably many Hall of Fame voters, including former players (I am looking at you, Mr. Anti-Ryno Joe Morgan!), can be a bit snobbish and unpredictable. Remember the fact that **no one** has been elected unanimously. Not *one* player voted unanimously, not Babe Ruth, Hank Aaron, Ted Williams, Nolan Ryan...*NO* one! But without reaching the magic number of 300 wins, I doubt Moyer has much of a chance.

Moyer will have to settle for the "Hall of Very Good," or the "Hall of Unbelievable Forty-Year-Old Achievements." Regardless of the Hall, Jamie Moyer had an astonishing Major League career.

CAFPR—25

Once again, I am going CAFPR *Back to the Future* style on this one. Jamie Moyer came up with the Cubs at the same time as **Greg Maddux**. Many of us Cubs' fans (old enough to remember) were elated to have *two* promising young starters. They were looked at as equals by some, and Moyer showed quicker promise.

Therefore, many Cubs' fans foresaw a future with these two pitchers as co-anchors of the Cubs' staff. Could the Cubs have had a similar combination of starters as Maddux had with Atlanta? The idea of Maddux and Moyer as career Cubs seems like a lovely alternative to the reality that took place: *both of these pitchers winning the majority of their games with other clubs.*

It took him until he was forty-five, but Jamie Moyer (**Reason 48**) won his World Series ring. Moyer is the epitome of perseverance, with an incredible "never quit" attitude. Qualities such as these have a positive effect on an organization of any kind, and they are attributes our beloved Cubs have not demonstrated much of in the last 104 years.

Jamie Moyer as a "career Cub" could have made a difference.

REASON 49

JON GARLAND

July 29, 1998: Traded to the Chicago White Sox for relief pitcher Matt Karchner.

WORLD SERIES CHAMPIONSHIPS
One (2005…yuck)

PENNANTS
One (2005)

POST-CUB CAREER ACCOMPLISHMENTS
Jon Garland made one All-Star appearance and had an excellent 2005 season to assist a *certain* team in winning the World Series in 2005. Garland has 132 career wins and a career ERA of 4.32.

OVERALL CAREER IMPACT
On the surface, Jon Garland's career stats show an average pitcher who had one outstanding season (18-10, 3.50 ERA). Garland had seven straight seasons in which he logged over 190 innings. The term "innings eater" may be overused in today's Major Leagues, yet pitchers like Garland are treasured for the innings they absorb. Garland was a major factor in the first White Sox championship since 1917.

As I grew up and matured (you know, in my early forties), I tried to avoid being a "White Sox-Hater." I liken the condition to a recovering alcoholic trying to avoid a drink. I avoid Hawk Harrelson at all costs, as he is an automatic trigger to *White-Sox Hater* regression. I try to observe the Sox as a baseball fan, and not just automatically dislike them. Nevertheless, for them to win that 2005 title… *that was tough.* I do find it funny how Sox fans act superior because of 2005, to which I say, "*Yes, you are so much better; it only took you eighty-eight years, and it would have been eighty-six had your team not thrown the World Series and almost ruined baseball!*" Sorry…I regressed a little there. I did say "*try* to avoid."

CAFPR—20

The current state of the Cubs has made the 2000s seem like ancient history, but the Cubs did have *three* play-off appearances during the decade. Jon Garland as a Cub would have added depth to a staff that was constantly hit with injuries. Garland may not have altered the 2003 NLCS, but his innings would have assisted the Cubs tremendously in 2004. Had Garland been part of the rotation in 2004, the Cubs probably would have made the play-offs… consequently giving the team a World Series chance in a CAFPR 2004. The 2005 Cubs, a team that was ravaged by pitching injuries, would have benefited greatly from Garland.

Jon Garland (**Reason 49**) would have given the Cubs a solid starter capable of pitching 200 innings every year…a commodity *every* Major League team needs. Perhaps had the Cubs kept Garland, the White Sox would still be suffering through their own World Series drought. The idea of White Sox followers equally distressed as Cubs' fans actually sounds quite appealing.

Sorry, I regressed a bit again.

REASON 50

JOE GIRARDI
November 17, 1992: Drafted by the Colorado Rockies from the Chicago Cubs as the nineteenth pick in the 1992 expansion draft.

WORLD SERIES CHAMPIONSHIPS
Three (1996, 1998, 1999)

PENNANTS
Three (1996, 1998, 1999)

POST-CUB CAREER ACCOMPLISHMENTS
Joe Girardi didn't win any Gold Gloves but was a solid defensive catcher for *three* World Champion New York Yankees' teams. In his post-playing career, Girardi has another World Series ring as manager of the Yankees.

OVERALL CAREER IMPACT

I will admit that something about Joe Girardi's haircut makes me uneasy. I guess it's that militaristic sort of look. Regardless of my silly insecurities, Girardi proved to be a valuable part of three World Series Championship teams.

Joe Girardi never hit .300, and he only hit above .280 twice. Girardi never hit ten home runs in a season, and never drove in sixty RBIs. Yet with all of these perceived negatives, the Yankees' teams he was a part of won.

I am not a Yankees' fan. In fact, I could give you numerous reasons why the New Yorkers have had a competitive advantage for much of their history. (Those reasons would be *money, money,* and more *money.*) Nonetheless, I will tell you what the Yankees have historically *rarely* been…*stupid.* Therefore, if Girardi was not beneficial to the team, or not a significant reason for their success, he would have been *gone.* Was Girardi statistically the best player on the team? No…not even close, but he brought *something* to the table that the Yankees valued.

Joe Girardi did finish up his career playing for the Cubs, and actually represented them in the 2000 All-Star game.

CAFPR—25

I used to argue with one of my Cubs' friends about Joe Girardi, and I was always taking the negative position. (I'm telling you…it's *that* haircut.) My inclusion of Girardi in this chapter is an obvious indication of my evolved position on the value of Joe Girardi as a baseball player.

Had Girardi stayed with the Cubs throughout the 1990s (instead of collecting championships with the Yankees), would he have made a difference? Girardi is another CAFPR where I will take a collective approach…including other players. Had the Cubs kept Joe Girardi *with* Greg Maddux and Jamie Moyer, an argument can be formed with the Cubs as a 1990s perennial contender. Maddux, Moyer, and Girardi would have given the Cubs three of the best baseball minds in the game. Perhaps Girardi's handling of the pitching staff would have made a substantial difference, as it did for the Yankees. Joe Girardi proved to be a winner with the Yankees, and with the right subsequent moves, Girardi may have contributed to a Cubs' title.

A secondary part of the CAFPR of Joe Girardi (**Reason 50**): Might he be managing the Cubs today had he been a career Cub? I cannot answer that for certain, but Girardi is a knowledgeable and solid baseball person who could have helped the Cubs' organization in many different ways.

A team that is still searching for a championship after 104 years should acquire as many players like Girardi as possible...*not* get rid of them.

REASON 51

L UIS GONZALEZ
December 19, 1996: Signed as a free agent with the Houston Astros.

WORLD SERIES CHAMPIONSHIPS
One (2001)

PENNANTS
One (2001)

POST-CUB CAREER ACCOMPLISHMENTS
Luis Gonzalez was a five-time All-Star after departing the Cubs. Gonzalez hit twenty-plus homers seven times after exiting the Cubs. In 1999, Gonzalez led the National League in hits with 206. Two seasons later in 2001, Luis Gonzalez hit 57 HRs, 142 RBIs, and had a .325 batting average. Gonzalez won a World Series title in 2001 with the Arizona Diamondbacks.

OVERALL CAREER IMPACT
From the 1990s until the mid-2000s, baseball's offensive numbers are a bit... *skewed?* Consider 2001, when Gonzalez hit 57 home runs, had 142 RBIs and batted .325...he did *not* lead the league in *any* of those categories! Gonzalez was *third* in the National League in homers beyond Barry Bonds (73) and Sammy Sosa (64). Yes...offensive numbers were *freakish* for about a ten-year stretch, and the Cubs benefited from that as much as any team. (I am looking at you, Sammy!) Consequently, we will treat Gonzo's numbers as any other player...in any era.

After never hitting more than fifteen homers in a season, Luis Gonzalez hit 23, 26, 31, 57, 28, 26, 17, and 24 over the next eight years. Gonzalez was an on-base machine posting an OBP of over .400 four times. Luis Gonzalez's OPS numbers were through the roof, with an astounding 1.117 in 2001. Gonzalez was simply one of the best left-handed hitters in the Major Leagues during this period.

CAFPR— 20

Just by our usual CAFPR assumptions, the Cubs would have had a lethal combination with both Sosa *and* Gonzalez. Assuming that Gonzalez's production remains constant, the Cubs would have had the *near* equivalent of a Maris/Mantle or Ruth/Gehrig type of duo over a four-year period. The early 2000s teams with Kerry Wood and Mark Prior at the top of the rotation would have had a 1-2 punch offensively to match. Considering that Sosa/Gonzalez in the same lineup provides marvelous protection…it's easy to project improvement throughout the lineup. Gonzalez played left field; perhaps in the '03 NLCS, Gonzalez makes a catch in Game 6 of a *certain* pop foul down the left field line. (I kid, I kid!) The potential effect that Luis Gonzalez could have had on a contending Cubs' lineup merits a CAFPR of twenty…regardless of if he would have made that catch. (Sorry…no more about *that*.)

I can't blame the Cubs for not predicting that Luis Gonzalez (**Reason 51**) would change from *below average power-hitter* to one of the most prestigious in the Majors. As a Cub, Gonzalez did not show anything close to the power he would eventually possess. These CAFPR ratings are not to ask *why* the player left, they are strictly to ponder what might have been. I can safely say that adding Luis Gonzalez to the Cubs' lineup from 2001 to 2003 would have greatly enhanced the team's chances at a World Series title.

No pun intended in using the term "enhanced."

REASON 52

Greg Maddux (Aaaaaaaaaahhhh!!!!)

December 19, 2002: Signed as a free agent with the Atlanta Braves.

WORLD SERIES CHAMPIONSHIPS
One (1995)

PENNANTS
Three (1995, 1996, 1999)

POST-CUB CAREER ACCOMPLISHMENTS
Would you be offended if I just labeled Greg Maddux the best pitcher ever and left it at that? Greg Maddux won three straight Cy Young Awards, after the one he achieved with the Cubs. (That gave him *four* straight, in case you were wondering.) Maddux won ten Gold Gloves, appeared in six All-Star games, and led the National League in innings pitched five straight seasons. Greg Maddux won four National League ERA titles. He had an amazing record of **19-2** with a **1.63** in 1995. Maddux has 355 wins (222 of the non-Cubs' variety). I could continue with more amazing Greg Maddux facts, but I think I will stop there.

OVERALL CAREER IMPACT
When looking at Greg Maddux's amazing career, it should be noted he pitched during the *greatest offensive explosion* in baseball history...commonly referred to as the "steroid" era. Looking over his career numbers, it is difficult to describe in words just *how* extraordinary his statistics are. So instead of just rattling off numbers, I am going to compare Maddux to one of the pitchers many people (not me) consider to be one of the most dominant of all time:

NOLAN RYAN VS. GREG MADDUX

CATEGORY	RYAN	MADDUX	EDGE
Seasons	27	23	Ryan
Wins	324	355	Maddux
Losses	292	227	Maddux
Winning %	.536	.610	Maddux
No-Hitters	7	0	Ryan
Shut Outs	61	35	Ryan
Career ERA	3.19	3.16	Maddux
Cy Young Awards	0	4	Maddux
Strikeouts	5,714	3,371	Ryan
Walks	2,795 (cough)	999	Maddux
15 Win Seasons	7	18	Maddux
Career SO/BB Ratio	2.04	3.37	Maddux
Led League in Wins	0	3	Maddux
Led League in ERA	2	4	Maddux
Career Hits per 9	6.6	8.5	Ryan
Career Ks per 9	9.5	6.1	Ryan
Walks per 9	4.7	1.8	Maddux
Hits + Walks per 9	10.8	10.3	Maddux
Career WAR	77.4	99.4	Maddux
Career ERA+	112	132	Maddux

The last two are "new" types of statistics; ERA-plus means the *league ERA divided by the player's ERA*. WAR, you may recall from CHAPTER 2, is *Wins Above Replacement player*. In twenty categories, you basically come to this conclusion: Nolan Ryan pitched longer, was better at striking people out, and had more no-hitters than Greg Maddux. By most *other* metrics, Maddux wins...and wins *big*. Why did I choose Nolan Ryan? For the sole purpose of pissing people off in Texas...*seriously*, because Ryan is often a Hall of Famer mentioned when discussions occur about the greatest pitchers of all time.

CAFPR—50

Greg Maddux leaving the Cubs was my personal "1969." I turned away from the Cubs for a couple of years and paid little attention. Imagine (I shudder to even utter this) if Michael Jordan had left the Bulls in his prime? (I guess he kind of did…but he came right back.)

Now critics may argue that Maddux won only one World Series title with the Braves…and they were loaded! How can I attest that the Cubs would have won a World Series with him?

Well…I can't.

I *can* say the Cubs would have had an extremely better chance; hence, Maddux's CAFPR of 50. Any team would have had an improved opportunity of winning a World Series if they added *one of the best pitchers of all time…in his prime!* That's what Maddux was when he was allowed to leave! (I need to calm down.) After the departure of Maddux, the Cubs struggled for over a decade to replace him…*because you can't replace the best bleeping pitcher in the game!*

Okay. I am calm now.

When Greg Maddux (**Reason 52**) came back to the Cubs in 2004, it took the sting away a bit. The 2004 return just wasn't the same as if Maddux had remained a career Cub. It's like comparing the Beatles 1996 "reunion" to a Beatles get-together taking place with John Lennon alive. Greg Maddux as a lifelong Cub could have altered the path of the franchise in numerous positive directions.

Career Cub Greg Maddux would have also meant a much greater chance of a Chicago Cubs' World Series title.

CHAPTER SUMMARY

Regrettably, there are other examples of successful ex-Cubs who could have appeared in **CHAPTER 4: ONES THAT GOT AWAY**. Rafael Palmeiro and Lee Smith are two players the Cubs…*maybe…should have…probably…*kept! Instead, I decided to limit the number of players to sixteen for a couple of reasons (not *just* because of my OCD):

The first reason is pretty simple, sixteen players just *sounds* better than seventeen, or eighteen. (Yes…OCD) Next, as I continued to work on this chapter, I concluded it would be more interesting (and more damning to the Cubs) to *only* include players that won World Series titles after departing the Cubs.

Listed below are the cumulative numbers of World Series titles won by the ex-Cubs featured in this chapter.

EX-CUBS' NUMBER OF WORLD SERIES RINGS (ASSUMING THEY WERE NEVER PAWNED)

Ken Holtzman	3
Joe Girardi	3
Fred Norman	2
Bill North	2
Lou Brock	2
Moe Drabowsky	2
Joe Carter	2
Greg Maddux	1
Bruce Sutter	1
Willie Hernandez	1
Manny Trillo	1
Jamie Moyer	1
Jon Garland	1
Dennis Eckersley	1
Bill Madlock	1
Luis Gonzalez	1

Total: *twenty-five* championships, including *twenty-three* different teams. Wow. When looking at the totals I can't shake the feeling that the Cubs are a very *generous* team. The Cubs helped twenty-three other teams win World Series titles…how nice of them! My semi-sarcasm aside, I realize that the sixteen players in this chapter were not all solely responsible for winning World Series titles. I would argue that they all *contributed*, and they could have been *contributing* to Cubs' success.

Of the sixteen players included in CHAPTER 4, there are three Hall of Famers (Brock, Eckersley, and Sutter) and soon to be a fourth (Maddux), there are All-Stars, batting champions, multiple-MVPs, and Cy Young award winners. *All* accomplished by these players upon leaving the Chicago Cubs. Can I state with certainty that any of these players would have guaranteed a World Series title?

No.

Can I say with confidence that these sixteen players would have given the Cubs a better chance at a World Series?

Yes.

Can I declare that these sixteen players are sixteen more reasons for the 104 year drought?

Absolutely.

CHAPTER 5

REASON 53—THE ENTIRE STARTING LINEUP OF THE 1930 CARDINALS
Every starter hit .300 or better…
no, I am not kidding.

REASON 54—MEL OTT
The New York Giants of the 1930s had one dominant hitter…
Mel Ott.

REASON 55—CARL HUBBELL
The New York Giants of the 1930s had one dominant pitcher…
Carl Hubbell.

REASON 56—DOCK ELLIS
Throwing no-hitters under the influence of LSD was one of his talents…
dominating the Cubs was another.

REASON 57—MIKE SCHMIDT
Project his numbers at Wrigley Field over a career
and he would have hit 1,000 home runs.

REASON 58—WILLIE STARGELL
With "Pops" playing first base,
the Pirates won two World Series titles in the 1970s.

REASON 59—STEVE CARLTON
The most dominant left-handed starter of his era…
can you guess what team he had his most career wins against?

REASON 60—THE ENTIRE NATIONAL LEAGUE:
(SPECIFICALLY THE NL EAST) 1975-82 AND 1986
From 1979 to 1986 FOUR of the six teams in the National League East
won a World Series Championship...just not the Cubs.

REASON 61—DWIGHT "DOC" GOODEN
Wait until you see his career numbers against the Cubs...
it will make you wish they selected him in 1982 instead of Shawon Dunston.
(Wait...you ALREADY wished that?)

REASON 62—TONY LARUSSA
He may get under Cubs' fans' skin, but you have to tip your cap to the guy...
but I don't have to like his glasses.

REASON 63—DAVE DUNCAN
Mr. LaRussa's right-hand man...
Duncan even turned former Cubs' cast-offs into successful starters.

REASON 64—ALBERT PUJOLS
Before bolting to St. Louis for a mega-contract,
he made Wrigley his personal playground.

SPECIAL OPS

It was quite a struggle for me to come up with a title for CHAPTER 5. I knew I wanted a section dealing with opposing players who "blocked" the Cubs from success. One problem, *ALL* opposing players the Cubs have ever lost to would fall into this poorly titled category. After many really lame ideas of a CHAPTER 5 title, I settled on a *mildly* lame title: SPECIAL OPS.

The OP stands for *opposing players*. For a player to be considered one of the 104 reasons, he had to meet "special" criteria; referring to how that player directly impacted the Cubs' ability to win, make the play-offs, or (chuckle, chuckle) make it to the World Series. The aforementioned criteria will be met in one of two ways: **1)** the player made outstanding contributions to a team that finished ahead of the Cubs or **2)** the player's performance against the Cubs was so prodigious, it impacted the Cubs' success over a period of years. There are players that will meet *both* criteria, yet here is a hypothetical situation to further explain the *first* criteria.

Pretend that there was an *alternative* 2012. (Stay with me here.) In the faux-2012, the Cubs were locked in a battle for the last play-off spot with the Los Angeles Dodgers. The Dodgers prevailed and garnered the last play-off spot. (The Cubs can't win even in my fake universe.) The Dodgers were led by Matt Kemp on offense (.406 average, 71 HRs, 189 RBIs) and pitcher Clayton Kershaw (28-3, 0.99 ERA, 310 Ks). When the Cubs played the Dodgers in this "alternate" 2012, they actually beat Kershaw and held Kemp in check. Nevertheless, even though neither player performed well *directly* against the Cubs, Kemp and Kershaw were integral to the Dodgers' ability to contend. Thus Kemp and Kershaw are Special OPS regardless of their performance against the Chicago Cubs.

The second measure in assessing a Special OP is how that player performed against the Chicago Cubs over a period of years. Posting tremendous career numbers against the Cubs, above and beyond the player's normal statistics, *may* qualify him as a Special OP. Consistent outstanding performances against the Cubs over a number of years, *will* qualify the player.

After watching the Cubs for decades, there always seem to be players who get labeled as "Cubs-Killers." As a child I remember my dad talking specifically about players, saying, "Oh, this guy always kills the Cubs" or "They can never hit this guy." In CHAPTER 5, I will use statistical data to identify these players, and add them to our list of 104 reasons why the Cubs have gone 104 years without a World Series title.

REASON 53

THE ENTIRE STARTING LINEUP OF THE 1930 CARDINALS

This chapter will consist of individual players who had incredible success against the Cubs or whose performance directly impacted the Cubs' ability to win a World Series title. **Reason 53** falls under the latter of those two categories, and it's more than *one* player. First, a brief recap of an earlier reason.

If you are reading this book from start to finish (not just skipping around), recall **Reason 5**; the tale of the 1930 St. Louis Cardinals. The Cards went on an improbable run to catch a Cubs' team that had been leading the National League for the majority of the summer. The Cardinals overcame a 7.5 game deficit in less than a month. In my quest to find Special OPS, the '30 Cardinals *had* to be represented. Upon perusing the hitting statistics of the 1930 Cardinals, I found something interesting. See if you can notice a pattern:

POSITION	'30 CARDINALS	ABS	BATT. AVG	OBP	OPS
C	Jimmie Wilson	362	.318	.368	.802
1B	Jim Bottomley	487	.304	.368	.860
2B	Frankie Frisch	540	.346	.407	.927
SS	Charlie Gelbert	513	.304	.360	.801
3B	Sparky Adams	570	.314	.365	.774
OF	Chick Hafey	515	.336	.407	1.059
OF	Taylor Douthit	664	.303	.364	.790
OF	George Watkins	391	.373	.415	1.037
OF	Showboat Fisher	254	.374	.432	1.019
C	Gus Mancuso	227	.366	.415	.965

POSITION	'30 CARDINALS	ABS	BATT. AVG	OBP	OPS
3B	*Andy High*	*215*	*.279*	*.349*	*.730*
1B	Ernie Orsatti	131	.321	.382	.848
OF	Ray Blade	101	.396	.504	1.118

After looking over these stats, I know what you are thinking: What kind of a name is *Showboat* Fisher and what must one do to garner such a moniker? Seriously, other than the shamefully italicized Andy High, every hitter with more than 100 at bats hit .300 or better. For you snobby "*Money Ball*-types" who question the validity of batting average, take a look at those on-base-percentages! Other than the aforementioned Mr. High, all OBPs are .360 or *high*-er. If you really like new "saber-stats," check out those OPS numbers! Using old metrics or new metrics, one thing is very clear; the 1930 Cardinals could really bleeping hit! Now, consider this:

TEAM	ABS	BATT. AVG	OBP	OPS
1930 Cardinals Team	5,512	.314	.372	.843

Wow! As a team the 1930 Cardinals hit over .300 and got on base 37 percent of the time! But wait, there's more:

TEAM	ABS	BATT. AVG	OBP	OPS
1930 Cards Minus the Pitchers' Hitting Stats	4,889	.334	.393	.874

Obviously with an offense like this, the Cubs had no chance…right? Remarkably, the Cubs' offense was surprisingly close. Take a look:

TEAM	ABS	BATT. AVG	OBP	OPS
1930 Cubs Team	5,581	.309	.368	.855

Wait a minute…that Cardinal team doesn't look *that* special now, do they? They did only finish *two* games ahead of the Cubs, yet there was a significant difference between the two 1930 slugging squads: the *balance* of their lineups. The Cubs' offensive numbers were buoyed by these four freakish seasons:

1930 CHICAGO CUBS	ABs	BATT. AVG	OBP	OPS
Hack Wilson	585	.356	.454	1.177
Kiki Cuyler	642	.355	.428	.975
Gaby Hartnett	508	.339	.404	1.034
Riggs Stephenson	341	.367	.421	.899

When four players have seasons like Wilson, Cuyler, Hartnett and Stephenson did, your team has a good chance to win ninety games as the 1930 Cubs did. Now, the rest of the 1930 Chicago Cubs:

1930 SEASON	ABs	BATT. AVG	OBP	OPS
All Other Cubs Players	3,505	.279	.334	.781

Statistics are easy to "cherry-pick" and manipulate to make a point. The Cubs did have those four players in their 1930 lineup; hence, looking at the statistics without them may seem irrelevant. However, in looking for reasons why the Cardinals finished *ahead* of the Cubs in 1930, the statistics of all players not-named Wilson, Cuyler, Hartnett or Stephenson *are* relevant.

The 1930 Chicago Cubs produced some of the greatest offense statistics in the team's long history. Unfortunately, the 1930 St. Louis Cardinals offense was a bit more balanced and just a tad better…*two games* better.

Two games, that placed the Cardinals in the 1930 World Series and the Cubs in second. Therefore the entire well-balanced, every player hitting over .300, lineup of the 1930 St. Louis Cardinals is **Reason 53**.

REASON 54

MEL OTT

The New York Giants won three National League titles in the 1930s. The Cubs finished closely behind the Giants in each year. In 1937, the Cubs had a record of 93-68 with a .604 winning percentage. Regrettably, the concept of a wild card entry into the play-offs was sixty years away. The Giants kept the Cubs from going to *four straight* World Series; a thought unfathomable to a non-1930 Cubs' fan. *Surely* (sarcasm implied), the Cubs would have won at least *one* of the four World Series.

Mel Ott was *the* dynamic player behind the Giants' offense. Ott is a Hall of Famer, an eleven-time All-Star, and he finished his career with 511 home runs. For fans of "new" stats, Ott had an impressive career *On-base plus slugging percentage* of .947. Let's see how Mel Ott performed against the Cubs in his career, and in years the Giants prevented the Cubs from winning the National League:

MEL OTT VS. THE CUBS	GAMES	HR	RBI	AVG	OPS
Career	402	77	251	.303	.939
1933	22	4	12	.238	.709
1936	22	3	16	.337	.927
1937	22	5	16	.301	.886

Mel Ott's numbers playing the Cubs are consistent with his performance against the rest of the National League. What makes Mel Ott a Special OP is his *performance* among the context of his team. Mel Ott *carried* (I really can't emphasize that bold-type enough) the Giants offensively. In fairness to Ott's teammates, the Giants played at the Polo Grounds, which had (to put it mildly) *spacious* dimensions. The center field fence was a whopping 483 feet from home plate, and the Polo Ground's power allies were a formidable 479 feet (left-center) and 458 feet (right-center) However, the left (279 feet) and right field (258 feet) line were easily reached by pull-hitters. The field played perfectly for a *left-handed* pull-hitter such as Ott. The discrepancies between Ott and his fellow hitters go beyond any advantages Ott received from playing in the Polo Grounds. Take a look at Mel Ott in 1933, '36 and '37 matched against the next two preeminent offensive players on his team:

NYG 1933 PLAYER	AB	R	H	2B	3B	HR	RBI	AVG	OPS
Mel Ott	580	98	164	36	1	23	123	.283	.834
Johnny Vergez	458	57	124	21	6	16	72	.271	.780
Bill Terry	475	68	153	20	5	6	58	.322	.798

NYG 1936 PLAYER	AB	R	H	2B	3B	HR	RBI	AVG	OPS
Mel Ott	534	120	175	28	6	33	135	.328	1.036
Gus Mansuco	519	55	156	21	3	9	63	.301	.755
Dick Bartell	510	71	152	31	3	8	42	.278	.773

NYG 1937 PLAYER	AB	R	H	2B	3B	HR	RBI	AVG	OPS
Mel Ott	545	99	160	28	2	31	95	.294	.931
Dick Bartell	516	91	158	38	2	14	68	.306	.836
Jo Jo Moore	580	89	180	37	10	6	57	.310	.804

Without Mel Ott, the New York Giants don't win National League titles in '33, '36, and '37; and consequently, the Cubs may have. The Cubs' second place finishes ('36 and '37) would have been two more World Series chances. Mel Ott and the Giants made sure that the Cubs never had those opportunities. These facts make Mel Ott a Special OP; and **Reason 54.**

REASON 55

CARL HUBBELL

The New York Giants' teams of the 1930s battled the Cubs throughout the decade for National League supremacy. The Giants were led by Mel Ott on offense and their pitching staff was led by Hall of Famer Carl Hubbell. Carl Hubbell was to the Giants' pitching staff what Mel Ott was to their offense... and then some.

Carl Hubbell may have even been more of a "one-man show" than Mel Ott was. First, let's take a look at Hubbell against the Cubs:

CARL HUBBELL VS. THE CUBS	IP	H	ER	BB	SO	W	L	ERA
Career	542.2	550	193	117	274	33	27	3.20
1933	34.2	36	7	8	14	3	2	1.82
1936	49.1	33	8	13	23	4	2	1.46
1937	50.2	68	30	15	19	3	2	5.33

In head-to-head matchups, Hubbell was about the equivalent of what he was against the league. In 1937 the Cubs rocked him twice, but notice Hubbell still had a winning record against the Cubs. Overall however, these numbers are not out-of-this-world impressive. The problem for the Cubs wasn't what Hubbell did against *them*, rather what he did against the *rest of the National League*.

Carl Hubbell led the National League in wins in 1933, '36 and '37, all of which were years that the Cubs finished behind the Giants. Hubbell also led the league in ERA in '33 (1.56) and '36 (2.31). When examining the Giants' pitching statistics from these seasons, only one extraordinary player emerges. Take a look at the 1936 rotation:

PITCHER	GAMES	STARTS	IP	HITS	SOS	W	L	ERA
Carl Hubbell	42	34	304	265	123	26	6	2.31
Al Smith	43	30	209	217	89	14	13	3.79
Schumacher	35	30	215	234	75	11	13	3.47
F. Fitzsimmins	28	17	141	147	35	10	7	3.32
H. Gumbert	39	15	141	157	52	11	3	3.89

Have you ever heard of any of the guys *not-named* Carl Hubbell? (Me neither!) Like Mel Ott on offense, Carl Hubbell was the only exceptional pitcher among the Giants' staff.

Mel Ott and Carl Hubbell were a dynamic duo for the New York Giants. The Giants had average to good talent elsewhere on the field, but Ott and Hubbell were **dominant** players. If *either* of these two players were not on the Giants, the Cubs win four straight pennants. Mel Ott and Carl Hubbell against the National League was a dominating duo. The two were a *bit* like Michael Jordan and Scottie Pippen (without the dunking, three-pointers, stifling defense and six NBA titles).

Mel Ott and Carl Hubbell are both justifiably in the Hall of Fame, and they are both deservedly two *reasons* for the Cubs' 104 year drought. Hubbell was the type of pitcher who could be counted on for a win virtually every time he took the mound. The 1930s' Cubs did not have a pitcher of Hubbell's ability...if they had, the World Series drought may only be 75-80 years.

The New York Giants of the 1930s could not get past their cross-town rivals, the Yankees. Perhaps the Giants spared the Cubs more World Series' losses at the hands of the Yanks. Special Op Carl Hubbell helped vault the Giants over the Cubs to challenge those Yankees...thus, he is **Reason 55**.

REASON 56

DOCK ELLIS
The 1969 season has taken a mythic and legendary place in the memories of Cubs' fans of that era. I was born one year prior, and I grew up thinking that 1969 was both one of the Cubs' finest moments and ultimate failures. 1969 has overshadowed the Cubs' seasons of 1970-1973. In the NEAR MISSES chapters I pointed out that the Cubs were actually *closer* to first place in 1971 *and* 1973. From 1970-72, the Cubs finished second, third, and second respectively. In each of those three seasons, the Pittsburgh Pirates won the National Eastern Division title.

Dock Ellis was a key member of the Pirates' pitching staff during all three National League East titles. Ellis, who died in 2006 of cirrhosis of the liver, is most famous for:

- Throwing a no-hitter in 1970.

- Claiming that he was under the influence of LSD while he threw that no-hitter.

- Declaring that he never pitched a game *not* under the influence of drugs.

- Throwing at all five batters he faced (hitting the first three) before being removed from a game against the Cincinnati Reds.

- Getting into an altercation with a Cincinnati security guard who refused to allow Ellis to enter the stadium because Ellis had no identification...except his World Series ring.

- Finding redemption later in life by counseling drug addicts and working positively with Major League Baseball.

Ellis was a remarkable and attention-grabbing figure who warrants more consideration. As fascinating as Dock Ellis tales are, we need to get back to our Cubs and how Dock Ellis dominated our Cubs. Ellis was particularly tough on the Cubs during the Pirates three-year run of 1970-72:

DOCK ELLIS VS. CHICAGO CUBS 1970-1972

7 Wins	1 Loss	67.33 Innings Pitched	17 Earned Runs	2.23 ERA

Dock Ellis' supremacy over the Cubs during that three-year stretch hindered the Cubs' attempts to capture the National League Eastern division title. Ellis was also dominant against the Cubs throughout his entire career.

CAREER VS. CUBS	W/L	IP	H	ER	BB	SO	ERA	CG
Dock Ellis	14-4	183	167	57	44	93	2.80	9

Ellis finished his career with 138 wins, 102 of them in the National League. Of course, in classic Cubs' fashion, Ellis' win total against the Cubs is his most against any Major League team.

The early 1970s' Pirates prevented the Cubs from having a chance at post-season play. While in broadcasting, Ron Santo would openly display his personal disdain for the Mets due to 1969. The Pirates may have been *more* responsible for preventing Ron's fine team from not winning a title, yet I don't ever recall him mentioning them. Dock Ellis was a big part of that, hence his inclusion on this list as **Reason 56**.

> *"I chewed my gum until it turned to powder. I started having a crazy idea in the fourth inning that Richard Nixon was the home plate umpire, and once I thought I was pitching a baseball to Jimi Hendrix, who to me was holding a guitar and swinging it over the plate."* **Dock Ellis on his no-hit game, in which he claimed he was on LSD.**
>
> ~Dan Epstein
> *Big Hair and Plastic Grass:*
> *A Funky Ride through Baseball and*
> *America in the Swinging '70s*

Whoa.

REASON 57

MIKE SCHMIDT

The Chicago Cubs in the mid- to late-1970s were not as awful as many teams' previous inclinations. In 1977, the team was in first place until late June. In '78 the Cubs finished third, albeit with a record of 79-83. In 1979 they were a *Cubs-respectable* 80-82, with Dave Kingman hitting forty-eight home runs and Bruce Sutter winning the Cy Young Award. I followed these seasons as an eight and nine year old, my "wheelhouse" of knowledge as a Cubs' fan. The Cubs were at least *entertaining* during this period. Regrettably, the Cubs had *no chance* in this era, as they were in the *National League East*. The *National League East* would produce the World Series Champions in 1979, 1980, and 1982... with three *different* teams!

During the mid-1970s and early 1980s the Philadelphia Phillies were the proverbial "team to beat" in the National League East. The Phillies won the division in '76, '77, '78, '80, '81, and 1983. The Phillies roster consisted of multiple eventual Hall of Famers, but there was one in particular who spelled doom for the Chicago Cubs: Michael Jack Schmidt.

Schmidt is often regarded as the greatest third baseman of all time. Schmidt hit 548 homers, won three MVP awards, and was a twelve-time All-Star. Mike Schmidt also won ten Gold Glove awards at third base. There is no denying this guy was one of the greatest, but believe it or not…Schmidt was even *better* against the Cubs.

In Mike Schmidt's career against the Chicago Cubs, he hit seventy-eight home runs, his most against any opponent (of course). Schmidt's seventy-eight home runs against the Cubs accounted for 14 percent of his career total. Schmidt also knocked in 207 runs, which is 13 percent of his career total of 1595. Schmidt's batting average was significantly higher against the Cubs too: a modest *.267* vs. *.292* against the North-Siders. I will appease sabremetricians/fans of new stats with Mike Schmidt's OPS numbers: career OPS .908 while .985 vs. the Cubs.

Mike Schmidt's numbers against the Cubs only tell part of the story. Mike Schmidt's numbers at Wrigley Field are just silly. Schmidt played in 138 games at Wrigley Field. In those 138 games, Schmidt batted .307, had fifty home runs, 124 RBIs…and a 1.048 OPS. Projected over a 162 game season, Schmidt would have hit fifty-nine HRs with 146 RBIs. Can you imagine if Schmidt had played his career with the Cubs? No. I couldn't imagine that either.

Mike Schmidt powered the Phillies, and the Phillies in the '70s and early '80s kept the Cubs from winning *any* division titles. If Schmidt had played his entire career against the Cubs, his numbers may have bested Babe Ruth and Hank Aaron. All the superlatives aside, Mike Schmidt may be one of the most deserved of our 104 reasons.

If you actually watched the carnage that was Mike Schmidt hitting against the Chicago Cubs take place like I did, you know he is quite worthy of **Reason 57.**

REASON 58

WILLIE STARGELL

If you ever saw Willie Stargell play when you were younger, you probably imitated his batting stance while playing Whiffle ball. Willie would wheel his arms up and around, creating a windmill effect before each pitch. An eventual Hall of Famer for the Pirates, Willie was a slugging outfielder turned first baseman. During the Pirates' three-year reign atop the National League East from 1970-72, Willie Stargell *was* Pittsburgh's preeminent offensive player. Before examining his numbers against the Chicago Cubs, let's look at how he did against the National League:

WILLIE STARGELL	AB	HITS	HRs	RBI	AVG	OBP	SLUG	OPS
1970	474	125	31	85	.264	.329	.511	.839
1971	511	151	48	125	.295	.392	.646	1.038
1972	495	145	33	112	.293	.373	.558	.930

Stargell was a colossal contributor to a Pirates' team that won three straight National League Eastern Division championships *and* the 1971 World Series. How did Stargell do specifically when playing against our Cubs?

CAREER VS. CUBS	AB	HITS	HRs	RBI	AVG	OBP	SLUG	OPS
Willie Stargell	942	276	50	167	.293	.366	.524	.890

Willie Stargell's performance against the Chicago Cubs was solid. The "friendly confines" of Wrigley were very good for Willie; he hit .307, and thirty-two of his fifty homers against the Cubs were hit on the North Side.

In 1979 the Pirates won their second World Series of the decade, defeating the Baltimore Orioles four games to three. Stargell was the MVP of the '79 World Series *and* the 1979 season at age thirty-nine. Stargell gets Special OPS status because he was a player who served as a "road block"…in the *way* of Cubs' success for an entire decade. As long as the man known as "Pops" was handling first base for the Pirates in the 1970s, the Cubs would finish below them…making Willie Stargell **Reason 58**.

REASON 59

S TEVE CARLTON

The National League East of the late 1970s and early 1980s was an absolute *beast* of a division. The Philadelphia Phillies won the division in '76, '77, '78, '80, '81, and '83. During that time period two teams *not named* the Philadelphia Phillies won the NL East: the 1979 Pittsburgh Pirates and the 1982 St. Louis Cardinals. Incidentally, both the '79 Pirates and the '82 Cardinals would win the World Series. The aforementioned Mike Schmidt was the strength of a very good Phillies' offense. Steve Carlton was the Philadelphia Phillies' pitching staff. Look at Carlton's numbers during the seasons in which Philadelphia won the National League East (1981 was a strike-shortened "split" season):

CARLTON	W/L	IP	H	ER	BB	SO	ERA	NOTES
1976	20-7	252.2	224	88	72	195	3.13	.741 winning pcg.
1977	23-10	283	229	83	89	198	2.64	won NL Cy Young Award
1978	16-13	247.1	228	78	63	161	2.84	....still really good
1980	24-9	304	243	79	90	286	2.34	won NL Cy Young Award
1981	13-4	190	152	51	62	179	2.42	3rd in Cy Young voting
1983	15-16	283	277	98	84	275	3.11	led NL in strikeouts

Carlton won a third Cy Young in 1982, when the Phillies finished behind the Cardinals. Steve Carlton's numbers on the Philadelphia Phillies NL East championship teams are incredible. Carlton was one of the most dominant pitchers of his era. Now, let's see how Carlton did against the Cubs. The number in parenthesis represents where the Cubs rank on Carlton's all-time lists:

- Wins: 41 (1ST)
- Winning Percentage: .672 (3RD)
- ERA: 3.11 (6TH)
- Complete Games: 29 (2ND)
- Shut Outs: 7 (1ST)
- Strikeouts: 421 (3RD)

Steve Carlton's numbers against the Cubs are extraordinary. (*Seven* shut outs?) Carlton is one player I watched dominate the Cubs, and when he was on the mound, I knew it was hopeless for my beloved Cubs. The perpetual sense of doom a Cubs' fan carries was intensified for me when the man nicknamed "Lefty" (creative, huh?) was on the bump for the Philadelphia Phillies.

The Philadelphia Phillies of this era benefited from having two Hall of Famers, in Steve Carlton and Mike Schmidt…in the **prime** of their careers. The Phillies may have indeed had the premier pitcher *and* position player in the Major Leagues. Carlton's and Schmidt's personal dominance over the Cubs notwithstanding, their mere presence in the division was enough to keep the Cubs from winning. Carlton and Schmidt would make sure the dearth of Cubs' World Series titles continued for the 1970s and into the early '80s.

Steve Carlton was the pitching counterpart to the offensive prowess of Mike Schmidt for the Philadelphia Phillies, which makes him a very Special OP and **Reason 59**.

REASON 60

THE ENTIRE NATIONAL LEAGUE: (SPECIFICALLY THE NL EAST) 1975-82 AND 1986

Reason 60 is not meant to sound like an excuse; the goal of this book is to get Cubs' fans to stop making excuses and rationalizations. However, during this time period (1975-1982) the Chicago Cubs played in a brutally tough National League and an equally as strong Eastern Division. Historically, the balance of power has shifted back and forth between the American and National Leagues. A more accurate statement is the balance of power has shifted between the National League and the *New York Yankees*. Here are the World Series Champions from 1975-82:

YEAR(S)	CHAMPION	LEAGUE
1975-76	Cincinnati Reds	National League
1977-78	New York Yankees	American League
1979	Pittsburgh Pirates	National League

YEAR(S)	CHAMPION	LEAGUE
1980	Philadelphia Phillies	National League
1981	Los Angeles Dodgers	National League
1982	St. Louis Cardinals	National League

The National League won six of eight World Series titles *and* the All-Star game *every* year during this period. This National League All-Star game dominance occurred when the leagues took great pride in winning the "midsummer classic." The supremacy of the National League East is apparent among the teams listed above. From 1979 to 1982, *three* of the *six* teams from the National League East won the World Series...three *different* teams. From 1975-82, the New York Mets and Chicago Cubs were the only team *not* to make the play-offs from the National League East.

However, even the *lowly* Cubs won the National League East in 1984 and the Mets won the division *and* the World Series in '86. Thus, from *1979-1986*:

- The National League East had *four different* teams win a World Series title.

- The National League East had *all six* teams reach the play-offs.

- The Eastern Division represented the National League in the World Series for seven of the eight years.

The facts above portray an incredibly competitive division. Consider that these Hall of Famers *all* played in the National League's Eastern Division: Willie Stargell, Bert Blyleven, Mike Schmidt, Steve Carlton, Andre Dawson, Gary Carter, Ozzie Smith, Bruce Sutter, Joe Morgan, and Tony Perez. Ponder as well that the following managers were leading teams in the National League East from 1979-86: Dallas Green, Dick Williams, Chuck Tanner, Joe Torre, Davey Johnson, and Whitey Herzog.

Reason 60 might appear to be a rationalization..."*Look at how tough these teams we are playing are*," does sound like an excuse (...at least a bit *whiney*). Yet I believe the extraordinary competitiveness of the National League East makes **Reason 60** a valid and fair example among the 104 reasons. By comparison to other futile periods in Cubs' history, winning a division in this time period seems *remarkable*.

"Remarkable" may seem too strong of a description, but for a team that wins as rarely as the Chicago Cubs, to win such a cutthroat division once qualifies as *remarkable*. Sadly, winning anything seems *remarkable* to Cubs' fans.

REASON 61

DWIGHT "DOC" GOODEN

In 1982 the New York Mets selected Dwight Gooden fifth overall in the first round of Major League Baseball's amateur draft. The Chicago Cubs had the first pick and drafted shortstop Shawon Dunston. CHAPTER 3 dealt with DAFT DRAFTS, so I am *not* second-guessing the pick of Shawon Dunston over Gooden. (Maybe I should have?) Just for fun though, think about this: Gooden won seventeen games and struck out 276 in 1984! Do you think Gooden may have contributed to the 1984 Chicago Cubs?

Okay, back from my foray into Cubs' fantasyland, I will illuminate why Dwight Gooden is a Special OP. Gooden was a gifted pitcher who battled substance abuse, which derailed what may have been a Hall of Fame career. Regardless, Dwight Gooden's career numbers are still impressive: 194-112, a .634 winning percentage with a career ERA of 3.51. Looking at Dwight Gooden's statistics you find some marvelous numbers:

1985 DWIGHT "DOC" GOODEN:
- 24-4 win/loss record for a .857 winning percentage
- 1.53 ERA
- 276 strikeouts
- 16 complete games, with 8 shut outs

Yikes! The Mets did not even win the division in 1985! They *did* win the National League East in 1986 and 1988, as well as a World Series in 1986.

For the '86 World Champion Mets, Gooden was 17-6 with a 2.84 ERA. In 1988 Gooden was 18-9 with a 3.19. 1986 and 1988 were outstanding years for Dwight Gooden, yet not as *freakishly* good as 1985. I bet you can guess which National League team Dwight Gooden was better than "freakishly" good against.

CAREER VS. CUBS	W/L	IP	HITS	BB	SO	ER	ERA	CG	SHO
Dwight Gooden	28-4	284	264	90	235	105	3.32	11	3

Holy blank! The above numbers certainly speak for themselves…yet I will expound on them further. A record of *28-4* calculates to a winning percentage of *.875*, or *.003 less* than that of the 72-10, 1996 Chicago Bulls. Why the reference to the greatest basketball team of all time…*because* .875 winning percentages don't happen very often. That percentage would have made you very rich if you wagered on the Gooden and Mets every time against the Chicago Cubs. The eleven complete games are extraordinary, as are the 235 strikeouts… yet, *28-4* declares dominance even more than any other astonishing numbers.

Dwight Gooden's lifetime performance against the Cubs makes him a *Special*, Special OP. Gooden may not have directly prohibited the Cubs from a World Series; nevertheless, he sure did kick their collective butts over forty career starts. The mental anguish from the beatings the Cubs took is enough to include Dwight Gooden on our list.

I have to go back to the 1982 draft. I need to pretend *one more time* that the Cubs drafted Gooden *instead* of Dunston. A Rick Sutcliffe and Dwight Gooden 1-2 punch at the top of the rotation would have been pretty, pretty intimidating. Maybe Doc's life would have turned out differently had he been drafted by the Cubs…avoiding the trappings of playing in New York. Had Gooden been drafted by the Cubs, 1984 could have been different.

Without the benefit of time travel, I cannot alter the 1982 draft. Dwight Gooden *was* drafted by the Mets, and he dominated the Cubs for most of the 1980s. Gooden's performances helped keep the Cubs from success, and greatly contributed to their continued lack of World Series titles.

Thus Dwight Gooden is a Special OP, and **Reason 61.**

REASON 62

Tony LaRussa

Tony LaRussa *was* a Major League Baseball player. Actually, Tony played a portion of his brief career with the Chicago Cubs. Tony LaRussa is not a Special OP because of his playing; Tony LaRussa is in it for his managing. If it seems like a bit of chicanery on my part including a manager in a chapter about "**special**" players, then define Tony as a *player (not a playa)* as the third definition in the Encarta Dictionary does:

> 3. **Participant in activity:**
> *A person, group or business that has an influential role in a political or commercial activity.*

Tony LaRussa took over as manager of the St. Louis Cardinals in 1996 and was definitely a *player* for the Cardinals' organization, managing the Cardinals for sixteen seasons. Many Cubs' fans don't care much for Tony. For me, it was his glasses; I really don't trust people that still wear those tinted glasses I wore for my fifth grade school picture in 1979. The majority of Cubs' fans don't like Tony because his Cardinals dominated their team.

Tony's teams always had two great attributes: his longtime pitching coach Dave Duncan and large (*ahem*) power hitters…usually first baseman. Somewhat kidding aside, Tony LaRussa has been one heck of a Major League manager. His arrival in the National League Central was not beneficial for the Chicago Cubs.

Tony managed the Cardinals for sixteen consecutive seasons. During that time, the Cubs' managers were Jim Riggleman, Don Baylor, Bruce Kimm (interim), Dusty Baker, Lou Piniella and Mike Quade. Not including Kimm, the Cubs had ***FIVE*** managers over the sixteen year period that Tony was in St. Louis. Here are some simple statistics:

1996-2011	TONY LARUSSA	THE CUBS' "FIVE"
Winning seasons	13	7
Play-off appearances	9	4
Play-off series victories	12	1
National League pennants	3	0
World Series titles	2	0

The numbers above don't indict any of the Cubs' managers as *terrible*; each had respective highs and lows during their tenures (okay, maybe not Quade). These numbers do reflect the (sorry, Cubs' fans) prominence of LaRussa as a manager. The numbers also reflect the Cardinals' supremacy over the National League Central Division during LaRussa's reign. I will hammer home Tony LaRussa's domination over the Cubs by asking a question:

- From 1996-2011, how many times did the Cardinals, managed by Tony LaRussa, finish ahead of the Cubs in the National League Central?

- Answer: twelve of the sixteen years

In 75 percent of the seasons he managed, Tony's Cardinals finished ahead of the Cubs…thus, LaRussa's Cardinals were consistently far superior to the Cubs. Tony is not solely responsible for all of the Cards' achievements during those sixteen seasons, but he *was* the leader. Tony LaRussa is a solid cause for the Cubs' lack of sustained success over a sixteen-year period, and subsequently another reason why the team has not won a World Series since 1908.

I guess I just have to get over my own silly insecurities about those glasses. Tony LaRussa is a Special OP, and **Reason 62.**

REASON 63

DAVE DUNCAN

Wait a minute…this guy is not *even* a Major League manager! How can Dave Duncan possibly qualify to be in this chapter? Wasn't he just a pitching coach?

Yes, Dave Duncan was the Cardinals' pitching coach for sixteen seasons. Using the definition of *player* we used for Tony LaRussa in **Reason 62**… Duncan definitely qualifies as a Special OP. Reason 62 examined the Cardinals' dominance over the Cubs under Tony LaRussa. Tony was the leader, but he had tremendous assistance from Duncan. Under LaRussa, the Cardinals had an uncanny ability of getting wins from starting pitchers that had moderate to little success early in their careers. Duncan deserves a large part of the credit for this ability to "mold" starting pitchers.

Baseball statistics are modified, debunked, debated and analyzed in much more detail since the early 2000s. I have heard and read many baseball experts attempting to devalue the "win/loss" statistic for pitchers. I agree with this…to a certain extent. The "win/loss" stat opponents would argue:

- Pitchers on teams with superior offenses will get "wins" many times even if they don't pitch well. Starter "A" goes five innings allowing seven runs…but his team was leading 11-7 when he left the game…he gets a win!

- A reliever comes in, blows a save, then his team bails him out and scores the next inning…he gets a win!

- If a pitcher is on a team that gives him minor run support…say only 3.3 runs a game when he pitches…he will automatically have a win/loss record not indicative of his performance.

I get it. The arguments above are all acceptable reasons to lessen the "win" statistic. Nevertheless, I still believe there is value in the "win/loss" statistic. Let me enlighten:

Only a few pitchers are skilled enough to even make it to the Major Leagues. Major League hitters are, for want of a better term, very good. They are so good in fact, that for a pitcher to get through five- or six-plus innings takes a level of ability that very few have. The ability to (baseball cliché alert) "give your team a chance to win" is a treasured talent. Have you ever watched a Major League Baseball game in which the starting pitcher could not last five innings? Of course you have, since you are a Cubs' fan. We can agree for the sake of argument, and for the validity of Dave Duncan being included, that "wins" do have value.

Tony LaRussa and Dave Duncan have an uncanny ability of finding pitchers who can get their teams wins. Let's look at some of their handiwork:

Kent Bottenfield

At the age of thirty, Bottenfield was with his sixth organization and had never won more than five Major League games in a season. In 1999 he went 18-7 with a 3.97 ERA for the St. Louis Cardinals. Bottenfield was chosen for the 1999 All-Star team. After the season, the Cardinals packaged Bottenfield and second baseman Adam Kennedy to the Angels for Jim Edmonds. Edmonds would be a COLOSSAL contributor to the Cardinals, while Bottenfield was out of baseball after two more seasons.

Woody Williams

When the Cardinals acquired Woody Williams in the middle of the 2001 season, he was thirty-four years old. Williams was 8-8 at the time with a career record of 58-64, and a career ERA of 4.30. In the second half of 2001, Williams went 7-1 with a 2.28 ERA for the Cardinals. In 2002, Williams went 9-4 with a 2.53 ERA, and in 2003 he was 18-9 with a 3.87 ERA. Woody Williams was a 2003 All-Star.

Chris Carpenter

In advance of Chris Carpenter becoming a Cy Young winner and World Series champion for the Cardinals, he was battling injuries and languishing in the Toronto Blue Jays' system. In six seasons with Toronto, Carpenter was 49-

50 with a 4.83 ERA. The Cardinals acquired him at age twenty-nine, and he proceeded to go 95-42 with a 3.06 ERA over the next eight seasons.

Todd Wellemeyer

The Cardinals were able to squeeze a 13-9, 3.71 ERA season out of this failed Cubs' prospect in 2008 at age twenty-nine. As a Cardinal, Wellemeyer was 23-21 with a 4.31 ERA. As a *non*-Cardinal Wellemeyer was 9-13 with a 5.65.

Kyle Lohse

Another former Cubs' prospect, Lohse had a career record of 60-74, with a career ERA of 4.83, when the Cardinals acquired him at age twenty-nine. In his first year with the Cards in 2008, Lohse went 15-6 with a 3.78 ERA. In the Cardinals' World Series title season of 2011, Kyle Lohse was 14-8 with a 3.39 ERA. In 2012, Lohse would win sixteen games for the Cardinals.

All of these pitchers were able to have the greatest year or years of their careers, at age twenty-nine or older. They all struggled in the majors, or had very moderate success with other organizations. Upon arriving to the Cardinals, their careers and fortunes changed dramatically. The similarities in these cases (I am going to use this word again) are **uncanny**. Major League teams all strive to cultivate starting pitching but most (of course including the Cubs) struggle terribly at developing pitchers. How can one team take so many cast-offs, at advanced ages, and consistently make them better than they ever were?

The Cardinals ability to magically develop these pitchers enabled them to dominate the National League Central and the Cubs during the LaRussa/ Duncan reign. Dave Duncan has to be given an enormous amount of credit for making this happen. Dave Duncan also deserves credit for keeping the Cubs from winning a World Series title during his tenure as pitching coach of the St. Louis Cardinals.

Dave Duncan may have "only" been a pitching coach, yet he is a worthy Special OP. Duncan is also **Reason 63** of our 104 reasons.

REASON 64

ALBERT PUJOLS

You may have noticed a bit of a St. Louis theme to these last three reasons. The explanation for that is simple: The Cardinals have been the dominant team in the National League Central for the last fifteen years. The Cubs and Astros have had periodic contending teams, with Houston making the World Series in 2005. The Milwaukee Brewers won the Central in 2011, but proceeded to lose to the Cards in the NLCS. The Reds won the division in 2010 and 2012. The Pirates are still looking for their first .500 season since 1992. Like it or not…the Cardinals have made the rest of the division seem second-rate.

The arrival of Albert Pujols to the St. Louis lineup in 2001 is equal in producing Cardinals' success/Cubs' failure as the aforementioned Tony LaRussa and Dave Duncan. Pujols won three MVP awards during his stint in St. Louis, and the Cardinals made the play-offs in seven of his eleven seasons in St. Louis. Unless Pujols has a horrible second half of his career, he is a Hall of Fame lock. When Albert Pujols left St. Louis for the Angels via free agency in 2011, Cubs' fans felt they had reason to rejoice. Yet, in typical Cardinal-fashion…even a Pujols-less Cards team made it to the 2012 NLCS.

At the outset of **CHAPTER 5**, I provided two criteria for a player to qualify as a Special OP: 1) the player's career kept the Cubs from winning or directly blocked potential Cubs' success, or 2) that player had incredible success against the Chicago Cubs. Albert Pujols absolutely fits the first criteria by winning two World Series…and making the play-offs in seven of eleven seasons. For the second criteria, let's look at how Albert has done against the Chicago Cubs.

CAREER VS. CUBS	AB	R	H	2B	3B	HR	RBI	AVG	BB	OPS
Albert Pujols	632	124	191	35	2	53	135	.302	103	1.020

The statistics above indicate a big *YES* on the question of Albert Pujols' success against the Chicago Cubs. Not surprisingly, Pujols' home runs, RBIs, walks and OPS are phenomenal when playing against the Chicago Cubs.

Pujols was an integral part to the Cardinals' success in the 2000s and he **pounded** Cubs' pitching. With Pujols in the lineup, the Cardinals only finished behind the Cubs *three* times in eleven seasons from 2001-2011. The astonishing head to head numbers Pujols produced against the Cubs were a factor in the Cardinals' advantage over the Cubs in the standings.

Albert Pujols easily met both criteria to be a Special OP, and he is also **Reason 64.**

CHAPTER 6

REASON 65—DICK DROTT
The Cubs had a young flame-throwing starter
who only had success for one season…sound familiar?

REASON 66—KEN HUBBS
A victim of a plane crash, had Ken Hubbs lived,
the Cubs' core of the late '60s would have been even stronger.

REASON 67—DICK ELLSWORTH
Ellsworth appeared to be a comparable pitcher to Sandy Koufax…
for one season.

REASON 68—JEROME WALTON
Walton was the catalyst of the 1989 Cubs and center field appeared to be filled.
It wasn't.

REASON 69—MIKE HARKEY
A top-flight Cubs' pitching prospect who battled injuries
and outfield tumbling.

REASON 70—Rick Wilkins
Wilkins had the greatest single offensive season by a Cubs' catcher not-named Gaby Hartnett. (Emphasis on the "single"…as in one)

REASON 71—Tuffy Rhodes
Rhodes hit three home runs off of Dwight Gooden on opening day, a feat he would never match on American soil.

REASON 72—Mark Prior
Sigh.

REASON 73—Rich Hill
Hill's lack of control earned him a trip to Iowa, from which he would never return… but did he deserve another chance?

ONE-HIT WONDERS

In 1976, Mark "The Bird" Fidrych of the Detroit Tigers was the Rookie of the Year in the American League. Fidrych won nineteen games, led the league in ERA (2.34), threw twenty-four complete games and had four shut outs. Fidrych would win ten games *total* over the next three seasons combined. Arm injuries had Fidrych out of the game by 1980 and had Tiger fans wondering, "what if?" In 1980, the Cleveland Indians had their own Rookie of the Year in outfielder Joe Charboneau. Charboneau hit .287 with 23 HR and 87 RBIs. Charboneau could not hit above .210 the next year, and was out of the majors by 1982.

What happened to these players? How did such promise disappear so suddenly?

Every baseball player who attempts to play is eventually told he can't play anymore. Baseball is a game that requires a set of specific skills. The skills baseball requires aren't always tied to physical abilities such as size and strength. If an athlete is 6'6" and 300 pounds, and can run…he will have a chance to play Division I football. If an athlete is 6'8" or above and has decent basketball skills, that player will likely get to extend his playing career. There are specific skills one must have to play football and basketball; however, certain physical attributes can mask the lack of those skills.

Baseball is different. Physical size and strength *are* advantages, yet not like in the other sports mentioned. Baseball specific "skills" must be at a level equaling physical abilities. If a player can't make contact with a pitched ball, his baseball career ends abruptly. An athlete will have a very short baseball career if he can't throw a ball with any accuracy. If one can't catch a moving sphere with his baseball glove, that player won't be *playing*. Baseball players who *can* hit, catch and throw will have *extended* careers, yet their time will be limited. I am not attempting to set apart baseball's superiority as a sport. Tremendous athletes, elite athletes play many different sports, yet, if the best athlete in the world can't hit a curveball or throw strikes…there is no career for him in baseball.

Okay, I am done lecturing about the difficulties of baseball. The references to Mr. Fidrych and Mr. Charboneau, and the previous three paragraphs were to preface **CHAPTER 6**. All baseball players fail. The disappointment may take place in little league, high school, college, the minor leagues, or the Major Leagues; but for *all* baseball players, the failure *will come*. Players reach a point where their skills are over-matched, or their talents erode due to injury or age. (This is a bit depressing.)

A fascinating occurrence in certain Major League careers is when a player shows incredible skill or ability above his perceived limits (i.e., Charboneau) for a brief period of time. Then as quickly as the skills have expanded, they evaporate and a career is over. I am referring to players who just seem to "lose it" all of a sudden…not due to injuries (which are obvious reasons, i.e., Fidrych). Players who have one shining year, perhaps two, and then for whatever cause… it's *gone*…and the player can't hit or pitch anymore.

The Cubs have a long history of players that fade out due to both injury *and* mystery. Cubs' fans are given false hope that the club has a star player at a certain position for the next decade…and quickly the decade becomes just a year or two.

CHAPTER 6 will examine some of the Cubs' most notorious examples of *One-Hit Wonders*…players who appear to be solid, only to disappoint rapidly. These types of players are not unique to the Cubs, yet like most things "Cubs," the club seems to have more of these types of player careers. These types of careers set organizations back to a starting point for a certain position, and leave a hole where the team thought it was set. Recurrence of these short careers has contributed to the Cubs' lack of long-term success.

These *One-Hit Wonders* have hindered the Cubs' chances at World Series titles, and unquestionably deserve to be among our 104 reasons.

REASON 65

DICK DROTT

Do you know what an archetype is? The concept of archetypes was developed by German psychologist Carl Jung, who believed human beings share a collective unconscious. Simply put, Jung believed human beings share many of the same thoughts, ideas, and concepts. He also held that as humans we have archetypes, or stories and traits that are passed down from generation to generation. These stories are told over and over, almost identical in plot, then retold under different circumstances. For example: The underdog story of David vs. Goliath has influenced stories from *Rocky* to the *Karate Kid*. These tales then share similarities to "new" sagas like *Rudy* and *The Rookie*. Many of the **One-Hit Wonders** I feature in this chapter share similar attributes, akin to archetypes. The Chicago Cubs have had their own examples of never-ending or repeating stories.

For example, let's say a twenty year old begins to pitch for the Chicago Cubs. The young hurler throws very hard and succeeds because of his extraordinary fastball. The pitcher has an outstanding rookie season. Cubs' fans believe they have the type of player who will be the ace of their staff for ten years. Regrettably, due to injury, ineffectiveness, or a combination of the two, the pitcher never again regains his previous form. Does this "Cub-type" sound familiar? In 1957 this Cubs' pitcher was Dick Drott.

Dick Drott was a hard-throwing righty nicknamed "hummer" for his blazing fastball. In 1957, Drott finished third in the National League Rookie of the Year voting. Here are Drott's 1957 statistics:

1957	W/L	IP	H	ER	BB	SO	CG	SHO
Dick Drott	15-11	229	200	91	129	170	7	3

Dick Drott had a *stellar* 1957 season. The 129 walks may have been a harbinger of what was to come, but Drott's other numbers excited many Cubs' fans into thinking Drott was an *ace*. They were wrong.

In thirty-nine games in 1958 Drott went 7-11, with a 5.43 ERA. In 1959 he battled injuries, and split the little time he did pitch between the Cubs and the minor leagues. In 1960 Drott was 0-6 with a 7.16 ERA over twenty-three games. In 1961 he pitched mostly relief for the Cubs, going 1-4 with a 4.22. Drott had gone from starter to a mop-up reliever...rarely used.

In 1961, Dick Drott was left unprotected by the Cubs and was drafted by the **Houston Colt .45s** in the National League expansion draft. In three short seasons, Drott fell from potential star and staff ace to insignificance...the

Cubs allowed him to leave for *nothing*. Drott's fortunes did not turn around in Houston (2-12, 4.98 ERA), and the 1963 season was his last.

Imagine if Dick Drott had pitched *similarly* to his rookie performance over an entire career. The Cubs then have a pitcher who ends his career with around 180-200 wins. Dick Drott won **nine** more games for the Chicago Cubs after winning **fifteen** in 1957. After the failure of Dick Drott, the Cubs had a hole in their starting rotation. This scenario seems to play out year after year for the Chicago Cubs…attempting to fill holes all over the baseball diamond. Imagine a ship springing a leak, and the people on board are frantically moving from hole to hole…struggling to patch them.

The Chicago Cubs are *always* springing leaks.

Dick Drott, **Reason 65**, gave Cubs' fans every inclination in 1957 that he was a good Major League pitcher. Unfortunately 1957 was the anomaly, making Drott our first *One-Hit Wonder.*

REASON 66

KEN HUBBS

Ken Hubbs was not a *One-Hit Wonder* in the traditional sense. Hubbs' career was not cut short by injury or failure. Ken Hubbs' career was tragically cut short by his death at age twenty-two.

Ken Hubbs died in a plane crash in February of 1964. Hubbs and a friend were returning to California after a brief stay in Provo, Utah. Hubbs was flying the plane upon receiving his pilot's license in January of 1964. Hubbs had resolved to take flying lessons between the 1963 and 1964 seasons. Why did Hubbs want to become a pilot? The answer is simple, yet surprising; Hubbs had an *intense* fear of flying. Hubbs' former teammates would remark later of Ken's extreme anxiety when the team flew on road trips. Courageously, Ken Hubbs wanted to meet his fright head on and learn to fly a plane.

The tragic loss of Ken Hubbs was a huge blow *on and off* the field to the Cubs' organization. At the age of twenty, Ken Hubbs was the National League's Rookie of the Year. Hubbs played 160 games for the Cubs at second base and was the National League Gold Glove winner. Ken Hubbs hit .260 with 5 HRs and 49 RBIs in his rookie season of 1961. In 1962, Hubbs' average dropped to .235, yet he upped his home runs to eight, and cut down his strikeouts tremendously. Hubbs' value as a defender was extraordinary, and I imagine the Cubs felt his offensive abilities would eventually be as well. I can make this assumption about Ken Hubbs' offense because the Cubs knew what kind of athlete and person they had in Ken Hubbs.

Ken Hubbs played in the Major Leagues at ages twenty and twenty-one in his only two seasons; ages that the vast majority of players (even in 2012) are still in the minor leagues. Ken Hubbs' athletic prowess suggests his offense would have improved as he aged. In high school, Hubbs was recruited to *play quarterback at Notre Dame*, and to *play basketball at UCLA*. Baseball was considered to be Hubbs' *worst* sport. However, in the early 1960s, baseball was *the* professional sport to play; professional football and basketball were years from the zenith they would attain. Hubbs declined the scholarships, and signed with the Cubs.

Imagine a Cubs' future for Ken Hubbs, and for the sake of argument, assume his offense would have progressed. Hubbs would have entered his prime along with Billy Williams, Ron Santo, Fergie Jenkins and other Cubs who made up the roster during the late 1960s and early 1970s. Envision a gifted athlete such as Hubbs continuing to win Gold Gloves, becoming a fielder on par with Hall of Famers Brooks Robinson or Ozzie Smith. Considering the age at which he made the Major Leagues and his athletic abilities, I am confident in assuming Ken Hubbs would have had a brilliant career with the Chicago Cubs.

The story of Ken Hubbs (**Reason 66**) is a sad one. The loss of Hubbs' life is more tragic than a baseball team that has an innate ability to continue to lose. Of the 104 reasons penned in this book...**Reason 66** is not the Cubs' fault. **Reason 66** is a horrifying twist of fate that cost a young man his life while he was attempting to conquer one of his weaknesses. A potentially great Major League career was cut short, and the Chicago Cubs were profoundly damaged on and off the field.

REASON 67

D ICK ELLSWORTH

Dick Ellsworth pitched for thirteen seasons in the Major Leagues, eight with the Chicago Cubs. Ellsworth pitched in 407 games throughout his Major League career. As a 6'3" left-hander, Ellsworth had good size, and threw with the hand that keeps players in the big leagues. Of his thirteen seasons in the majors, only two of them could be considered "hits" or statistically aesthetic. One of those seasons was 1968 with the Boston Red Sox when Ellsworth was 16-7 with a 3.07 ERA over twenty-eight starts. Ellsworth's 1968 season pales in comparison to his 1963 season with the Cubs. Take a look:

1963	W/L	IP	H	ER	BB	SO	ERA	SHO
Dick Ellsworth	22-10	290.2	223	68	75	175	2.11	4

How many teams would like to have the season above from a twenty-three year-old left hander? Yes…every baseball team that has ever existed. If a lefty starter put up those kinds of numbers in 2012 at age twenty-three, he would be looking at attaining a contract of $100 million. After Dick Ellsworth's 1963 season, it appeared the Cubs had a *true* left-handed ace! Then this happened:

DICK ELLSWORTH	W/L	ERA	HOME RUNS ALLOWED
1964	14-18	3.75	34
1965	14-15	3.81	22
1966	8-22	3.98	28

Oops…so much for Dick Ellsworth being considered an ace. In two of the seasons listed above Ellsworth led the league in *hits allowed*. In 1966 he allowed an amazing 321 hits in 269.1 innings. The fellow was apparently pitching batting practice, after dominating the league just three years before. Imagine witnessing the kind of greatness displayed so briefly in 1963 and watching it vanish so quickly? It's no wonder the Cubs let Ellsworth struggle for three full seasons, undoubtedly hoping he would rediscover whatever "magic" or stuff he had in 1963. After waiting for three years, and seeing nothing close to the performance of 1963 return, the Cubs had to wonder... what happened?

If you look at Dick Ellsworth's total career numbers, a reasonable answer *can* be found. Ellsworth's career record was 115-137, a winning percentage of .456. If I remove Ellsworth's two "hit" seasons of '63 and '68, his career record drops to 77-120...a winning percentage of .390. Ellsworth finished his career with an ERA of 3.72, but that number jumps to 4.07 sans 1963 and 1968. Dick Ellsworth's career mirrored the pitcher he was in eleven of his thirteen seasons, not the player he was in 1963 and 1968. Those two seasons were statistical anomalies for Dick Ellsworth, a phenomenon that has fooled many a baseball observer. If "new" statistics (unavailable at the time) were applied to Ellsworth's 1963 and 1968 seasons, they might provide some answers. Maybe Ellsworth was just really lucky in those two seasons?

Dick Ellsworth's one tremendous season for the Cubs, and his subsequent disappointing seasons tell a conflicting tale. The idea behind CHAPTER 6: ONE-HIT WONDERS was not to prioritize them, yet Ellsworth is the type of player the Cubs really need to compete. Starting pitchers have continuously been of short supply, and left-handers who flash the success Dick Ellsworth displayed in 1963 are particularly uncommon. Consequently, when it appears you have such a valuable asset, it makes it a considerably tougher disappointment when the asset turns out to be worthless. The Cubs may have rightfully assumed they had another Sandy Koufax-type lefty after Ellsworth's 1963 season. The Cubs never get the "Sandy Koufax's" of the MLB, they get an abundance of "Dick Ellsworth's."

Dick Ellsworth was a classic *One-Hit Wonder* for the Chicago Cubs in 1963, and he is quite worthy of being **Reason 67.**

REASON 68

JEROME WALTON

When the Cubs made the play-offs in 1984, it had been thirty-nine years since the team's last post-season appearance. Cubs' fans only had to wait five years after 1984 as 1989 saw the Cubs reach the post-season again. The Cubs weren't expected to contend in 1989, so the 1989 National League Eastern Division title came as quite a surprise. The Cubs still had three holdovers from the 1984 division winners in Rick Sutcliffe, Scott Sanderson and Ryne Sandberg. In addition, the 1989 Cubs had Greg Maddux, who won nineteen games and combined with Sutcliffe to give the Cubs a formidable 1-2 rotation punch. Furthermore, the '89 Cubs had a still-productive Hall of Famer in Andre Dawson and a budding star in Mark Grace, who hit .314 and was an on-base machine with a .405 on-base percentage. Much of the rest of the team was made up of surprises, career years and regrettably, *One-Hit Wonders.*

Jerome Walton was the 1989 National League Rookie of the Year. The Cubs' fortunes turned about in 1989 when Walton was installed as the center fielder and lead-off man. With Sandberg hitting second, the Cubs had a similar 1-2 combination at the top of the order to 1984's Bob Dernier and Sandberg. In fact Harry Carry quickly dubbed them the new "Daily Double;" the title he affectionately used on Dernier and Sandberg in 1984. Walton hit .293, scored sixty-four runs and stole twenty-four bases in only 116 games. Walton slugged .385, with twenty-three doubles, three triples and five home runs. A flaw in Walton's '89 numbers was his .335 on base percentage...he only drew twenty-seven walks in 515 plate appearances. Despite his inability to draw walks out of the lead-off spot, Walton's positive numbers outweighed his negatives and contributed significantly to the 1989 National League Eastern Division title.

After Jerome Walton's stellar 1989 Rookie of the Year campaign, the Cubs appeared to have a long-term solution in center field. In characteristic Cubs' style, Walton's 1989 season proved the *exception* rather than the *rule.* The center field position was only solved for a very short time for the Chicago Cubs. In his sophomore season of 1990, Walton battled injuries and ineffectiveness as his batting average dropped to .263. Walton's walk total (50) and on-base percentage (.350) rose, yet his slugging percentage dipped to .329.

In 1991, at the age of twenty-five, Walton appeared in 123 games, and hit just .219 in 270 at bats. The Cubs began to employ Walton solely as a pinch hitter, pinch runner and fourth outfielder. After appearing in only thirty games for the Cubs in 1992 (hitting .127), Walton signed with the Angels as a free agent. Walton bounced around with four more organizations, becoming an effective fourth-outfielder hitting over .290 in five straight seasons. In those five seasons Walton had 100 at bats only once. Walton was out of baseball by 1998, at age 32.

In examining a career such as Jerome Walton's, a number of questions arise:

1. Was Walton's 1989 rookie year a fluke?
2. Did the Cubs give up on Walton too soon?
3. Did Walton deserve another adequate chance to prove himself?
4. Why does this type of scenario always seem to happen to the Cubs?

Jerome Walton was probably *not* as good as 1989 indicated, yet he was perhaps better than he displayed in 1990 and 1991. Walton may have indeed deserved another chance to prove himself, but the Major Leagues are an unforgiving place. Many players only get one shot at success, and if it doesn't happen, they are quickly gone and forgotten. Combined with a fan-base as impatient and hungry for achievement as the Cubs, time works against players such as Jerome Walton.

In **CHAPTER 9**, center field will be exposed as a position in which Chicago Cubs' players have historically failed. The Cubs rarely have players consistent enough to man the position for more than a year or two, let alone a *long-term* solution. Could Jerome Walton have been the longstanding answer he appeared to be in 1989? The Cubs' cynic in me says it is decidedly doubtful.

Cubs' fans can't be held accountable for wishing for something that seems doubtful or impractical. Perhaps that is the reason the Cubs' appear to have so many **One-Hit Wonders**. Cubs' fans are so thirsty for success; we often find it in unlikely and illogical places. When that success *appears* to be legitimate, as Jerome Walton (**Reason 68**) did for one season…we drink it down.

REASON 69

Mike Harkey

Did you ever collect baseball cards? I know, I know, if you are over fifty...your mom threw them all out and you would have had a *fortune* had she kept them. If you are under forty, you may have started collecting at the *worst possible* time; the late 1980s. In the card-collecting industry, this is when the market was flooded with over-produced and unrealistically valued cards. As a collector with a bit of knowledge, I can tell you that considerable money was spent during those years on *crap*. You may have paid $10-$15 for a Greg Jeffries' rookie card! How about $5 for a Kevin Mass rookie? Jose Canseco and Mark McGwire...the *safest* "investments," turned out to be...crap. One of the cards you may have bought during this time: a 1989 Donruss Rated Rookie of Mike Harkey.

Mike Harkey was the fourth overall pick of the first round for the Chicago Cubs in 1987. Harkey quickly ascended through the Cubs' minor league system. By 1990, at the age of twenty-three, Harkey had a spot in the Cubs' starting rotation. Take a look at Mike Harkey's 1990 season:

1990 SEASON	GAMES	W/L	IP	H	ER	BB	SO	ERA
Mike Harkey	27	12-6	173.67	153	63	59	94	3.26

I hope you sold all of your Mike Harkey rookie cards *after* the 1990 season, as that would have been the only time you could have gotten *any* return on your "investment." Injuries to his arm and an ill-advised cartwheel would cause a downward spiral for Mike Harkey's career. Shoulder and elbow problems limited Harkey to just four games in 1991, and seven in 1992. Harkey and the Cubs suffered through two completely *lost* seasons after his breakout season of 1990.

In September of 1992, Harkey damaged his knee while attempting to do a cartwheel (why?) before a game. Harkey was able to recover enough from his outfield gymnastics to start twenty-eight games for the Cubs in 1993. The results for Harkey in 1992 displayed that perhaps he should try his hand at gymnastics:

1993 SEASON	GAMES	W/L	IP	H	ER	BB	SO	ERA
Mike Harkey	28	10-10	157.33	187	92	43	67	5.26

Hmmm…I hope it wasn't *just* because of the cartwheel. Harkey left the Cubs after 1993 and signed as a free agent with the Colorado Rockies. In 1994 Harkey went 1-6 with a 5.79 ERA. Mike Harkey's arm was apparently shot. He struggled for three more seasons with the A's, Angels, and Dodgers…but by age thirty-one, he retired.

Mike Harkey's arm injuries abruptly ended a once-promising career. Like Dick Drott before him, Mike Harkey's injuries created a hole in the Cubs' rotation. Once again, the Cubs would be looking for starting pitching. As with Dick Drott, Mike Harkey seemed to have tremendous potential. One good year would be all the Cubs would receive.

Don't feel *too sorry* for Mike Harkey. He got his World Series ring as a member of the New York Yankees coaching staff in 2009. He currently holds the position of bullpen coach for the New York Yankees under Joe Girardi. Coming up in the Cubs' system *with* Joe Girardi gave Harkey a wonderful opportunity at a post-playing career.

Mike Harkey's one successful season makes him a prototypical *One-Hit Wonder.* The demise of Harkey's pitching career as a Chicago Cub places him as **Reason 69** out of 104.

If you would still like to "invest" in some Mike Harkey rookie cards, there is a lot of 50 for $2.95 for sale on ebay right now! I am not an expert, but I wouldn't advise it.

REASON 70

RICK WILKINS

As a *young* baseball fan, did you ever wonder why pitchers couldn't hit? I couldn't comprehend this when I was a young lad. It boggled my little mind. Pitchers are Major League ballplayers…why can't they hit? It took a while before I could logically understand why the majority of pitchers struggle to hit at the Major League level. I had to grasp the concept that it requires an entirely different skill set to pitch, an ability that requires constant repetition and practice. *Hitting a baseball* requires a different skill set entirely, necessitating just as much practice. Only exceptional players have the skills to compete at the Major League level as *both* a hitter and a pitcher.

Catcher is a position that also requires a specific skill set for success; it is a demanding *defensive* position. Due to the immense defensive skills catching requires, it is *almost* as hard to find a catcher with both Major League offensive and defensive skills. When examining catchers in Cubs' history, only one truly stands out: Hall of Famer Gabby Hartnett. An OPS is now accepted as a reflective and relevant offensive statistic. Gabby Hartnett's numbers from the twenties and thirties are still the greatest in team history. Of the top five offensive seasons by a catcher in Cubs' history, Gabby has four of the top five. Take a look: (we will throw in home runs, RBI, and batting average since they are "sexier" statistics, more identifiable to the average baseball fan).

TOP 5 OFFENSIVE CUBS' CATCHERS	HR	RBI	AVG	OPS
1930 Gabby Hartnett	37	122	.339	1.034
1937 Gabby Hartnett	12	82	.354	.971
1935 Gabby Hartnett	13	91	.344	.949
1993 *Rick Wilkins?*	30	73	.303	.937
1928 Gabby Hartnett	14	57	.302	.928

If I kept ranking Cubs' catchers, Gabby would garner the next two spots on this list as well. Geo Soto's recent 2010 (.890) would rank eighth overall in Cubs' history. Yet, of the top *five* catchers listed above, who stands out? I am deducing you detected the same oddity I did; the inclusion of one Rick Wilkins.

After the 1993 season, I remember thinking what an outstanding year Wilkins had. I did not grasp how *historically* significant it was until embarking on this project. Jody Davis was a solid offensive and defensive (Gold Glove winner in 1986) catcher for the Cubs...yet his OPS never broke the .800 mark. Former Cubs' catcher Randy Hundley, acknowledged as one of the Cubs' best catchers, also *never* had an OPS above .800. Jody Davis and Randy Hundley are familiar names to most Cubs' fans, yet it was *Rick Wilkins* who had the fourth best offensive season in the Cubs' 137 year history!

Rick Wilkins was twenty-six in 1993, and the Cubs' appeared to have an extraordinary player. In typical Cubs' *One-Hit Wonder* fashion...Wilkins followed up his phenomenal '93 with a dud of a season in 1994. Wilkins hit just .227 with seven home runs and thirty-nine RBIs. After struggling again in 1995, the Cubs quickly shipped Wilkins to Houston for Luis Gonzalez and Scott Servais. Perhaps the Astros felt Wilkins could revert to his 1993 form. In 1996, despite being in the middle of a decent offensive season (.743 OPS), the Astros traded Wilkins to the Giants. Beginning in 1996, Wilkins would play for five more teams, primarily as a back-up catcher.

In CHAPTER 9 I will examine the historic dearth of left-handed power from the Cubs. I will also investigate the Cubs' inability to discover solid catchers *not-named* Gabby Hartnett. In Rick Wilkins, it initially appeared the Cubs had a solution to *both* of these long-term problem areas. The 1993 "appearance" of Rick Wilkins was quite deceiving.

Why was Rick Wilkins so good in 1993 compared to the rest of his career? If you have those answers, I am confident a Major League team would hire you as a hitting coach or as a team psychologist. As with most things Cubs, there are no answers...only questions.

There is *no* question regarding the *One-Hit Wonder* status of Rick Wilkins. (**Reason 70**)

REASON 71

TUFFY RHODES

Karl "Tuffy" Rhodes was the starting center fielder for the 1994 edition of the Chicago Cubs. The Cubs acquired Rhodes in a three-team deal with the Royals and Yankees at the 1993 trade deadline. Rhodes was a highly touted prospect in the Houston organization, yet had failed to ascend to the Major League level. Rhodes saw limited action for the Cubs in '93, but it was enough to impress the Cubs' brass. Rhodes hit .288 with three HRs with an impressive .413 on-base percentage in sixty-three plate appearances. At twenty-four, "Tuffy" Rhodes was a part of the Cubs' plans for the 1994 season.

On April 4, 1994, Rhodes made the Cubs look pretty clever. Rhodes was on-base in all five plate appearances and scored three runs. The bigger story was that Tuffy hit *three* home runs...all off of Mets' ace Dwight "Doc" Gooden. Rhodes' impressive debut was for naught as the Cubs lost 12-8. Even when the Cubs actually *hit* Dwight Gooden (5 IP, 11 hits, 5 ER), they still managed to lose to him.

Rhodes followed up his opening day performance with two hits in four at bats in Game 2 of the season...another Cubs' loss. The rest of April went pretty well for Rhodes, and Rhodes had impressive numbers for a lead-off hitter at the end of the month:

APRIL 1994	AB	R	H	2B	3B	HR	RBI	BB	SO	AVG	OBP
Tuffy Rhodes	80	16	25	5	0	6	10	10	16	.313	.396

Rhodes slugged .600 in April, which gave him an impressive .996 OPS. Regrettably for Tuffy and the Cubs, the season did not end in April.

REST OF 1994	AB	R	H	2B	3B	HR	RBI	BB	SO	AVG	OBP
Tuffy Rhodes	189	23	38	12	0	2	9	23	48	.201	.287

Rhodes was no longer playing regularly by the end of July, and a strike would end the only season that did not crown a World Series champion. Rhodes was traded to the Boston Red Sox in 1995 and was out of the Major Leagues by the end of 1996.

Tuffy Rhodes' career is just significant enough for inclusion on our list of 104 reasons. In Rhodes' case, I am not just examining the player, but the Cubs' decision as well. Rhodes' brief performance at the end of 1993 may have had the Cubs believing they possessed a legit Major League lead-off man. They gambled a portion of their potential success the following season on Tuffy Rhodes...and they lost. The Cubs were wrong about Tuffy Rhodes...but *how* were they wrong?

In 1996 Karl "Tuffy" Rhodes signed a contract to play for the Kintetsu Buffaloes of Nippon Professional Baseball in Japan. NPB has produced such Major Leaguers as Ichiro Suzuki, Hideki Matusi and most recently... Yu Darvish. Tuffy Rhodes would play thirteen seasons in Japan. Among his extraordinary accomplishments:

- Rhodes tied the single season home run mark of fifty-five and was pitched around in the final days of the season, protecting the record from a foreign player.

- Rhodes hit 474 career home runs.

- Rhodes had .286 lifetime batting average.

- Rhodes earned the right after ten years to be considered a Japanese player, not counting against his teams' foreign player cap.

- Rhodes drove in 1,292 runs.

Rhodes had tremendous success in the NPB. He was a popular player and adapted well to Japanese culture. Rhodes' great seasons in Japan were comparable to Ichiro Suzuki. In 2007, the Chicago Cubs would give Kosuke Fukudome a four-year $48 million contract to play right field. Fukudome's numbers in Japan did not compare to Tuffy Rhodes, against the same competition.

So *how* were the Cubs wrong? Were they wrong to have given Rhodes a chance, which helped ruin their 1994 season? Should the Cubs have given one of the greatest hitters in Japanese baseball history more of an opportunity? In the case of Karl "Tuffy" Rhodes, it appears the Cubs were wrong *either* way. In either case, Karl Rhodes was a *One-Hit-Wonder* and is **Reason 71** of our 104.

REASON 72

MARK PRIOR
This one hurts.

I was fortunate enough to be at the first game Mark Prior ever pitched for the Chicago Cubs in 2002. Prior earned his first Major League victory as the Cubs defeated the Pirates 7-4. Prior threw six innings, allowed two runs and struck out ten. Upon seeing Prior, I was amazed at the size of this twenty-one-year-old "kid." I left the game very content that night. Combined with Kerry Wood, I felt the Cubs' staff was set for many years to come.

When I was growing up, it was common for people who grew up in the 1960s to state that they could recall their exact location upon hearing of John Kennedy's assassination. I can tell you exactly where I was when Mark Prior had *two* significant injuries. I was standing directly in the middle of my living room when Prior collided with Atlanta second baseman Marcus Giles. Prior would spend time on the disabled list after the collision, yet he came back strong going 10-1 to finish 2003. In 2005, I was going to lunch when a co-worker said, "Prior's done; he just got hit in the elbow with a line drive…they are saying his career is over." My friend was a bit overdramatic, but his prediction of Mark Prior's demise wasn't totally inaccurate. Mark Prior *was* just about done.

After Prior recovered from the linedrive that nailed him (estimated to be traveling at **117** MPH), he returned to finish 11-7 in 2005. Prior was shut down in the spring of 2006 with a sore shoulder, and when he pitched in 2006…he was shelled. Prior finished 1-6 with a 7.21 ERA and the Cubs did not offer him a contract for 2007.

In 2003, Mark Prior went 18-6 with a 2.43 ERA and 245 strikeouts in 211 innings. It was Mark Prior who was on the mound (and in control) when the Cubs were a mere five outs away from going to the 2003 World Series. After the myriad of injuries Prior incurred, he never approached his 2003 performance levels. Mark Prior is a **One-Hit Wonder** due to his injuries, and his inclusion in this chapter requires "what if?" analysis.

What if Mark Prior had pitched more than one or two healthy seasons for the Chicago Cubs? Mark Prior was one of the most highly touted prospects to come out of college…**EVER.** The pitcher Mark Prior was often compared to Tom Seaver. Prior's delivery produced "easy heat," as his fastball consistently sat in the mid-1990s. Prior had exceptional command and control of his pitches. *Had* Prior stayed healthy with consistency *close* to his 2003 season, the idea of this book may have been obsolete. Mark Prior is significant enough that he appears in more than one of my 104 reasons. The cause for that is simple: Mark Prior may be the player whose demise impacted the fate of the Chicago Cubs more than any other.

Imagine the Cubs having a healthy Prior over the last nine seasons. (I know, I know, it's tough…but just do it.) It's depressing and sad, but the entire decade would have been altered for the Chicago Cubs. In 2003 Mark Prior was one of the two or three best pitchers on the planet...and he was twenty-two years old. Cubs' players often cannot repeat a great year, and Cubs' fans are left to ponder if the season was legitimate. Prior was different because he had genuine talent...he wasn't a fluke or a flash in the pan. Mark Prior *was* the real deal, only all too briefly.

Mark Prior may pitch again in the Major Leagues, as he is still attempting to pitch at age thirty-two. Regardless, Prior has left a legacy in Major League Baseball that will last a long time. Teams are more cautious than ever with prized pitching prospects, even shutting pitchers down upon reaching innings limits. Teams now realize the need to protect young pitchers as valuable assets, something the Cubs did not do with Mark Prior.

I don't mean to sound overdramatic, but **Reason 72** was difficult for me to write. Labeling Mark Prior a *One-Hit Wonder* seemed a bit harsh and cold. Conversely, it's only because of the immense talent that Prior briefly displayed that makes him the most significant player included in this chapter.

REASON 73

R ICH HILL

The Cubs' rotation that had showed such promise in 2003-2004 was almost completely turned over in three short years. Kerry Wood, Mark Prior and Matt Clement would all succumb to arm injuries, and pitch sparingly or not at all. When the Cubs fell out of contention in 2006, Greg Maddux was traded away at the July 31 deadline. As the promise of Wood/Prior was vanishing, Cubs' fans were given a glimmer of hope upon hearing of a new prospect. This prospect was striking out batters in the minors at an *astounding* rate...*and* he was left-handed. In 2005, this pitcher struck out 194 batters in just 130 innings between A-AA stops...a rate of 13.4 per 9. At AAA Iowa in 2006, the prospect went 7-1 with 135 strikeouts in one-hundred innings. The Cubs could not hold back their new "Kid K" any longer, and Rich Hill came up to the Major Leagues at the end of 2006.

Rich Hill finished out the 2006 season going 6-7 with a 4.17 ERA. Hill struck out ninety batters in ninety-nine innings, and showed enough promise to be a lock for the 2007 rotation. In 2007, Hill started thirty-two games, and went 11-8 with a 3.92 ERA. Hill struck out 183 batters in 195 innings. On the down side, Hill did walk sixty-three batters and allow 27 HRs. However, 2007 was promising enough that Hill was counted on to be part of the Cubs' starting rotation again in 2008.

After the promise of 2007, Rich Hill would only start *five* games for the Chicago Cubs in 2008. Hill's control issues did not endear him to manager Lou Piniella, and he was quickly gone from the rotation. Here are Hill's first five starts in 2008:

2008 RICH HILL	TEAM RESULT	IP	H	ER	BB	SO	W/L
vs. HOU	Cubs lose 4-3	6	4	2	3	4	ND
vs. PIT	Cubs win 7-3	3	3	3	4	3	ND
vs. PIT	Cubs win 3-2	5	3	1	3	4	WIN
vs. COL	Cubs win 7-6	5	3	2	4	3	ND
vs. STL	Cubs lose 5-3	.2	0	1	4	1	ND

Hill was sent down to the minors after walking four in the first inning against St. Louis. For the rest of 2008, Hill would struggle in the minors to regain his control and never earned a return trip to the Cubs' rotation. Rich Hill's career with the Cubs would come to an end the next winter when they allowed him to leave via free agency. Over the next four years Hill would bounce around the league with the Orioles and Red Sox. Hill also battled arm injuries for the latter part of his professional career.

Rich Hill is a player of whose career path I had already forgotten. When I began this project, I knew Hill would be featured in my *One-Hit Wonder* section, yet now I feel Hill merits a second look. In just four short years, my recall about Rich Hill was not completely accurate. Rich Hill had to better command his pitches to remain at the Major League level, yet the Cubs did *win* three of his starts in 2008. Hill's overall numbers were decent enough to warrant another start. Hill's last start with the Chicago Cubs occurred on May 2, 2008...the Cubs were 17-12, 1.5 games out of first place. Was it necessary to send Rich Hill to the minor leagues after only five starts?

(BASEBALL CLICHÉ ALERT) Baseball is a game of confidence, and I am assuming/guessing/speculating that Rich Hill's self-assurance was shot in 2008. Lou Piniella was seemingly tired of Hill's performances, and his patience with Hill may have worn out. A different manager may have treated Rich Hill with more patience, which may have produced improved results. Perhaps a diverse approach causes Rich Hill to rebound. It was May 2; the twenty-seven year-old threw 195 solid innings the year before. Why not give Hill one or two more starts? How about ten starts before sending him down??

Frankly, I have no idea why Rich Hill was not given another opportunity or if he even deserved one. I do know that left-handed starters are difficult to cultivate, and his abrupt termination was unfortunate for Hill and the Cubs. Is it such a stretch to believe Hill may have regained his confidence? What if Hill began to resemble the pitcher who struck out 13.4 per 9 in the minors? Does a dominant Hill give the Cubs an enhanced opportunity to win in the 2008 play-offs?

Rich Hill (**Reason 73**) may have lacked the mental make-up to be a starting pitcher in the Major Leagues. Lou Piniella's impatience with Rich Hill may have ruined a once-promising career. The truth may lie somewhere in between those scenarios. Regardless, the Chicago Cubs lost a spot in the rotation they thought was accounted for. Resources and assets would have to be diverted, weakening the Cubs in another area to make up for Rich Hill's rotation spot. The unfortunate result is Rich Hill becoming another *One-Hit-Wonder* for Chicago Cubs.

One-Hit Wonders

The term *One-Hit Wonders* is most often used to describe musicians who have one chart-topping song. Popular music is chock-full of musical acts that come and go in a flash. With this analogy in mind, I am going to have a little fun with the players listed here in CHAPTER 6. I am going to count down a Cubs' One-Hit Top Five! I will prioritize them in terms of relevance and how big of a "hit" they were. Here are the four *honorable* mention players, who do not merit a position on the Cubs' One-Hit Top Five: Dick Drott, Dick Ellsworth, Tuffy Rhodes, and Rich Hill.

5. **Mike Harkey**

    While pitching in high school, Harkey drew comparisons to Bob Gibson. The Cubs were hoping Harkey would be the next Dwight Gooden. The Cubs received one solid year...and an ill-advised pre-game cartwheel.

4. **Jerome Walton**

    Lead-off center fielders with speed that can hit...are hard to find. The Cubs found one...for *one* season.

3. **Ken Hubbs**

    One of the most tragic stories in all of Cubs' history. This gifted athlete would have been a big part of the Chicago Cubs from the early 1960s until the mid-1970s.

2. **Rick Wilkins**

    He produced the greatest offensive season by a catcher for the Chicago Cubs not-named Gabby Hartnett. After that outstanding season...*not so much.*

1. **Mark Prior**

    Prior may have had the most talent of any Cubs' draft pick/prospect ever. He was talented enough to get the Cubs five outs away from a World Series, and who knows where else he might have taken them, if he could have remained healthy.

Taking this music one-hit wonder analogy one step further, I am going to take our top five players and connect them with an appropriate song. These may seem a bit silly, but we need to end with a bit of levity after such a depressing chapter.

Mike Harkey
"It's Raining Men"
by the Weather Girls

I picture Harkey as a big, lovable goof (maybe it was the cartwheel). I also picture Harkey being a man secure enough to admit he would dance around to this guilty pleasure. With all of Harkey's injuries, he always landed on his feet...except once.

Jerome Walton
"Ice, Ice Baby"
by Vanilla Ice

All right, stop. Collaborate and listen. It's the right time period, and I am sure Walton had Ice's trademark fade haircut at one time. As a fleet-footed center fielder, I am sure Walton could match Ice on the dance floor.

Ken Hubbs
"American Pie"
by Don McLean

If you know this old tear-inducing anthem, then you know why I made this choice.

Rick Wilkins
"I'm Too Sexy"
by Right Said Fred

I can't explain it...I just find something funny about associating this former catcher's career with this song. It's actually funny picturing anyone singing this song, including Right Said Fred.

Mark Prior
"My Sharona"
by the Knack

I will never forget the comment one of my college roommates said about this song. He said if an alien arrived on Earth and wanted to hear what rock 'n roll sounded like...this would be the perfect song. Upon its release, this song was a monster success...just like Prior. The Knack's first album **GET THE KNACK,** had other minor hits, and the group appeared to be the "real deal." Like Mark Prior, this group had one remarkable accomplishment... and then irrelevance.

Injuries, luck, lack of skill and even death permitted these players from fulfilling their potentials as Major League players. I am not labeling any of these *One-Hit Wonders* players as responsible for the Cubs' lack of World Series titles. Regrettably, the circumstances, outcomes, decisions, and results that accompanied these careers undoubtedly meet those criteria.

CHAPTER 7

REASON 74—THE CUBS *HAD* THEIR RIGHTS...
THEY JUST DIDN'T SIGN THEM (*SIGH*)
Did you even know the Cubs had the rights to
Darrell Evans and Tim Lincecum? Me neither.

REASON 75—THE 1970S AND 1980S TRADE COINCIDENCES?
The Cubs traded away many solid players who ironically
made much more money on the teams who acquired them.

REASON 76—LATE TO THE FREE AGENT PARTY
Many teams were quick to take advantage of free agency...
the Cubs? Not one of them.

REASON 77—NOT SO *FREE* AGENTS (1):
TWO BAD PITCHERS
Danny Jackson and Dave Smith pitched very poorly
upon signing with the Chicago Cubs.

REASON 78—NOT SO *FREE* AGENTS (2):
THE GREG MADDUX REPLACEMENTS
Cubs' GM Larry Himes spent the money that would have gone
to Maddux on Juan Guzman, Candy Maldonado, and Randy Myers.
How'd that work out?

REASON 79—Not So *Free* Agents (3): Jeff Blauser

I still can't figure out if I forgot he was even on the Cubs, or if I blocked the whole thing out.

REASON 80—Not So *Free* Agents (4): Todd Hundley

Sometimes you can go home again. Other times, it turns into a catastrophic disaster.

REASON 81—Not So *Free* Agents (5): Alfonso Soriano

It's usually not a good idea for contracts to equal two presidential terms.

REASON 82—Kosuke, Milton, and the Cubs

The Cubs' search for a left-handed bat led them to Japan, and to one very stupid signing.

REASON 83—Money Matterz: The Cubz Crazy Extenzion of Big Z

Who would have thought giving almost $100 million to a guy who punched things…and people…was a bad idea?

REASON 84—The 2010 Season: The Worst Team Money Could Buy?

The 2010 Chicago Cubs had the highest payroll in team history… they were not good.

MONEY MATTERS

L et's pretend that I wrote (and you read) a long introduction on money in society. The introduction stated the evils of money, its benefits, how it makes the world go 'round, why it doesn't buy happiness and blah, blah blah! You already realize the importance of money in the United States. Money has always mattered a great deal in the United States…as has Major League Baseball.

Yankees' fans may want to cover their ears for this next section. The New York Yankees have benefited more than any team in the history of the universe because of their huge financial advantages. The Yankees have done *many* things right, so *it's* not *all about the money*…but it's helped. Consider this:

- The Yankees bought Babe Ruth from the Red Sox.

- The Yankees were able to offer Lou Gehrig the most money to sign as an amateur.

- Ruth and the team's success allowed them to build Yankee Stadium, which produced a great amount of revenue.

- Without a draft in Major League Baseball…they just had to outbid teams for amateurs…so Mantle, DiMaggio, Berra…were bought.

- From the 1930s-1960s the Yankees were really the only *big* market team.

- Then a funny thing happened…the MLB amateur draft was installed in 1965…allowing *all* teams the chance to acquire the rights to players. Oddly enough, from 1965 to 1975, the Yankees did make the play-offs once.

- The Yankees' revival in '76-'78 (three straight World Series appearances, with two wins) coincided with the purchase of the team by shipping magnate George Steinbrenner and the advent of free agency. The 1977 Yankees, with Reggie Jackson, Catfish Hunter, and Don Gullett all signed as free agents, were the first team to essentially buy a championship.

- The Yankees recent success in the 1990s and 2000s *has* combined great scouting and development with the Major's highest payroll. Just consider this: In 2012 the Yankees' payroll will be over $200 million for the fifth straight year. Of the twenty-nine other teams, only twelve have payrolls above *$100 million.* Money does not guarantee winning; hence, the Yankees don't win every year. It helps significantly, and affords teams the luxury of paying for mistakes.

Enough about the Yankees; let's get back to the Cubs! CHAPTER 7 will examine reasons that money has prevented the Cubs from winning a World Series...in 104 years. I will observe money as a resource, and the decisions, consequences and outcomes that have accompanied money and the Chicago Cubs.

In the 1970s, the Cubs had the reputation of being cheap (does frugal sound better?). The Wrigley family ownership was ill-equipped to lead the Cubs into the era of free agency. As someone who attended games in the late '70s, things were a lot different around Wrigley Field. Parking was free on the street and just a few blocks away from Wrigley. "Walk-up" tickets were always available the day of the game and great seats they were. My dad took me into the Cubby Bear as a child and it doesn't remotely resemble the place it is today. The differences in "Wrigleyville" cannot be understated...because there was no *Wrigleyville.*

As unpopular as the Tribune ownership may have eventually become, its purchase of the Cubs was met with great joy. The team had successes, and by the end of the 1980s, the Cubs were no longer considered cheap.

The 1990s and 2000s saw a new money problem for the Cubs: having it, but spending it unwisely. In a span of a decade, they went from cheapskates to dumb spenders. The team made a plethora of money mistakes in free agency, contract extensions, and players they chose not to sign. By 2010, the team had one of the largest payrolls in baseball, yet the money was tied up in terrible long-term deals.

After 2012, some of the contracts that saddled them for the end of the decade were "coming off the books." The team's payroll has decreased in each of the last three seasons. Under new ownership…are the Cubs going back on the cheap? It's a question that will be answered over the next decade.

The Chicago Cubs have an uncanny ability at finding ways to avoid success and fail…and their history with money mirrors that description. Money can be a great resource, and can be a hindrance when spent unwisely. The Cubs' success with money is comparable to their success on the field over the last century.

I think you have a good idea how that has worked out.

REASON 74

The Cubs *Had* Their Rights… They Just Didn't Sign Them… (*sigh*)

Since the inception of the MLB draft in 1965, high school and college players are now drafted. If a team drafts a college senior with no eligibility left, that player has to sign with the team, or languish in the independent leagues (or somewhere else) until the next draft. If a player has college eligibility left, or if he is a high school player with a scholarship waiting for him, then the situation gets unpredictable. When an MLB team drafts a player, it has the *exclusive* rights to sign that player. The window of time to sign that player has changed throughout the respective collective bargaining agreements (in 2012 it was around two months). The new collective bargaining agreement (CBA) that was signed over the winter of 2011-2012 has tighter budgetary controls regarding how much a team can spend on a specific draft pick. Prior to the 2012 draft, a team could "overpay" at a draft spot, where the MLB "recommended" a different, lower amount. Thus, players re-entering the draft gamble that there will be a lucrative spot for them in the *next* draft.

The Cubs are not the only team with examples of players who do *not* sign. Mark Prior was drafted by the New York Yankees out of high school, but chose to take his scholarship at USC. In a game where money matters, examining picks the Cubs could not sign is a valid exercise. We don't *know* the magic amount of money it might have taken to sign these players; we do *know* the Cubs did not hit that amount. The cynic in me believes there *was* an amount in most of these cases. Here is a list of players the Cubs had the rights to…many of whom, I bet you did not know about:

1965 Darrell Evans (13ᵀᴴ Round, Number 241)

Baseball stat-guru and current Red Sox employee Bill James has called Evans one of the most under-rated players of all time. Evans played in an era when batting average was king, and his great on-base percentage was completely discounted. Evans slugged 414 career home runs and had five seasons of more than 100 walks. To put that in perspective, all-time great Cubs' hacker Shawon Dunston walked 203 times…in his entire career! Evans was a man ahead of his time, as his OPS (*on-base plus slugging*) would make him a very rich man in today's game. Darrell Evans did something he *wouldn't* have done with the Cubs; he won the 1984 World Series with the Tigers. Ouch.

1974 Bob Welch (14ᵀᴴ Round, Number 317)

Welch burst on the scene as a twenty-one year old in the 1977 World Series, striking out Reggie Jackson (Reggie did get his revenge in Game 6). Welch won World Series titles with both the Dodgers and A's, and was awarded the 1990 Cy Young after a 27-6 record! Welch finished his career with 211 wins, and was a dominant starter from the late 1970s until the early 1990s.

1978 Mark Langston (15ᵀᴴ Round, Number 377)

Mark Langston never *won* a World Series; however, he did pitch in the 1998 World Series for the Padres. Mark Langston was a hard-throwing, left-handed starting pitcher who led the American League in strikeouts three times. Langston won 179 games over sixteen Major League seasons. Mark Langston would have looked very good…in *any* Cubs' rotation.

1986 Ray Lankford (January Draft; 3ᴿᴰ Round, Number 62)

Lankford is one of those double whammy type picks…after not signing with the Cubs, he was drafted by the Cardinals. Lankford was an outstanding power and speed outfielder for the Cardinals for twelve of his fourteen Major League seasons. How about Lankford's 1998 numbers: .293 AVG, .391 OBP, 31 HRs, 105 RBIs, and 26 SBs. In the modern era, Ryne Sandberg is the only Cubs' player to come close to those kinds of numbers.

2003 Tim Lincecum (48TH Round, Number 1,408)

Tim Lincecum won back to back National League Cy Young Awards in 2009 and 2010. Lincecum helped the Giants win the 2010 and 2012 World Series. Over his short career, Tim Lincecum has *averaged* 9.9 strikeouts per nine innings. He might resemble a female on the mound (dude, cut the hair), but he has been one of the best pitchers in all of baseball over the last five years.

It would be unfair to assert the Cubs were totally at fault for not signing *all* of the players listed above...yet the ever-present Cubs' skeptic in me says they blew it with a few of them. The Cubs were clever enough to see the potential in all of these players...and they were right! The problem lays somewhere between the player wanting to go to or stay in college and the Cubs not offering enough money. If they would have signed just *one* of these guys, it would have made a significant difference. Considering that *three* of the five would go on to win World Series championships, they would have been great additions to *any* Cubs' team. Every Cubs' team since the inception of the draft in 1965 would have been improved by any of these five players.

Missing out on these five guys is a valid example of why the Cubs still have not won a World Series. The scouts did their jobs, the team made the picks; the Cubs just couldn't close the deal with any of them. I am just guessing (sarcasm implied), but a little more money might have done the trick. Just imagine these scenarios:

- Tim Lincecum coming up to pitch for the Cubs at the end of 2008 and dominating like he did that year for the Giants.

- Mark Langston on the 1989 National League Eastern Division title team, pitching with Maddux and Sutcliffe.

- Bob Welch on the 1984 National League Eastern Division title team, pitching with Sutcliffe and Trout.

- Ray Lankford or Darrell Evans in any Cubs' lineup throughout their entire careers.

In any of the above scenarios, the Cubs are much improved, and their chances of winning would be greatly enhanced. **Reason 74** is the fact that the Cubs *had* the rights to these players (Evans, Langston, Welch, Lankford and Lincecum) and were not able to sign them…no matter what the reason.

REASON 75

THE 1970S AND 1980S TRADE COINCIDENCES?

I was eight years old when I began to closely follow the Cubs in 1976. With innocent and fresh thoughts on the Cubs, I vividly remember asking my dad a question. Upon learning the Cubs had just traded away Bill Madlock, the twenty-five-year-old batting champion, I asked my dad why. His reply was simple, "He wanted too much money." I didn't ask how he knew this; I took it as gospel as kids tend to do until their teens. I even recollect talking to him at dinner that night about how baseball was kind of like a business. He said yes… and then expounded on numerous things about the Cubs. My dad would always complain about the cheapness of the Cubs in the 1970s. Was my dad right?

I have already mentioned these players in CHAPTER 4: ONES THAT GOT AWAY; **Reason 75** is examining the circumstances and *not* the players. First, I will investigate the case of the aforementioned Bill Madlock. Displayed below is Madlock's salary in his final season with the Cubs compared to his first post-Cubs' salary. In parenthesis, the numbers will be adjusted for inflation to reflect 2013 amounts…we can all learn some economics!

PLAYER	SALARY LAST YEAR WITH CUBS	POST-CUBS' SALARY
Bill Madlock	1976—$80,000 ($310,200)	1977—$260,000 ($1,008,156)

Bill Madlock "got paid" upon leaving the Cubs. Considering that the Cubs took back Bobby Murcer in the deal, who was making $320,000, it may not initially indicate "cheapness" by the Cubs. Yet, Murcer was nearing the end of his career while Madlock's was just beginning, pointing to an attempt by the Cubs to control their long-term costs. The 1976 season was a *very* different era, and I doubt those old enough to remember would argue the statement I am about to make: *A twenty-five-year-old African-American asking for more money was not the same in 1976 as in 2013.*

I will next look at the situation of All-Star and Cy Young Award-winning closer Bruce Sutter. In Sutter's first two breakout seasons (1977-78), Sutter was making $50,000. The Cubs gave Sutter a raise in 1979 and paid him $225,000. Sutter's 1980 salary escalated to $700,000. Here are those numbers for readers who prefer them in chart form…along with the 2013 inflation adjusted amount for more economics fun:

BRUCE SUTTER	SALARY	2013 DOLLARS
1977	$50,000	$181,000
1978	$50,000	$181,000
1979	$225,000	$750,000
1980	$700,000	$2,300,000

After the 1980 season the Cubs would trade Sutter to (of all teams!) the St. Louis Cardinals for 3B Ken Reitz and prospect Leon Durham. Let's compare the 1981 salaries of Bruce Sutter and the players they received:

1981 PLAYER	SALARY	2013 DOLLARS
Bruce Sutter	$975,000	$2,400,000
Ken Reitz	$95,000	$228,000
Leon Durham	$60,000	$140,000

The Cubs were able to slice off around $820,000 from the budget ($2.2 million in 2013 dollars)…a nice bit of savings! The Wrigley family might not have to sell as many packs of *Juicy Fruit* in 1981. I can't *prove* the Sutter deal was motivated by money, but Sutter was young and only going to get more costly. Sutter unquestionably still had ability…as his World Series title with the Cardinals just *two* years later would attest.

Let's look at one more example, former Cubs' second baseman Manny Trillo. Like Bill Madlock and Bruce Sutter, you recall Manny was also featured in CHAPTER 4: ONES THAT GOT AWAY. Why did Manny *get away*? Maybe because of this:

PLAYER	SALARY LAST YEAR WITH CUBS	POST-CUBS' SALARY
Manny Trillo	1978—$50,000 ($181,700)	1979—$375,000 ($1.2 million)

In retrospect, I should have been very happy for Manny in 1979; he received over a 700 percent raise! In 1979, I naively believed the Cubs felt the players they received in return...Barry Foote, Ted Sizemore and Jerry Martin...would win them a World Series title. You know, like the World Series title Manny *won* with the Phillies in 1980...just *one* year later!

In all three of these circumstances, the Cubs made significant financial gains by trading away the player in question. I can't prove these deals were motivated by the bottom line, yet the cynic in me suspects it. In the span of four seasons, the Cubs:

~TRADED AWAY~

A twenty-five-year-old batting champion at a position of weakness for the Cubs

A Cy Young Award-winning relief pitcher that was still dominant

A Gold Glove caliber defender at second base who hit well for the position

~AND RECEIVED~

A power hitting right-fielder at the end of his career

A good first base prospect that later would have five productive seasons

The rest...pretty much nothing of significance...at all.

If money was not a factor in these decisions, then stupidity is the only explanation. All of the players traded away would win a World Series rather quickly:

BILL MADLOCK
World Series Champion 1979
with Pittsburgh Pirates

MANNY TRILLO
World Series Champion 1980
with Philadelphia Phillies

BRUCE SUTTER
World Series Champion 1982
with St. Louis Cardinals

What about the players the Cubs got back?

ALL OF THEM
No World Series Champions
with the Chicago Cubs

Like Cubs' fans, these players never experienced a World Series with the Chicago Cubs. **Reason 75** may seem cynical, but I believe *Money Mattered* in all of these deals.

*All the salary information listed above was obtained from
Baseballreference.com. In some cases, salaries had to be estimated
using the last salaries on record.*

REASON 76

LATE TO THE FREE AGENT PARTY

Have you ever seen the movie *Stripes* starring Bill Murray? In the film, Murray plays John Winger, a late twenty-something slacker who regrettably joins the army. After his brief experience with Winger, Winger's commanding officer Sgt. Hulka expresses his dissatisfaction with him:

HULKA:
"I've noticed something, soldier. You're always last."

WINGER'S RESPONSE:
"I am pacing myself, Sergeant."

Perhaps this is what the Cubs have been doing for 104 years...pacing themselves. Like John Winger, the Cubs seem to be last...*a lot*. I am not just referring to the standings, I am talking about *everything!* I can relate to the importance of tradition, yet I feel the Cubs and their fans value tradition *over* success. If the DH rule was instituted in the National League, it wouldn't surprise me if the Cubs refused to use it, putting their own team at a disadvantage.

The Chicago Cubs were the last team to get lights, and after twenty-five years *still* can't play a game on a Friday night in their own park. In 2012, the Cubs installed a Jumbo-tron in right field; it's more like a big TV. Simply, the Cubs have been historically slow to evolve in a number of areas...including free agency.

In 1976, Dodgers' pitcher Andy Messersmith signed the first ever free agent contract with the Atlanta Braves. Many teams, specifically the Yankees and other high-revenue teams, immediately embraced the concept of free agency. Forty years later, free agency in Major League Baseball has proven to be a very slippery slope; failure is as common as success. Some Major League teams are *still* reluctant to dip their toes in the free agent pool. The Cubs, as usual, were deliberate in their approach to free agency.

In **Reason 76** I am NOT going to include years in which the Cubs re-signed their own free agents (i.e. Rick Sutcliffe and Dennis Eckersley after 1984). In any sport when a team re-signs its own players, I don't view it in the same way. It bothers me when general managers take credit for re-signing their own free agent players, or attempt to spin it like it is an addition to the team. Fans never feel the team is signing a *new* player; they rightfully think *"we had that guy last year!"*

Discounting their own players, over a fourteen-year period (1976-1990), the Cubs signed two "major" free agents. The first was Dave Kingman who signed with the Cubs in November 1977. (The *same* Dave Kingman who gave a certain substitute batboy a "high five" after a spring training home run in March of 1978!) In 1979 Kingman had a **HUGE** year for the Cubs; hitting .288 with forty-eight home runs and 115 RBIs. When Kingman hit home runs that summer, he *hit* them. The buildings and houses on Waveland Avenue were getting peppered with Dave Kingman shots all season. Kingman had a hard time dealing with the Chicago media (actually he had a hard time with all media), and he was traded to the Mets just two years later. The year 1979 would be Kingman's only significant season with the Cubs. Kingman wasn't necessarily a free agent bust, but he certainly wasn't a long-term success.

The Cubs' second major free agent signing (their first *real* one in my opinion) was Andre Dawson prior to the 1987 season. Andre pursued the Cubs as much as the Cubs chased him. Dealing with bad knees from the poor artificial turf in Montreal, Andre longed to play at least eighty-one games on natural grass. The potential signing of Dawson was my off-season obsession that year...I can remember drawing a Cubs' hat on a picture of him during one of my college courses. (For some reason, the *Chicago Tribune* sports section usually accompanied me to class.) I followed the saga closely, and Andre basically gave the Cubs a blank check to sign him to what they deemed fair. Andre wasn't pleased when GM Dallas Green wrote $500,000 on that check. Dawson did earn another $200,000 in incentives by hitting forty-nine home runs and winning the 1987 MVP. Andre was a significant part of the Cubs' 1989 Eastern Division Championship team and was a rock solid leader in the clubhouse.

As with most changes to the game of Major League Baseball, the Cubs were very slow to embrace free agency. The Cubs' initial tepid response to free agency can be excused, but over a fourteen-year period, they should now be more active. An earlier or more aggressive approach to free agency may have helped them win a World Series title. In 1982, the Cubs were one of the finalists to sign free agent first baseman Steve Garvey. Garvey eventually signed with the Padres, who the Cubs later played in the 1984 NLCS (need reminding on how that turned out?). Here is just a sampling of players who were available via free agency from 1976-1990: (I only included players who had productive years after signing...in other words...they were not washed up.)

1976—1979

Sal Bando, Don Baylor, Bert Campaneris, Darrell Evans, Don Gullett, Gary Matthews, Joe Morgan, Pete Rose, Joe Rudi, NOLAN RYAN, and Luis Tiant.

(I felt Nolan Ryan had to be in capital letters.)

1980—1989
Joaquin Andujar, Jack Clark, John Denny, Steve Garvey, Kirk Gibson,
Rich Gossage, Ron Guidry, Reggie Jackson, Dennis Martinez,
Jack Morris, Dave Winfield, and Robin Yount

There were dozens of other significant players that I could have included in the lists above. I restricted the lists to Hall of Famers and players the average fan may have heard of. Any one of the players listed above...if signed at the time they were free agents...would have enhanced the Cubs' chances at a World Series.

Free agency has doomed many teams that have spent in reckless and unintelligent ways. The Cubs' own recent history (Soriano, Fukudome, and Bradley) is a very good example. Even the Yankees are not immune, as after 2012, the $114 million and five years still owed to Alex Rodriguez appears to be a huge albatross.

Mistakes like those listed above give pause regarding free agency, yet in the initial fourteen years of free agency, the Cubs were too cautious. **Reason 76** states that the Cubs' careful (or cheap) approach to free agency certainly cost them opportunities to win a World Series.

REASON 77

Not So *Free* Agents (1): Two Bad Pitchers

In the winter of 1990, the Cubs *finally* took a plunge into the free agent pool...a *big* plunge. The Cubs still had Ryne Sandberg, Mark Grace, Greg Maddux, Andre Dawson, and Rick Sutcliffe on the roster, and general manager Larry Himes saw the potential in adding to this strong core. The Cubs signed a trio of free agents: outfielder George Bell, starting pitcher Danny Jackson, and closer Dave Smith. Two of the three turned out to be colossal busts, money poorly spent for the Chicago Cubs. Actually "poorly spent" is too kind, how about: The Cubs could have just burned the money in a big fire at Wrigley Field and it would have accomplished the same results!

Danny Jackson was signed to be the left-handed complement to Maddux, Sutcliffe and Mike Bielecki. Jackson was coming off a subpar 6-11, 5.60 ERA performance for the 1990 World Champion Reds. Himes and the Cubs must have been convinced that Jackson could revert back to his 1988 form, in which Jackson went 23-8 with a 2.73 ERA, and pitched fifteen complete games and *six* shut outs. Jackson signed a four-year deal with the Cubs for around $10.5 million, working out to about $2.625 million per year. That contract would be a pittance today; adjusting for inflation, it would be $4.4 million per year in 2013. Regardless of the year, the Cubs *really could have* just burned that money in a big pile...or given it to me.

Jackson pitched in only seventeen games due to injuries in 1991. In 1992 he pitched in nineteen games before he was traded to the Pirates for 3B Steve Buechele. (This trade took place on my wedding day...and pathetically, I knew about it.) Here are the career numbers for Danny Jackson as a Cub:

CUB CAREER	GAMES	W/L	IP	H	ER	BB	SO	ERA
Danny Jackson	36	5-14	183.2	206	106	96	82	5.19

How can I put this delicately...these numbers are atrocious! Jackson's strikeout to walk numbers are horrible! In any form of organized baseball, it's awful when a pitcher walks more guys than he strikes out. 206 hits and ninety-six walks over 183 plus innings equals a ratio of 1.6 hits/walks to innings pitched. On average there were at least one and a half runners on base in *every* inning Danny Jackson pitched for the Cubs! After Jackson's thirty-six games for Chicago, the Cubs had to be relieved in finding a taker for him in the Pirates.

In typical Cubs' fashion/luck, Jackson rebounded and helped the Philadelphia Phillies reach the 1993 World Series. Jackson went 12-11 and 14-6 over two years with the Phillies respectively. As a Cub, Danny Jackson was a poor financial investment.

Dave Smith, who unfortunately passed away in 2008, was a very successful closer for the Houston Astros. The Cubs signed Smith to a two-year $4.9 million contract. (Two years at about $8.3 million in 2013...more economics!) Let's just compare Dave Smith's career with the Astros and Cubs:

DAVE SMITH	GAMES	SAVES	W/L	IP	H	ER	BB	SO	ERA
With Astros	563	199	3-47	762	646	240	260	529	2.53
With Cubs	46	17	0-6	47.1	54	26	23	19	4.94

I think the Cubs should have let Mr. Smith finish out his fine career with the Houston Astros. Instead, the Cubs sank $4.9 million into those numbers listed above. For two years of Jackson and Smith, the Cubs spent close to $10 million and received horrific pitching in return.

In their first major foray into free agency, the Cubs proved to be very poor gamblers when it came to the pitchers they chose. Over the next two decades the Cubs would continue to "gamble" in free agency. Regrettably, the Cubs' level of aggressiveness in pursuing free agents was often either too great, or not quite enough, rarely getting a player for the right price. The Cubs always appear to be "chasin' it," a gambling term that means *following bad bets with worse bets, and failing to recognize good bets*. This method is not a successful way to gamble, or to run a Major League Baseball team.

Danny Jackson and Dave Smith were two bad pitchers for the Chicago Cubs, and their signings are **Reason 77**.

REASON 78

Not So *Free* Agents (2): The Greg Maddux Replacements

"According to Maddux, a no-trade clause and the Cubs' tardiness at returning a phone call meant the difference between signing or rejecting a five-year, twenty-five million dollar extension. Maddux went into 1992 without the extension, made 4.2 million for the season, while Scott Boras continued negotiations with the Cubs."
~*The Wall Street Journal*, 11/6/92

Greg Maddux was not a greedy man in 1992 (…and I doubt he is a greedy man today). Greg Maddux *wanted* to re-sign with the Chicago Cubs. If this situation were handled with just a bit more precaution, Maddux would have signed that five-year, $25 million extension with the Cubs. Pitching without a long-term deal in place, Greg Maddux won the 1992 National League Cy Young Award while pitching for the Cubs. The Cubs reportedly offered Maddux a five-year contract totaling $27.5 million. The Braves were offering $28 million over five years, while the Yankees were reported to be offering $34 million with a $9 million signing bonus. (*New York Times*–12/10/1992.) Maddux chose the Braves because according to Boras, "Above all, Greg wanted to win." I told you he wasn't greedy.

Reason 78 isn't about Greg Maddux; it examines what the Cubs did with the money that *should* have been spent on Maddux. I recall reading articles after Maddux signed with the Braves in which Cubs' GM Larry Himes rationalized how the Cubs could spread the money around on more players. In November of 2012, it had been twenty years since Greg Maddux left the Cubs for the Braves. Enough time has passed that the players the Cubs signed *instead* of Maddux can be accurately analyzed. Did "spreading the money around" work better than keeping one of the best pitchers in the history of all of baseball? Here is a look at what the Cubs did with the "Maddux Money":

	YEARS/TOTAL	REPLACEMENTS	YEARS/TOTAL
Greg Maddux	5/$28 million	Jose Guzman	4/$14.35 million
		Randy Myers	3/$12 million
		Candy Maldonado	2/$2.6 million
		Willie Wilson	2/$1.4 million

After Maddux signed with the Braves, the Cubs signed four players for $30 million, with the longest commitment being Jose Guzman at four years. The immediate results for Maddux and the Atlanta Braves were *three straight* Cy Young awards and a World Series! How did Greg Maddux's replacements do for the Chicago Cubs?

Jose Guzman

Guzman wasn't horrible in 1993, going 12-10 with a 4.34 ERA and 163 strikeouts over 191 innings. In 1994 Guzman threw in only four games due to a serious arm injury, going 2-2 with a 9.15 ERA. Guzman would never pitch again for the Chicago Cubs. The Cubs paid Guzman around a million dollars a win for his fourteen victories. They paid him $3.675 million in '95 *and* '96 while he was not able to pitch. (*Another* economics lesson: Guzman's money works out to about $24.5 million today.)

Randy Myers

The Cubs received their money's worth out of Myers, who led the league in saves in two of the three seasons he pitched for the team. Myers had an impressive fifty-three saves in 1993. Myers was not a complete waste of the Cubs' resources.

Candy Maldanado

Candy Maldanado hit .186 with three HRs and 15 RBIs in 140 at bats with the Cubs. Maldanado was traded in August to the Cleveland Indians for Glenallen Hill. Glenallen Hill would have moderate success with the Cubs. Candy Maldonado was a complete bust for the Chicago Cubs.

Willie Wilson

The Cubs acquired a player past his prime...*way* past his prime. At thirty-seven, in 105 games Willie Wilson could only muster up a .301 on-base percentage and steal seven bases for the Cubs. He still played a decent center field, but by May of 1994 Wilson was out of the majors.

Therefore, for about $30.35 million, the Cubs got:

- a decent year out of Guzman, then paid him for three years of injuries
- three solid years of Randy Myers as a closer
- a dreadful half season out of Candy Maldonado
- an aging player in Willie Wilson who did make it through his contract

The Braves getting Greg Maddux at five years and $28 million was phenomenally better than how the Cubs spread out their $30 million. It is difficult to describe just how horrible this was for the Cubs' franchise. I am grateful for my self-imposed two-year "semi-boycott" due to Maddux's departure; thus I rarely saw the replacements play. The Cubs let the best pitcher in baseball walk away in the prime of his career, even though he wanted to stay.

I will finish with a quote from the December 19, 1992, edition of *The New York Times* from Yankees' GM Gene Michael after his team lost out on Greg Maddux:

"This one hurts," said Yankee GM Gene Michael.
"He's the best one out there. I never thought I could say this,
but he's a steal at 28 million. He's a steal."

1. I think he was right.
2. Do you think he thought the same of Guzman, Myers, Maldanado and Wilson? The players who collectively are **Reason 78**.

REASON 79

Not So *Free* Agents (3): Jeff Blauser

As a member of the Atlanta Braves, Jeff Blauser *killed* the Cubs:

CAREER VS. CUBS	G	AB	R	H	HR	RBI	AVG	SLUG	OPS
Jeff Blauser	78	262	45	92	15	48	.351	.611	1.023

The above numbers don't express just *how* amazing Blauser was against the Cubs. Consider some of these facts:

- Blauser's fifteen career homers against the Cubs were the most against any team he faced.

- Blauser's .351 batting average against the Cubs was eighty-nine points higher than his career average of .262.

- Blauser's career OPS of 1.023 against the Cubs was 263 points higher than his career OPS of .760.

- Blauser had forty-eight career RBIs against the Cubs...he had six more (fifty-four total) against the Reds...in fifty-three more games!

Against the Cubs, Jeff Blauser transformed from "scrappy little shortstop" into a Honus Wagner-type shortstop. When Blauser became a free agent after the end of the 1997 season, it made sense for the Cubs to pursue him. Blauser had hit well in Wrigley Field (insert own joke about facing Cubs' pitching), was only thirty-one years old, and was coming off this season:

1997 BRAVES	AB	R	H	HR	RBI	AVG	OBP	SLUG	OPS
Jeff Blauser	519	90	160	17	70	.308	.405	.482	.887

Blauser won the Silver Slugger award for shortstops and was an All-Star. The Cubs signed Blauser to a two-year, $8.4 million deal after the 1997 season.

Apparently I blocked out Blauser's 1998 performance (before embarking on this project I had even forgotten he was a Cub). I bet *you* can guess where the story of Jeff Blauser as Cubs' shortstop is going:

1998 CUBS	AB	R	H	HR	RBI	AVG	OBP	SLUG	OPS
Jeff Blauser	361	49	79	4	26	.219	.299	.340	.639

Yikes! That's what the Cubs received for their $4.2 million investment for the 1998 version of Jeff Blauser?! Ironically, the Cubs would face the Braves in the NLDS. Blauser was relegated to a reserve role in the series, and the Cubs were swept three games to zero. As he was watching his former team celebrate, I wonder if Jeff Blauser regretted taking the money and signing with the Cubs. Surely, Cubs' fans were wishing he would have stayed with his old team.

In 1999, the Cubs used Blauser primarily as a platoon second baseman. In 200 at bats, Blauser hit .240 with nine home runs. Blauser was released/retired after the season...he was thirty-three.

Jeff Blauser was a solid player for the Atlanta Braves. He won a World Series title with the Braves in 1996. His terrible performances in 1998 and 1999 make Jeff Blauser a worthy nominee for our list, and his contract clinches it! In a year that the Cubs won the wild card, Blauser's $4.2 million could have been better allocated. ("Better allocated" is too kind, "not *bleeping* wasted!" is probably more accurate.) After his brutal 1998, the Cubs had to pay Blauser *another* $4.2 million for 1999.

As poor of a decision as the Cubs' signing of Jeff Blauser proved to be (**Reason 79**); it is doubtful that anyone could have predicted the rapid descent of Jeff Blauser's career. Regrettably, it was the Cubs who paid $8.4 million to watch it happen.

REASON 80

Not So *Free* Agents (4): Todd Hundley

Randy Hundley was a much-beloved player for the Chicago Cubs. Randy was a Gold Glove winner, an All-Star, and hit eighteen homers and knocked in sixty-four runs for the 1969 Cubs. Randy has occasionally worked on Cubs' radio broadcasts, and I find him an absolute joy to listen to. His knowledge of the game is remarkable, and (please don't hang me for saying this) his insight was a nice break from Ron Santo's Super-Cubs' homerism. Randy's son Todd... is a different story.

Todd was one of the best offensive catchers in the 1990s, having seasons of 24, 30, and 41 home runs. Hundley was a switch-hitter and in 2000, he hit .284 with a .375 on-base percentage, 24 HRs and 70 RBIs. At thirty-one years old, Hundley was now a free agent. (*BACK-IN-TIME RED-FLAG ALERT... SAME AGE AS BLAUSER, SAME AGE AS *BLAUSER!!!*)

The Cubs signed Hundley prior to the 2001 season. Hundley received a four-year $23.5 million contract ($30.5 in 2013 dollars). The signing of Todd Hundley *seemed* to be a good fit. Hundley was returning *home* and was coming off a year where he posted an OPS of .954. After seventy-nine reasons, you know that *nothing* is ever as it seems for the Cubs.

Full disclosure: Todd Hundley might have been one of my least favorite Cubs of all time. I will attempt to be as impartial as possible. I was suspicious of Todd's sudden power (...*cough*...his name is in the Mitchell report, linking him to steroids...*cough)* and I was never fond of how he had the top buttons of his shirt open. Strikingly similar to the Jeff Blauser situation, the player the Cubs paid for was far from the player they received:

TODD HUNDLEY	G	AB	R	H	HR	RBI	AVG	OBP	SLUG	OPS
2000 w/Dodgers	90	299	49	85	24	70	.284	.375	.579	.954
2001 w/Cubs	79	246	23	46	12	31	.187	.268	.374	.642
2002 w/Cubs	92	266	32	56	16	35	.211	.301	.421	.722

The slight uptick in Hundley's 2002 numbers did little to excite Cubs' fans, and most were happy to see Todd traded back to the Dodgers following the 2002 season. I remember thinking it was miraculous (yes, I just compared the trade to a miracle) that general manager Jim Hendry received Eric Karros and Mark Grudzielanek in return. The deal was described as "bad" contract for "bad" contract, yet Karros and Grudzielanek proved to be valuable pieces for the 2003 Cubs. Hundley only played in twenty-one games for the Dodgers in 2003 due to injuries. After that season, Todd Hundley would never again play in the Major Leagues.

As well as the trade of Hundley worked out for the Cubs, we still have to view his signing as a gigantic failure. The Cubs' teams of the early 2000s were some of the most talented of all time. The team had a productive Sammy Sosa, a healthy Kerry Wood, and young stars Carlos Zambrano and Mark Prior. What if the Hundley money had been allotted to other pieces to be used in the 2001-2003 seasons? Could the 2003 NLCS have turned out differently? Might 2001 or 2002 have been play-off seasons?

Once again the Cubs received virtually nothing for their money. The money spent on Todd Hundley (**Reason 80**) could have been used in a multitude of different ways...all superior to the reality of how it was used.

At the dawn of the new century, the Cubs were about to wade deeper than ever into free agency. A generous $23.5 million would soon seem like a drop in the bucket to the Cubs and their fans. Hundley's contract was about to be dwarfed in terms of length and money. In terms of bad play, Hundley's contract will always rank near the top.

REASON 81

Not So *Free* Agents (5): Alfonso Soriano

Quick trivia question...who was the first Major League player to have an illustrious 40-40 season of home runs and stolen bases? If you guessed Jose (reality star/celebrity boxer/steroid supporter/celebrity mug-shot participant) Canseco, give yourself a point. Can you name the other three players to achieve 40-40? The other members of the 40-40 club are Barry Bonds, Alex Rodriguez and Alfonso Soriano. Alfonso Soriano accomplished the feat in 2006, hitting forty-six home runs and stealing forty-one bases. Soriano came close to 40-40 earlier in his career, finishing just *one* home run shy in 2002. Soriano's 2006 40-40 season was the last attained in Major League Baseball, and it occurred at an opportune time for Mr. Soriano.

Soriano became a free agent after the 2006 season, and the Cubs would be one of the teams chasing him. Different tales abound of who in the Cubs' organization was pushing hardest for the deal, yet there is little doubt everyone wanted Soriano as a player. The details of the contract itself are where the responsibility of whom was most in favor of the deal gets...murky. Was it general manager Jim Hendry or those above him attempting to add an asset prior to the sale of the team? If Soriano had led the Cubs to multiple World Series appearances, we would have our answer. The fact that matters is that the deal *was* completed.

What a deal it *is* (yes, the Cubs are still paying); the Cubs signed Soriano to an *eight*-year $136 million contract. "You're talking about the best lead-off hitter in all of baseball," Cubs' manager Lou Piniella said at the time. (*USA Today* 11/20/2006.) Before assessing the finer points of the contract, let's examine Soriano's performance.

Soriano, limited to 135 games in 2007 due to injuries, performed well in his first season with the Cubs. Soriano hit thirty-three home runs, knocked in seventy, hit .299, slugged .560 and had an OPS of .897. (Soriano's OPS was only fourteen points lower than 2006.) The biggest drop off was in Soriano's running game: his stolen base total dropped to nineteen. Nonetheless, the Cubs received *almost* the same player they paid for…during the 2006 regular season. Next, the National League Divisional Series against the Diamondbacks took place…and *this* happened:

2007 NLDS	AB	R	H	2B	3B	HR	RBI	AVG	OBP	SLUG	OPS
Soriano	14	0	2	0	0	0	0	.143	.200	.143	.343

Hmm…okay, any player can have *one* bad series. Conversely the 2007 NLDS was astonishingly brutal for Soriano. He had two singles, no extra-base hits, and not one single run knocked in. In 2008 the Cubs won the National League Central Division, winning ninety-eight games.

Soriano played in 105 games:

2008 REGULAR SEASON	AVG	HRs	RBIs	SBs	OPS
Alfonso Soriano	.280	29	75	19	.876

Soriano nearly duplicated his 2007 numbers…during the regular season. Then the NLDS against the Dodgers took place, and *this* happened (again):

2008 NLDS	AB	R	H	2B	3B	HR	RBI	AVG	OBP	SLUG	OPS
Soriano	14	0	1	0	0	0	0	.071	.071	.071	.143

Alfonso Soriano has played in two play-off series as a Chicago Cub and has three singles and a walk to show for them. These results are not the type of production anticipated from a player with a contract like Soriano's. Alfonso's pitiful play-off performances in 2007 and 2008 are one of the reasons Soriano *lost* many Cubs' fans. The failure of the team in back-to-back play-offs, coupled with Soriano's extremely weak production, has made him a lightning rod for criticism. Soriano has never recovered in the minds of most Cubs' fans.

From 2009-2011 Alfonso Soriano's numbers were pretty consistent, as he averaged around twenty-three home runs and hit between .241 and .258. The speed was gone (16 SBs combined over the three seasons) and his sub-par play in left-field had fans screaming for his exit from Chicago. Soriano rebounded nicely in 2012, slugging thirty-two home runs and driving in 108 runs. That year did not redeem Soriano and he will never satisfy Cubs' fans for one reason: THE CONTRACT.

I "first guessed" this contract signing. I hated the length and didn't like that the Cubs were not filling a premium defensive position. I felt (and still do) that if you allocate that much money, you need to fill an important defensive spot. Soriano has been a constant defensive liability with the Cubs, and not worth what the Cubs are paying him.

By all accounts, Soriano is a hard worker and a good teammate. Alfonso Soriano, the man and the player, is not a reason why the Cubs haven't won in 104 years; Alfonso Soriano's contract is. As of this writing, in 2013 and 2014 the Cubs are "on the hook" for $18 million per season as Soriano turns thirty-seven and thirty-eight. The Cubs will be paying most of that money regardless if Soriano is traded to another team. Soriano may continue his resurgence and have two solid offensive seasons; they just won't be worth $18 million per year.

The Cubs made a colossal error in long-term judgment in November of 2006. Perhaps by an ownership that knew they weren't going to be around to pay the bills...like maxing out someone else's credit card. The Cubs also had a general manager who had come *so close* to a championship, that he made a desperate move, throwing caution to the wind. The reality for the Cubs post-2008 has been an incredible albatross of a contract that rears its ugly head any time the Cubs have tried to improve the team. The odds of Alfonso Soriano being traded may fluctuate over the next two years depending on American League teams' needs for designated hitters. The odds of the Cubs getting a team to take on the last two years of the contract are 0 percent.

It's amazing that a decision made in the winter of 2006 (**Reason 81**) could still be affecting the Cubs' probabilities of winning in 2013 and 2014. Like a prison sentence without parole, the contract has hovered over the Cubs for almost a decade. Considering the impact the contract has had, it is included as a significant reason for the Cubs' inability to win in the last six years, and likely 2013 and 2014.

REASON 82

KOSUKE, MILTON, AND THE CUBS

If you think "Kosuke, Milton and the Cubs" sounds like a bad sitcom, then my title accomplished its goal. After a quick exodus from the 2007 playoffs, one of Jim Hendry's goals for the off-season was to get balance in the lineup. This meant acquiring left-handed hitters to balance out the Cubs' right-handed dominated lineup. (*Foreshadowing alert* The Cubs have historically been very right-handed.) The decisions that resulted may not have been the correct ones, but the Cubs *were too* right-handed. One of the complications, left-handed power hitting is a scarce commodity in the Major Leagues.

The Cubs went outside the Major Leagues and set their sights on Japanese free agent outfielder Kosuke Fukudome. There was significant demand for Fukudome among Major League teams, and the Cubs had to pony up a four-year $48 million contract to land him. The signing seemed to be a good match, and the Cubs were able to beat out such teams as the White Sox for Fukudome's services.

Kosuke Fukudome proved a very good defensive outfielder and displayed the ability to draw a walk. Fukudome's other skills appeared to be middling at best. In his first four seasons, Fukudome hit 10, 11, 13 and 8 home runs. His batting averages in the four seasons: .257, .259, .262, and .263, remarkably consistent, *average* production. The Cubs had not solved their left-handed power dilemma; instead the Cubs received a solid defender with offensive capabilities resembling a team's *fourth* outfielder.

In the winter of 2008, the Cubs tried again; enter switch-hitter Milton Bradley. After leading the American League in OPS in 2008, the Cubs and GM Jim Hendry sought the left-handed solution in Bradley. Unfortunately, Milton Bradley came with more red flags than...you have anything? 'Cause I don't...let's just say he had a *lot* of red flags. Bradley seemed a problem for the Dodgers, *and* the Padres, *and* the Rangers, *and all* teams he played for. The Cubs did not adhere to the warning signs, and Jim Hendry felt they had a good match. The Cubs signed Bradley to a three-year $30 million contract. Milton Bradley said all of the right things at the introductory press conference, and the Cubs went into 2009 with Bradley in right field.

Milton Bradley almost lasted a *whole* season with the Cubs before being dismissed from the team on September 20. Along the way he punched some Gatorade coolers, threw the second out of an inning into the stands allowing two runners to score, and got into a few altercations with manager Lou Piniella. Bradley's .999 OPS from the previous season dropped to .775. Bradley hit twelve home runs and knocked in forty runs. The offensive production was hardly worth tolerating the collective pain in the a$$ Milton was with the Chicago Cubs.

Bradley was a bust that most baseball observers could have easily predicted. It was a very ill-advised gamble on Hendry's part. Kosuke Fukudome was not as easy to forecast. There were numerous teams interested in Fukudome's services; the Cubs were just unfortunate to *win*. Fukudome was/is not a bad player. Fukudome always seemed to hustle and was fundamentally sound in areas. Fukudome was a victim of his contract far exceeding his abilities, which is not his fault. Those same excuses do NOT apply to Milton Bradley. If the Cubs' solicited advice on this venture, they would have been hard-pressed to find any supporting the Bradley signing.

In the span of fourteen months, the Cubs had allotted $78 million to two players who were not going to assist them in winning a World Series. One was an average player, a serviceable fourth outfielder. The other was a talented malcontent who could get in a fight in an empty room. Neither of the players was worth near what the Chicago Cubs paid them. Both Bradley and Fukudome became two more contract impediments for the Cubs to overcome.

CHAPTER 7 has displayed that the Cubs' financial decisions have mirrored their worst on-field performances. Allotting this absurd amount of money ($78 million) over a period of four years, for virtually nothing, ranks near the top. (*Obvious alert*) $78 million is a ton of money and could have been used for numerous other productive resources. Even in the modern era of baseball, teams have won World Series titles with less than $78 million as a *total* team payroll.

Hendry's decisions in these cases will be reexamined in CHAPTER 8. The Cubs and Hendry were desperate in making these two decisions. Desperation tends to trump rational and logical thinking. I think I have made it abundantly clear that I give Hendry a pass on Fukudome, *not* on Bradley. The notion that a guy, who had constantly been a problem for so many teams, was going to help contribute to the Cubs winning a World Series was ludicrous…as ludicrous as wasting $30 million.

Kosuke and Milton (**Reason 82**) will be forever linked due to the proximity of their signings and the motives behind them. They will also be connected as two of Jim Hendry's last gasp efforts at getting the Cubs a World Series title. For the purposes of this book, Kosuke and Milton are coupled as one collective reason for the 104-year dearth of Chicago Cubs' World Series titles.

REASON 83

Money Matterz: The Cubz Crazy Extenzion of Big Z

During the stretch drive of 2003, I felt sorry for Carlos Zambrano. Kerry Wood and Mark Prior were garnering all of the headlines. Zambrano was nearly matching them on the field, and in my observations was going slightly unnoticed. Zambrano did not match them in the 2003 play-offs, yet in subsequent seasons he proved to be much more durable than Wood and Prior. Zambrano was the Cubs' top starter from 2004-2006. The only thing that ever gave me pause as a fan was Zambrano's "volatility." I felt he always had a bit of a crazed look in his eye, kind of like an unstable, unpredictable animal. Zambrano consistently gets especially feisty with umpire's calls and swings the bat like a possessed, switch-hitting Babe Ruth. That said, Zambrano finished off a very good 2006 season in which he went 16-7 with a 3.41 ERA, and 210 strikeouts in 214 innings.

During the 2007 season, the Cubs and general manager Jim Hendry decided to lock up their "ace" to a long-term contract extension. There were warning signs before the contract signing…for those paying close attention:

- Zambrano led the National League in walks in 2006, and he was leading the league in walks again in 2007 when the Cubs signed him to the new deal.

- Of Zambrano's first ten starts of 2007, only three were "quality starts" (6 IP, 3ER).

- Zambrano's strikeout rate was down 1.5 per nine from the previous season.

- In his last start before the extension was signed, Zambrano pitched seven innings, allowed thirteen hits, walked two and struck out none.

The year 2007 was also the season in which Zambrano's trademark instability boiled over. For instance, Zambrano got into an altercation with his own catcher, Michael Barrett. Zambrano also started the selfish act of staring down defenders when certain plays were not made. Despite these potential red flags, the Cubs and Jim Hendry must have feared the idea of Zambrano hitting the open market. The new contract was announced on August 17, 2007; five years at $91 million. Carlos Zambrano would still pitch well at times after the contract signing, but he was far from a long-term ace worthy of $91 million. Let's take a look at the years following the signing year of 2007:

2008

Zambrano went 14-6, but saw his ERA jump from 2.78 at the beginning of August to 3.91 by the end of the season. Zambrano did throw the Cubs' first no-hitter in almost thirty years on September 14. In his lone play-off start, he allowed three runs over six innings against the Dodgers.

2009

In May, Zambrano was ejected for arguing balls and strikes, tossed the ball and his glove into the stands, and then took out his frustrations on a poor, unsuspecting Gatorade dispenser. Zambrano finished 9-7 with a 3.77 ERA.

2010

On opening day, Zambrano allowed eight runs, two home runs over an inning and a third in a 15-6 loss to the Braves. After three more starts, manager Lou Piniella made the curious decision to move "Big Z" to the bullpen. Carlos did *not* like the move. The Cubs put Zambrano back in the rotation in late May. On June 25, he gave up four runs in the first inning against the White Sox and then exploded in another dugout tirade (I am sure the Gatorade dispensers were hiding). Zambrano was screaming at his fellow players, including team-leader Derek Lee. Zambrano was suspended by the team and forced to partake in anger management sessions. Lou Piniella announced that upon his return, Zambrano would be back in the bullpen.

Zambrano was in and out of the rotation until mid-August where his record stood at 3-6 with a 5.46 ERA. With the Cubs far out of contention, the team put him back into the rotation where he went 8-0 over his next ten starts. To state that Zambrano's year in 2010 was inconsistent would be an insult to other inconsistencies.

2011

Zambrano's Cubs' career finally came to an end. Zambrano's on-field performance was extremely unpredictable...again. Zambrano's record stood at 9-6 with a 4.46 ERA on August 12 when he took the mound against the Atlanta Braves. After five home runs, eight earned runs, and two pitches thrown at Chipper Jones, Zambrano was ejected from the game. Zambrano left the game, cleaned out his locker, either *did or did not* say he was retiring (depending on whom you believe) and left the team. The Cubs suspended him for thirty days and announced on September 2 that he would not be back with the team...and he wasn't.

Zambrano would never pitch again for the Cubs, as they traded him in January of 2012. The Cubs would have to pay all but about $2.6 million of Zambrano's $18 million salary for the 2012 season. The Cubs essentially paid Zambrano almost $16 million to go away...hardly what most teams do with an "ace." For the Marlins in 2012, Zambrano made twenty starts before being relegated to the bullpen (...hmm). Zambrano's 2012 numbers: seven wins, ten losses, a 4.49 ERA, and almost as many walks per nine innings (5.1) as strikeouts (6.5).

Carlos Zambrano's up and down performance as a Cub was not an unusual career path for many pitchers. Zambrano's antics and outburst *were* uncommon and unacceptable for any player, particularly one getting paid $91 million. The Cubs made a huge error in judgment by allotting this amount of money to a player with the character flaws that Zambrano displayed. The length and amount of Zambrano's contract were preposterous considering the warning signs. These actions were not a surprise to the Cubs, who had either hoped or wished that Carlos would eventually grow up. They should have known better.

The fact that Carlos Zambrano pitched poorly while being paid $91 million may seem like reason enough to be included on this list. What is more worthy of his inclusion is the fact that the Cubs gave a $91 million contract to a player who acted like a selfish, petulant child. The Cubs knew the type of character they were investing in, and they stuck their proverbial heads in the sand.

Carlos Zambrano's extension (**Reason 83**) in the summer of 2007 was a preventable blunder. Zambrano's last four seasons with the team, as well as the absurd amount of money that was wasted on him, prevented the Cubs from contending during this period.

REASON 84

THE 2010 SEASON: THE WORST TEAM THAT MONEY COULD BUY?

The 2010 Cubs finished the season with a record of 73-89. The only thing that kept the team from a ninety-loss season was an inexplicable 24-13 run under interim manager Mike Quade. One very noteworthy fact about the 2010 version of the Chicago Cubs: the team had the highest payroll in team history at $144,359,000. That's over $144 million if you are not good with all of those zeros.

Let's take a look at this mess, and it was a *mess*:

PLAYER	'10 SALARY	2010 HIGHLIGHT/STATS
Alfonso Soriano	19.0m	24 HRs, 79 RBIs, 123 strikeouts
Carlos Zambrano	18.9m	11-6 after bullpen demotion...don't be fooled
Aramis Ramirez	16.7m	strong finish to get to 25 HRs/83 RBIs, .241 AVG

Kosuke Fukudome	14.0m	.264 13 HRs, 44 RBIs...we already covered this
Ryan Dempster	13.5m	very good starter, 15-12, 208 Ks in 215 IPs
Ted Lilly	13.0m	3-8 when traded to the Dodgers
Derek Lee	13.0m	hitting .251 with 16 HRs when traded to ATL
Carlos Silva	12.75m	started 8-0, finished 10-6, last year in Majors

Now consider this, the Cubs had eight guys making at least $12.75 Million, *and*:

- Not one of these players was in the top ten in MVP voting. (It almost seems comical to even mention MVP and these players in the same sentence...none of these guys were remotely close!)

- None of the hitters were in the top ten in the NL for either home runs or RBIs.

- None of these hitters finished in the top ten in the league in runs, hits, batting average, on-base percentage, slugging percentage, walks (should I keep going?).

- The only top ten offensive player was Soriano, sixth in doubles (*whoopee!*).

- Not one pitcher in the top ten in Cy Young voting.

- Not one pitcher in the top ten in ERA.

- Ryan Dempster finished ninth in the league in wins, tenth in innings pitched.

- Not one of these guys was an All-Star (I can't read that without snickering).

- Not one of these players won a major award (and this statement constitutes more than a snicker.).

Wow...the Cubs were paying a whole lot of money for a whole lot of nothing! The only debatable thing might be *which* of these players was the *most* ridiculously overpaid? Ryan Dempster was the only player who produced remotely near his pay! I chose the above categories and statistics because when you compensate players like the Cubs were...you *expect* All-Stars, stat leaders, award winners, or at the very least...winners.

Let's use another metric to measure the absolute crummy-ness of this $145 million pile of goo that was the 2010 version of the Chicago Cubs; WAR (these numbers include defense as well):

2010 Chicago Cub Player	WAR
Alfonso Soriano	0.6
Carlos Zambrano	2.5
Aramis Ramirez	-0.9
Kosuke Fukudome	1.1
Ryan Dempster	2.4
Ted Lilly	1.9
Derek Lee	0.5
Carlos Silva	1.7

Let's refresh your memory on WAR values: an average Major League player *should be* at least 2.0, a very good player is usually around 4.0 to 5.0. Here are the top position players and pitchers in WAR for 2010:

1. Albert Pujols	7.3		1. Roy Halladay	8.3
2. Joey Votto	6.7		2. Ubaldo Jimenez	7.3
3. Troy Tulowitzki	6.5		3. Josh Johnson	6.8

The Cubs did not have a position player or pitcher *remotely close* to the best WAR performers in the league. Just gaze at those amazing differences between the top guys and the slop that was the 2010 Cubs and it becomes evident why a team with a $145 million payroll won only seventy-five games.

Historically there are other Major League teams with payrolls this large and performances this poor, but in the Cubs' case this is the absolute worst. Considering that the Cubs were still paying four of these players in 2011, and *three* of them entering 2012, the performances on the field had slim hopes of improving. And indeed, the Cubs' win totals sunk to seventy-one in 2011 and sixty-one in 2012.

When comparing the WAR numbers between the Cubs' players and the league's top performers, it's clear why 2010 and 2011 were lost seasons... seasons in which the Cubs had virtually no chance of having a winning season, let alone a World Series.

Reason 84 is the unbelievably overpaid Chicago Cubs' 2010 team and its terrible performance. A team so foul that its awfulness has stretched into multiple seasons.

CHAPTER SUMMARY

CHAPTER 7 was not intended to be a lesson about the evils of capitalism. In all professional sports, money has always *mattered*. Money is entwined with a team's success on the playing field. The Cubs' lack of success with money has been a factor in their shortage of World Series titles (an extreme shortage!).

To have fun with the last section, I decided to assemble the worst possible/most expensive Cubs' team ever. The team will consist of many recent players because of the rise in salaries over the last thirty years. All numbers will be put into 2013 values (one last economics lesson).

Here goes:

POS.	PLAYER	SALARY	STATS/COMMENTS
P	Carlos Zambrano	18.875m	anger issues trumped talent
P	Jose Guzman	5.8m	played one year, Cubs paid for four
P	Carlos Silva	12.5m	trash-for-trash deal for Bradley
P	Dave Smith	4.2m	0-6, 6.00 as a closer
P	Danny Jackson	4.4m	1-5, 6.75 as a starter
P	LaTroy Hawkins	5.5m	lasted only one season with Cubs
P	Rich Harden	7.0m	Mark Prior dressed in an A's uniform
P	Kevin Gregg	4.2m	lots of blown saves to go around
P	Jason Marquis	6.3m	eats innings and lots of money
P	Glendon Rusch	2.75m	3-8 ,7.46, tie your son's right hand
P	John Grabow	4.8m	seriously, *make* your kid be a lefty!
C	Todd Hundley	8.4m	button your shirt until you hit .200!
C	Jason Kendall	*about* 5.0 m	for half a season of no hitting
1B	Matt Stairs	4.1m	not a 1B, but was a pro-hitter
2B	Eric Young	5.8m	looked a lot better on the Dodgers
SS	Jeff Blasuer	6.0m	looked a lot better on the Braves
3B	Aramis Ramirez	16.75m	you have to hit in April and May too
IF	Aaron Miles	3.2m	like feeding a dog prime rib
UT	Xavier Nady	3.3m	we pay to make *sure* guys are done
OF	George Bell	6.6m	long line of DHs in left field for Cubs
OF	Marlon Byrd	6.5m	traded in 2nd year, released by June 1
OF	Kosuke Fukudome	14.0m	not even including translator's cost
OF	Juan Pierre	5.75m	looked a lot better on the Marlins
OF	Milton Bradley	10.3m	...speechless
OF	Jaques Jones	5.6m	one great year, then totally lost it
OF	Alfonso Soriano	19.0m	nice guy, awful deal

The price tag for this twenty-five man roster: **$196,625,000**. Many of these players had decent seasons with the Cubs, just not worth the money that was paid. How many games do you think this team would win?

The Cubs' payroll has run the gamut...from pointlessly low to one of the highest in baseball. Over the past twenty-five years, teams that have won come from both ends of the payroll spectrum. Throughout their long, sorry history, the Cubs have proven to be able to struggle no matter what their financial status.

Like it doesn't guarantee happiness (yeah, right), money also does not guarantee success. *Money* does *matter* in Major League Baseball though, and it has contributed to successes and failures for most teams. The Chicago Cubs have had many failures on the field...and have been equally as poor with money.

CHAPTER 8

REASON 85—ONE GRIMM DECISION
In 1945, the Cubs and Tigers needed a seventh game to determine
the outcome of the World Series and Cubs' manager
Charlie Grimm had one big decision to make.

REASON 86—P.K. WRIGLEY TAKES THE CUBS TO COLLEGE
No team has ever tried to do what the Cubs did in the early 1960s…
and for good reason.

REASON 87—GM JOHN HOLLAND
Yes…the man who made the infamous Brock for Broglio trade.

REASON 88—NOT NICE GUYS FINISH SECOND
(THREE OUT OF FOUR YEARS)
The 1969 Cubs weren't managing themselves during
their historic fade down the stretch.

REASON 89—BOB KENNEDY AS GENERAL MANAGER
(NOT AS "HEAD COACH")
Kennedy did not make many moves during his short tenure,
yet the ones he did had a lasting impact on the franchise.

REASON 90—FREYED

Where to begin…how about trading Lee Smith
for Calvin Schiraldi and Al Nipper?

REASON 91—THE CRIME(S) OF LARRY HIMES

Letting Greg Maddux go is enough to warrant him a spot on this list…
but that wasn't his only crime.

REASON 92—ANDY MACPHAILED

The Cubs came close under MacPhail,
but he had more than enough time and still came up empty.

REASON 93—JIM HENDRY'S SECOND TERM

He was five outs away from immortality…
seven seasons later he left the Cubs in ruins.

REASON 94—TOTAL INSTABILITY

Over the last thirty-five years the Cubs have averaged
a new manager every 1.6 years. No, that is not typical.

MANAGING...GENERALLY AND BAD

In the long history of the Chicago Cubs, they have had fifty-eight field managers and fifteen general managers. Only one of their field managers, Frank Chance, has ever won a World Series title. Mr. Chance actually guided the Cubs to back-to-back titles in 1907 and 1908. Frank Chance also took the Cubs to the 1906 and 1910 World Series, both losses. I intended to interview Mr. Chance for this project and get his unique perspective on managing the Cubs in *four* World Series; regrettably, Mr. Chance died in September 1924, forty-four years before I was born. The Cubs have never had a general manager win a World Series. The Cubs' first general manager was not hired until 1934, twenty-six years after their last title. In CHAPTER 8, we will examine which general managers and field managers impeded the Cubs' ability to win a World Series title.

Back in CHAPTER 4: ONES THAT GOT AWAY, I did not question or second-guess the trades or moves that allowed the players to leave the Cubs. In CHAPTER 4, we examined the ex-Cubs' career, and if his presence on the Cubs would have made a difference in the never-ending quest for a World Series title. In CHAPTER 8, I *will* "second-guess" the deals that led to players' departures. Throughout this project, I have attempted to back-up reasons with numbers and facts. In judging the careers of managers of the Cubs, my *opinion* will be inflected more than in previous chapters.

In CHAPTER 8, I will not judge a general manager or manager based on one poor decision, unless that decision directly led to the Cubs not winning a World Series. (This will not be difficult as the Cubs have won *three* games in a World Series once since 1908...1945.) Instead, I will be determining inclusion on this list based on patterns of moves. If a general manager or manager consistently made moves that prevented the Cubs from winning the title, he will be included. Here is an example regarding field managers:

In the 2007 NLDS, Lou Piniella was strongly criticized for removing Carlos Zambrano from Game 1 early and saving him for *a potential* Game

4 or 5. In my opinion, it is silly to assert this move cost the Cubs a title since they lost the series 3-0. If I discover a number of moves by Piniella that I feel collectively cost the Cubs a chance at a title, then he is fair game.

The same standard will be used in judging general managers on this list, with a bit more of a qualitative standard. As with the managers, one move will not put a GM on this list. Example: In 1983, Dallas Green traded Willie Hernandez to the Phillies for starting pitcher Dick Ruthven. One year later, Hernandez was the Cy Young of the World Series-winning Tigers. Using our standards, this one bad move would not tarnish Green's record. To simplify the analysis of trades, free agent signings and other player personnel moves, I will use the grading categories below:

PUSH:
A move that was either insignificant for both teams or equally beneficial for both clubs.

HIT:
A move in which the Cubs definitely had an upper hand, gaining a significant player without giving up much.

HOMER:
A move in which the Cubs acquired a Hall of Fame player who made significant contributions to the Cubs.

BUST:
A move in which the Cubs gave up significant resources for a player that turned out to be nothing.

CATASTROPHIC WHIFF:
A move in which the Cubs traded Hall of Fame caliber or gave up massive resources (i.e. money) for a player/s who did virtually nothing.

Using this rubric (fancy word that basically means grading system), I will more accurately be able to judge the moves. The reader may not agree with my analysis, but if it's between a **bust** and a **catastrophic whiff** we can agree the move was pretty bad. If a GM has a significant number of moves that fall on the negative side of the ledger, he will be included.

One silly little disclaimer before we begin this chapter: a person's inclusion on this list is not a personal attack on the character of that individual. Therefore, family members, loved ones, or friends of these individuals who may happen to read this book (not bloody likely), I apologize up front. It's nothing personal; I am analyzing decisions, not people.

Okay...it might be a little personal with a couple of them. Sorry.

REASON 85

O NE GRIMM DECISION

In the beginning of this chapter I stated I would not include field managers because of one poor decision...*unless* that decision directly led to a World Series loss. Regrettably for Charlie Grimm, he made one of those judgments in 1945. In **Reason 10**, I examined why the Cubs lost the 1945 World Series; now I will evaluate the team's decisions and who made them.

Charlie Grimm was in his second year with the Cubs, and the team was playing the Detroit Tigers in the World Series for the second time in ten years. World War II had recently ended, yet the 1945 World Series was still viewed in a negative light as many Major Leaguers were still under military obligations. In **CHAPTER 1**, I explained that Cubs' pitcher Hank Bowory pitched in Games 1, 5, *and* 6. Here are Bowory's cumulative statistics for those games:

GAMES 1, 5, 6 (1945 W.S.)	W/L	IP	H	ER	BB	SO
Hank Borowy	2-1	18	18	5	6	8

These games were played on Wednesday, Sunday, and Monday, October 3-8, 1945. Borowy threw four innings of relief on Monday to propel the Cubs into Game 7. Borowy was selected by Grimm to start the deciding game on Wednesday. Sixty-seven years later, this seems like a poor choice; apparently it was viewed much the same in 1945. Here is an excerpt taken from BaseballAlmanac.com's recap of the series:

> "As the Tigers prepared to close the door on the Cubs and the 1945 season, Chicago's newest hero (Borowy) was selected to win Game 7. The Chicago press had questioned the decision and printed that Grimm was making a serious mistake by pitching Borowy who was going on one day of rest after pitching the final four innings of Game 6. He had also pitched into the 6th inning of Game 5, and many wondered if his arm would hold up."
>
> ~1945 World Series Recap, BaseballAlmanac.com

Borowy's arm would not hold up. He allowed three solid hits to start game seven, and Grimm soon realized Borowy's arm was toast. The score was 5-0 Detroit before the Cubs even came to the plate. Tigers' ace Hal Newhouser would make those runs hold up in a 9-3 Detroit win. Did Grimm have any choice other than Borowy? Let's take a look:

1. **Claude Passeau**—Grimm could have started Passeau, the Game 3 winner and Game 6 starter on *two* days rest...not optimal but perhaps better than Borowy pitching three out of four days.

2. **Hank Wyse**, who won twenty-two games for the Cubs during the regular season, had only logged seven innings during the World Series...but he did allow six runs. Wyse had thrown one inning in Game 6. Pitching Wyse *probably* would have been the most prudent thing to do.

3. **Paul Derringer** won sixteen games during the season, and had only thrown five innings in the 1945 World Series...but walked seven.

4. **Hy Vandeberg** who eventually threw in relief in Game 7 and did not allow a run in six innings of work during the entire World Series. Vanderberg only started seven games during the season but was clearly throwing well during the Series.

All four of these selections would have been better than throwing in a guy who had thrown five innings on Sunday and four innings on Monday. Charlie Grimm is the only Cubs' manager that has made such a big decision in a seven-game series...ever!

Unfortunately for the Cubs and Mr. Grimm, it was the wrong decision and is **Reason 85** of our list of 104.

REASON 86

P.K. WRIGLEY TAKES THE CUBS TO COLLEGE

P.K. Wrigley deserves credit for some "out-of-the-box" thinking in 1960... *way* out of the box. After the Cubs finished 60-94 in 1960, Wrigley decided it was time to do something drastic to shake the Cubs out of the worst multiyear stretch in team history. 1960 was the *fourteenth straight* year in which the Cubs finished fifth or lower in the eight-team National League. Perhaps Wrigley felt he had to do something...*anything*, as things for the Cubs couldn't get much worse. Unfortunately, things tend to "get worse" in regards to the Chicago National League ball club.

In December of 1960, Wrigley announced that the Cubs were going to an eight-man committee as opposed to having a single field manager. The concept called for the eight coaches to rotate through the entire organization from the low minors to the Cubs, ensuring one standard system of play. In announcing the experiment, Wrigley argued, "Managers are expendable. I believe there should be relief managers just like relief pitchers." He also contended that the managerial system led to constant turnover. (Neyer) At the Major League level there would be four coaches, and the position of "head coach" would be rotated among the men. Here is a logical question to ask at this point:

"By rotating leaders *during* the season, aren't you creating the 'constant turnover' that you didn't like in the managerial system by rotating head coaches?"

From 1961-1965 the Cubs had twenty-four different coaches participate in the "college of coaches." I would list them all, but that would be boring and you have only heard of one of them (maybe). Instead, let's just look at the predictably awful results:

1961

The team finished with a record of 64-90 which was a *slight* improvement over the previous season. Here is the breakdown of the four "head coaches" and their records: Vedie Himsl 10-21, Harry Craft 7-9, El Tappe 42-54, and Lou Klein 5-6. If I researched enough, I could find out the answer to the following question, yet it's more fun to speculate: How did they determine who was head coach when? Did they draw out of a hat? The number of games for each head coach is *so* random. Did they arm wrestle for it? Perhaps Mr. Tappe, who managed (sorry...*head coached*) sixty-three more games than Mr. Himsl (second highest number), had some distinct advantage over the other men.

1962

Yikes! The 1962 version of the Chicago Cubs had the worst record in franchise history: 59-103. Thank goodness for the first-year Mets who lost 120 games and finished a full seventeen games behind the Cubs in the race for ninth place. The breakdown of head coach records for the 1962 season: El Tappe 4-16, Lou Klein 12-18, and Charlie Metro 43-69.

An anonymous Cubs' player told the *Chicago Tribune* he had never been on a team with lower morale. (Golenbock)

After two disaster-like seasons, Wrigley decided the Cubs would have just one head coach for the upcoming 1963 and 1964 seasons: Bob Kennedy.

1963

Under head coach Kennedy, the Cubs finished 1963 at 82-80, their first winning season since 1946! What a novel idea...one guy in charge for the whole season. But wait a minute, isn't that then a "manager?" Is there more than just a semantic difference between the title of head coach and manager? I am confused now.

1964

Oops, the Cubs had a bit of a step back as they finished 76-86 under head coach Kennedy, or could he be called a manager now?

1965

After the Cubs got off to a slow 24-32 start under Coach Kennedy, they fired…err, *rotated* him with Assistant Coach Lou Klein. The Cubs would finish 72-90, which landed them in eighth place in the National League.

After the 1965 season the Cubs would hire Leo Durocher as manager, thus ending the debacle that was the college of coaches. The hiring of Durocher also concluded one of the silliest ideas ever in professional sports. The concept is really quite ridiculous when you consider it. I see only *one* way this idea would work: if you have a really freaking talented team. Even with a talented team, the four men would need to be totally in sync with each other, care little of their own egos, and be totally committed to the good of the whole organization. *None* of these traits were overtly present during the failed seasons of the college of coaches. (Golenbock)

Had the Cubs employed a single manager for these four seasons, they would not have won a World Series title. Consequently, one might wonder why this strange and unsuccessful idea lands on our list of 104 reasons the Cubs have not won since 1908. Here are two simple reasons:

1. It was embarrassing! This idea may have tarnished the Cubs' image as much as the losing that precluded the concept. Quality baseball people, talented enough for positions in the Cubs' organization, may not want to even associate themselves with the team that was ridiculed for doing this.

2. The four years essentially were years of "wheel spinning": no progression was made at all. Player development was likely hindered in a system in which they adjusted to different leaders, even if (in theory) they were teaching the same philosophies. 1961-65 were four *lost* years. Consider: might the talented core of Billy Williams, Ron Santo and Ernie Banks developed into a winning team earlier than 1969 without the college of coaches?

I am a fan of creative and "out-of-the-box" thinking in all sorts of different endeavors. Many people make the same mistakes over and over again by repeating ineffective but accepted behavior. However, the "out-of-the-box" or novel approach should make *some* sense...or at least be a fairly logical idea. The Chicago Cubs are the only team in any sport to attempt *this* idea.

The fact that no other team has attempted the plan described as **Reason 86** should not be surprising. The plan itself mirrors the amazing stretch of futility that led to its inception...and the idea contributed to the continuance of the longest title drought in all of professional sports.

1. Neyer, Rob. *Rob Neyer's Big Book of Baseball Blunders.* New York City: Fireside, 2006. ISBN 0-7432-8491-7

2. Golenbock, Peter. *Wrigleyville: A Magical History Tour of the Chicago Cubs.* New York City: St. Martin's Press, 1996. ISBN 0-312-15699-5

REASON 87

GM John Holland

John Holland was the Cubs' general manager from 1957 to 1975. Holland holds the record for longest term of any Cub GM; therefore, the length of his tenure may force him on this list. As noted in the prologue, we will give each GM a fair shake. So let's look at some of Holland's major moves with our rating system:

~TRADE HISTORIES~

June 15, 1964
Traded Lou Brock, Jack Spring, and Paul Toth to the
St. Louis Cardinals for Ernie Broglio, Doug Clemens, and Bobby Shantz.
GRADE: Catastrophic Whiff

December 2, 1965
Acquired Bill Hands and Randy Hundley from the Giants for
Don Landrum and Lindy McDaniel.
GRADE: Push +

April 21, 1966
Acquired Fergie Jenkins, John Hernstein, and Adolfo Phillips from the
Philadelphia Philles for Bob Buhl and Larry Jackson.
GRADE: Homer

April 26, 1967
Traded Fred Norman to the Los Angeles Dodgers
for Dick Calmus.
GRADE: Bust

November 29, 1971
Traded Ken Holtzman to the Oakland A's for Rick Monday.
GRADE: Push -

November 21, 1972
Traded Bill North to Oakland A's for Bob Locker.
GRADE: Bust

August 31, 1973
Traded Larry Gura to the Texas Rangers for Mike Paul.
GRADE: Bust

Drafts/Signings
The Cubs signed amateur free agent Ron Santo in 1959.
GRADE: Homer

1965 Draft
Drafted Ken Holtzman in the 4th round.
GRADE: Hit

1965 Draft
Drafted and failed to sign Darrell Evans.
GRADE: Bust

1966–1969 Drafts
NO players of any significance were drafted.
GRADE: Catastrophic Whiff

1970 Draft
The Cubs drafted Rick Rueschel.
GRADE: Hit

1971–1972 Drafts
The Cubs drafted *NO* players of any consequence.
GRADE: Bust

1973 Draft
The Cubs drafted Mike Krukow.
GRADE: Push

1974 Draft
The Cubs drafted, but did not sign Bob Welch.
GRADE: Bust

1975 Draft
The Cubs drafted Lee Smith.
GRADE: Hit

Holland's record is not one of *total* failure. The Lou Brock trade was not so good (yes, an understatement), but he stole a Hall of Famer from the Phillies in acquiring Fergie Jenkins. If those moves cancel each other out, Holland still dealt away three left-handed starters who would have success in the Major Leagues: Ken Holtzman, Larry Gura and Fred Norman. (…ouch.)

I can only speculate on the inner workings of the Cubs' front office during the years of the MLB draft, but Holland *has* to be held accountable. Over a ten-year period, the Cubs drafted Holtzman, Rick Reuschel, Mike Krukow, Ray Burris, and Lee Smith. These five players are the **ONLY** Major League contributors…encompassing ten drafts!

Holland is not the worst Cubs' general manager, but he has to be included on this list. The trade of Brock, the drafts, and eighteen years without one single play-off appearance all make John Holland deserved of inclusion in this book.

John Holland assembled a Cubs' team with four Hall of Famers, two of which he acquired. Holland got the Cubs close, but under his watch the amateur drafts were awful and contributed to future Cubs' failure. Holland's influence on the club was greater than his eighteen-year tenure because of the drafts…likely more than a quarter of a century. This lands him squarely as **Reason 87** on our list of 104.

REASON 88

Nᴏᴛ Nɪᴄᴇ Gᴜʏs Fɪɴɪsʜ Sᴇᴄᴏɴᴅ (Tʜʀᴇᴇ Oᴜᴛ ᴏғ Fᴏᴜʀ Yᴇᴀʀs)

If I ever get a chance to write another baseball book, I may choose to write about the idiocy of Hall of Fame voting. I love the concept of the Hall of Fame, and I adore baseball history, yet there are serious flaws in the voting system. I will state it for the second time in this book: *no player in the history of baseball has ever been unanimously elected to the Hall of Fame.* If *you* had a Hall of Fame vote, why would you not vote for Hank Aaron after hitting 755 homers and getting 3,000 hits? The only explanation would be idiocy.

The reason I bring up Hall of Fame voting is because of the case of Ron Santo. Santo was posthumously elected to the Hall and inducted in 2012. I will not argue whether Ronnie had a rock-solid case for the Hall of Fame; I will point out one of the dumbest arguments against him. Ron Santo's teammates: Ernie Banks, Billy Williams, and Fergie Jenkins are *all* Hall of Fame members. The argument was *how can a team that never made it to the World Series have four Hall of Famers?* This idea led to much reluctance in Ron Santo's candidacy. Was it written somewhere that the Cubs' were allowed three, but not four? Unfortunately for Ron Santo, he was that fourth.

Here is a different approach...I say all four of them *were* good enough. In CHAPTER 2, I pointed out that 1969 was not the only Cubs' team from this era that was close. Ernie Banks, Billy Williams, Fergie Jenkins, *and* Ron Santo probably should have made the play-offs at least once or twice. Here is an interesting way to look at 1969 and 1970:

YEAR	DATE	CUBS' PLACE	END OF SEASON GAMES BACK
1969	Sat., August 16	up by 9 games (43 to play)	2nd place 8 games back
1970	Tues., Sept 15	1 game back (16 to play)	2nd place 5 games back

In CHAPTER 2, I examined some logical reasons why the Cubs were caught by the New York Mets in 1969. The Mets played superior baseball down the stretch. While true, this doesn't preclude anyone from blame for the 1969 Cubs' fade. Blame frequently lies with leadership, and in this era, Leo Durocher was the manager of the Cubs.

Leo "the Lip" Durocher was about as "old-school" as you could get. Leo Durocher was as "hard-nosed" as you could get. Durocher is credited with the saying, "Nice guys finish last." Durocher took over the Cubs in '66 and bluntly stated, "I don't manage eighth place ball clubs." Leo was right...in 1966 the Cubs finished ninth place. By the late 1960s, Leo had the Cubs contending for the National Eastern Division title.

Now to that "four Hall of Famer argument" at the beginning of this piece; the Cubs were a very talented team in 1969 and 1970. Ernie Banks was in the latter part of his career, but Ron Santo, Billy Williams, and Fergie Jenkins (*three* Hall of Famers) were in their prime. Perhaps the argument should be, "How could this team have *four* Hall of Famers and not win?" When a team is in prime position to win (nine games up with forty-three to play is *really* prime position) in two consecutive years and *doesn't* win, the manager warrants some blame.

"Old-school" Durocher may not have been the best equipped to handle a struggling yet talented team. Leo "the Lip," known for berating players and umpires, was not the calming influence the Cubs needed. Leo clashed with players, including a "near riot brawl" with Santo. At the time Durocher was said to be out of touch with the modern high-priced athletes. Really?! When the league minimum was below $35,000 and the reserve clause kept the players as property of the owners, Leo couldn't relate? I wonder how Durocher would handle athletes in the twenty-first century.

A sports cliché that has developed over the last quarter century is "getting a team from point A to point B" in regards to a coach or manager. The cliché refers to a leader who advances a team to *just* a certain level and no further. Leo Durocher was a man who could only get the Cubs so far. Successful leaders can adapt to their players, and Leo expected his guys to adapt to him.

The Cubs were nine games ahead of the Mets with forty-three games to play in 1969. The Cubs were one game behind the Pittsburgh Pirates with sixteen games remaining in 1970. In both years, the Cubs would finish at least five games behind the first-place club. The leader in both cases deserves some responsibility.

Leo Durocher may be a Hall of Famer, but as manager of the Chicago Cubs, he is **Reason 88** of our 104.

REASON 89

Bob Kennedy as General Manager (Not as "Head Coach")

One of the most notorious ideas in Cubs' history, and in baseball itself, was Cubs' owner P.K. Wrigley's idea of a "college of coaches." Bob Kennedy served as "head coach" for two and a half seasons. Kennedy was the only head coach who finished above .500, finishing 82-80 in 1963. Bob Kennedy returned to the Cubs as general manager in 1977. Kennedy's tenure as GM was short, but it did not lack for long-term destruction to the franchise. There are not many **HITS** or even **PUSHES** in Kennedy's record:

MLB Drafts from 1977-1980

A team's amateur draft involves many people, yet it transpires on the general manager's watch. During this period the only significant players drafted were Mel Hall and Craig Lefferts. The Cubs drafted but did not sign Mark Langston.

GRADE: Catastrophic Whiff

~TRADE HISTORY~

January 11, 1977

The Cubs traded Mike Garman and Rick Monday to the Los Angeles Dodgers for Bill Buckner and Ivan DeJesus.

GRADE: Hit

February 11, 1977

The Cubs traded Bill Madlock and Rob Sperring to the San Francisco Giants for Bobby Murcer and Steve Ontiveros.

GRADE: Bust

(This is hard for me to admit though, as Murcer was my favorite player at the time.)

June 10, 1978

The Cubs reacquired Ken Holtzman from the New York Yankees for a player-to-be-named later. That player turned out to be Ron Davis, who went 14-2 with 9 saves and a 2.85 ERA...the *very next* year for the Yankees. Davis would be a solid set-up reliever and closer in the American League for the next seven seasons.

GRADE: Catastrophic Whiff

February 23, 1979

The Cubs traded Manny Trillo, Greg Gross and Dave Rader to the Philadelphia Phillies for Barry Foote, Jerry Martin, Ted Sizemore and Derek Bothello.

GRADE: Catastrophic Whiff

October 17, 1979

The Cubs traded Donnie Moore to the St. Louis Cardinals for Mike Tyson (not the boxer). Moore would close for the Angels in the 1980s.

GRADE: Bust

December 9, 1980

The Cubs traded Bruce Sutter and Ty Waller to the St. Louis Cardinals for Ken Reitz and Leon Durham.

GRADE: Push - - -

~OTHER MOVES AND SIGNINGS~

November 30, 1977

The Cubs signed Dave Kingman as a free agent.

GRADE: *minor* Hit

May 7, 1980

The Cubs sold Miguel Dilone to the Cleveland Indians. The rest of 1980, Miguel Dilone hit .341 in 528 at bats. Dilone also had an .807 OPS, with 61 stolen bases.

GRADE: Minor Bust

I can't sugarcoat this one, Bob Kennedy's four-year career as Cubs' GM was a colossal disaster. The four-year stretch of acquiring virtually *nothing* from the MLB amateur draft is brutal. In CHAPTER 3: DAFT DRAFTS, I listed some of the players the Cubs could have selected from 1977-1980. (Refer back to them at your own risk.)

Kennedy's trade record is almost as miserable. Kennedy did only trade *one* Hall of Famer in Sutter; however, he traded Trillo and Davis for virtually nothing. The only trade that is considered a hit is acquiring Bill Buckner and Ivan DeJesus for Rick Monday. Monday did star in and win a World Series championship with the Dodgers in 1981. Why is it that so many players win *after* they leave the Chicago Cubs? It's like they get released from a baseball prison.

Kennedy's tenure as GM was short compared with others included in this section. As brief as it was, Kennedy's tenure inflicted long-term damage to the Chicago Cubs. Imagining Kennedy winning a championship in his four-year span is unrealistic, yet his moves left the Chicago Cubs in an inferior position to win a World Series after his departure. Therefore, Mr. Kennedy rightfully deserves to be **Reason 89**...even after only four years.

REASON 90

F**REYED**

In January of 1989, I was attending Illinois State University. During my tenure there, the Cubs' Caravan would make a stop on the campus each January. The Cubs' Caravan at that time would feature major stars, prospects and other members of the organization. In January of 1989, Shawon Dunston, Greg Maddux, and GM Jim Frey made the trip to Normal, Illinois. (Fill in your own oxymoron joke about *Normal*, Illinois) Being dutiful Cubs' fans, my future wife, a couple of friends, and I attended the event.

After autograph sessions, Jim Frey had a question-and-answer period with the crowd. Keep in mind this was *way* before the time of instant media… there were no cell phones, Twitter accounts, or Facebookers in attendance. I remember Frey being defensive, arrogant and condescending. When questioned about the trade of Rafael Palmeiro, he sounded extremely self-justifying. Frey stated how Palmeiro was just an "average" hitter, runner and fielder. Frey then delivered a quip about Palmeiro's defense that I will **never** forget. When talking about Palmeiro losing a ball in the sun in left field, Frey stated, "How can a Mexican lose a ball in the sun?" My first thought, even as a dumb twenty-one year old, was... *Wait, what?! Palmeiro is Cuban.* My next consideration was that it seemed to be a pretty racist comment...even in 1989. I am sure Mr. Frey has no recollection of that event, but my wife and friends certainly do. Regrettably, we older Cubs' fans have a *strong* recollection of Mr. Frey's time as general manager.

Jim Frey had some success as a manager, leading the Kansas City Royals to the 1980 World Series (losing to the Philadelphia Phillies). Frey was also the manager of the 1984 division-winning Cubs, but was fired two years later after consecutive losing seasons. In Frey's defense as a manager, the Cubs were decimated by injuries in '85 and '86. After a brief stint in the WGN broadcast booth, Frey was hired as GM in December of 1987 after Dallas Green had resigned the post. Now I will examine Frey's record and start with the trades because Frey got busy right away:

~TRADE HISTORY~

December 8, 1987
Frey traded Lee Smith to the Boston Red Sox for
Al Nipper and Calvin Schiraldi.
GRADE: Catastrophic Whiff

February 12, 1988
Frey traded Keith Moreland and Mike Brumley to the San Diego
Padres for Rich Gossage and Ray Hayward.
GRADE: Bust

March 31, 1988
Frey acquired Mike Bielecki from the Pittsburgh Pirates
for Mike Curtis.
GRADE: Hit

July 14, 1988

Frey traded Dave Martinez to the Montreal Expos for Mitch Webster.

GRADE: Minor Bust

December 5, 1988

Frey traded Rafael Palmeiro, Jamie Moyer and Drew Hall to the Texas Rangers for Paul Kilgus, Steve Wilson, Curt Wilkerson, Mitch Williams and two names that would only be wasting ink.

SHORT-TERM GRADE: Push

LONG-TERM GRADE: Catastrophic Whiff

~FREE AGENT SIGNINGS~

November 21, 1990

The Cubs signed Danny Jackson.

GRADE: Catastrophic Whiff

December 6, 1990

The Cubs signed George Bell.

GRADE: HIT

(Only because Bell was traded for Sammy Sosa...just not by Frey)

December 17, 1990

The Cubs signed Dave Smith.

GRADE: Bust

~MLB Drafts Under Frey~

1988–1990 Drafts
The Cubs had three consecutive terrible drafts…
not one significant player was selected.
Ty Griffin over Robin Ventura in 1988…three completely wasted drafts.
GRADE: Catastrophic Whiff

1991 Draft
The Cubs drafted Doug Glanville and Steve Trachsel.
GRADE: Minor Hit

Jim Frey's first deal, trading Lee Smith, may have been his worst move. The absence of Smith set in motion a series of bad moves: trading for Gossage, the mortgaging of Palmeiro and Moyer for Mitch Williams, and the horrendous signing of Dave Smith. The Cubs won the 1989 division title with Frey as their general manager, yet I will never give him credit for that victory. In my opinion, the '89 Cubs were still Dallas Greens' Cubs. Frey's trades were awful, his draft classes dreadful, and he failed miserably in his free agent signings.

Jim Frey will always be remembered positively for managing the 1984 Cubs. Jim Frey *as a* GM earned his place on this list as much as any one individual. It is difficult to collectively calculate the damage to the franchise he inflicted…how far he set the Cubs back. The Cubs were in a much worse position upon his departure regarding Major League talent, the minor league system, and the payroll. Frey was allotted financial resources that no other Cubs' executive prior had been allocated…and he wasted them.

Jim Frey (**Reason 90**) was an awful general manager. And his geography skills are poor.

REASON 91

THE CRIME(S) OF LARRY HIMES

George W. Bush has been quoted numerous times saying that approving the trade of Sammy Sosa to the White Sox when he was a managing partner of the Texas Rangers was one of his biggest mistakes. The future president's trading partner was White Sox General Manager Larry Himes. Himes was fired by the White Sox after the 1990 season and found himself in the same job with the Chicago Cubs one year later. In spring training 1992, Himes traded for Sosa again by sending George Bell to the Sox. I will spare future analysis and just give this trade a grade of a **HOMER** right now. Unfortunately for Mr. Himes, the Sosa/Bell deal is where the praise will end.

Actually, I could have just titled this piece the "crime" of Larry Himes, and he would have qualified for inclusion on this list. Before examining Mr. Himes' major crime, here are a few minor ones:

The 1992-94 Drafts

Himes and his brain trust did not select any players of consequence in 1992. They selected Brooks Kieschnick in 1993, a left-handed reliever disguised as a power hitter...a few short picks before Chris Carpenter, Derek Lee and Torii Hunter. The 1994 draft was a total failure except for Kyle Farnsworth in the 47th round.

Trade for Anthony Young

Only the Cubs would trade for a pitcher coming off of a 1-16 season. Himes traded Jose Vizcaino, a middle infielder who would play eighteen seasons in the Major Leagues, for Anthony Young. While Vizcaino was never spectacular, his career was superior to Young's.

Ryne Sandberg Retirement

While Himes certainly wasn't the *only* reason for Sandberg's abrupt first retirement, he was most definitely a factor.

"He (Sandberg) had little use for former Cubs'
General Manager Larry Himes. He hated the atmosphere
he claims Himes brought to the team."
~*Chicago Tribune,* October 31, 1995

The crimes above are minor compared to the biggest transgression of Larry Himes' tenure as general manager of the Chicago National League ball club. The most heinous offense of Himes' would be the departure of one Greg Maddux.

I think I made my feelings clear on this in Maddux's *Ones That Got Away* piece in CHAPTER 4; I declared his departure was my own personal 1969. Make no mistake, Greg Maddux could have stayed with the Cubs; he even *wanted* to stay with the Cubs! Larry Himes is the man most responsible for the exit of Greg Maddux. The following (depressing) excerpt is from the November 22, 1992, edition of the *Rome Daily Times*:

"The Chicago Cubs decided Saturday to give up bidding for 1992 Cy Young winner Greg Maddux. General manager Larry Himes said that a $27.5 million, five-year offer which Maddux rejected in July still stands—but maybe not for long. Himes said the offer will be withdrawn as soon as he signs someone else. 'I looked at myself bidding against myself and decided to stop,' Himes said."

Himes wasn't bidding against himself, he was bidding against the Yankees and the Braves. Himes' "bidding against myself" statement may have been an attempt to paint Maddux and agent Scott Boras as unreasonable or greedy. A few facts shred any argument that Himes would make in that regard:

1. Maddux was ready to sign a five-year, $25 million extension the previous winter until it was Himes who dragged his feet on the deal and did not return a call to Maddux. This event prompted Maddux to go into the season without a deal in place.

2. Maddux eventually signed with the Braves for $28 million over five-years...a whopping $500,000 more than what the Cubs were offering.

3. The Yankees were offering Maddux a reported $9 million more than the Braves; if Maddux were greedy, he would have taken the Yankees' deal.

Mr. Himes made a horrendous mistake that cost Cubs' fans the prime years of arguably the best pitcher of all time. Maddux is without a doubt the best pitcher ever to come up through the Cubs' system, and Himes let him go. (Writing this is really making me angry...again!)

I am not sure if Mr. Himes was lacking intelligence, was too arrogant, or let his pride get in the way. A simple solution was right there for the taking. Maddux did not want to play for the Yankees. If Himes would simply beat the Braves' offer by $1 to $2 million over five years, Maddux likely would have remained a Cub. The Tribune Company had the money; Himes spent it on the wonderful Guzman/Myers/Maldonado combo.

Greg Maddux did everything right as a member of the Cubs both on and off the field. Maddux was twenty-six years old and coming off his first of *four straight* Cy Young Awards. The Chicago Cubs decided they didn't want him anymore, and that decision was made by Larry Himes. This idiotic decision earns Larry Himes the distinction of being **Reason 91**.

Ugh...I *am* angry now.

REASON 92

ANDY MACPHAILED

It didn't take long after Andy MacPhail joined the Cubs as president/ CEO for some members of the Chicago sports media to *cleverly* (implied sarcasm) spell Andy's name Mc F-A-I-L. Andy was doomed to fail in Chicago; many factors were working against him. Andy didn't necessarily help himself, and bears plenty of responsibility for his demise with the Cubs.

Andy MacPhail was a third-generation baseball man, whose father (Lee) and grandfather (Larry) are the only father/son members of the Hall of Fame. The MacPhails were not players; they operated Major League franchises. Andy MacPhail had a difficult time winning over many Chicago fans because of his appearance and persona. As a Chicago sports fan for almost forty years, I can tell you there is an element of meathead-ism among Chicago fans. A bookish-looking guy such as Andy was not going to get many free passes in Chicago. Chicago is a sports town in which many people (*not me*) still worship a football coach like Mike Ditka who once broke his hand punching a locker.

MacPhail was hired on September 9, 1994, and resigned on October 1, 2006. Andy came from the Minnesota Twins where he served as general manager, winning two World Series championships within a four-year span. MacPhail's accomplishments were considered impressive because of the Twins' status as a small market team with a minor budget.

The Cubs *did* make the play-offs twice during MacPhail's reign; 1998 and the ill-fated 2003 season. By traditional Cubs' standards, two play-off appearances in twelve years isn't that bad. However, for organizations that readily compete for championships, two out of twelve would be totally unacceptable. Having twelve years to succeed and only coming close once...Andy belongs on this list. MacPhail served as Cubs' president, CEO, and even GM for a brief period. Let's take a look at the eleven seasons under Andy MacPhail's watch:

- From 1994-2006 the Cubs had four winning seasons and seven losing seasons.

- The Cubs won *one* play-off series...2003 vs. Atlanta.

- In those seven losing seasons, the Cubs lost ninety games *five* times! (Repeat *five times* in your head...like hearing Ed Rooney say *"Nine Times"* from *Ferris Bueller's Day Off.*)

- The Cubs finished higher than third place only twice in those eleven seasons, in a division often regarded as one of baseball's weakest.

- MacPhail may not have directly selected them, but under his watch the Cubs had thirteen first-round draft picks. Kerry Wood, Corey Patterson, Mark Prior, and Jon Garland you have heard of; the rest of the picks either never made it to the Major Leagues or never did anything of significance.

- Of those four "good" first-round picks, Wood showed flashes of brilliance between injuries, Prior's injuries shortened his once-promising career, and Jon Garland was traded for Matt Karchner and won himself a World Series. Corey Patterson (once a top prospect) became a serviceable fourth outfielder/occasional starter.

- The *horrendous* signing of Todd Hundley also took place under MacPhail.

Next let's look at positional stability under MacPhail's reign; here is the number of different players who started for the Cubs from Opening Day 1995 *until* Opening Day 2006:

C: Wilkins, Servais, Santiago, Girardi, Hundley, Miller, Barrett (7)

1B: Grace, Stairs, McGriff, Choi, Lee (5)

2B: Sanchez, Sandberg, Morandini, Young, DeShields, Grudzielaniek, Walker (7)

3B: Buechelle, Hernandez, Orie, Gaetti, Andrews, Mueller, Stynes, Bellhorn, Ramirez (9)

SS: Dunston, Sanchez, Blauser, Hernandez, Nieves, Gutierrez, Gonzalez, Garciaparra (8)

LF: Bullett, Gonzalez, Brown, Rodriguez, White, Alou, Hollandsworth, (7)

CF: McRae, Johnson, Buford, Patterson (4)

RF: Sosa, Burnitz (2)

SP: Bullinger, Navarro, Mulholland, Tapani, Trachsel, Lieber, Wood, Zambrano (8)

Over an eleven-year period, there should be *some* stability at a *couple* positions. Just gaze again at the positional changes listed above...what a mess! These year-to-year changes were not due to rampant player movement; these positional changes followed a pattern of failure...new guy...*he* fails...another new guy...*he* fails...etc.! This amazing lack of continuity has many consequences:

- Constant locker room chemistry changes
- Constant changes in double-play combinations
- Pitchers getting used to different catchers...almost every year
- Catchers getting used to different pitchers...almost every year
- Managers understanding of their players' talents, abilities and limitations
- Constant quitting of uniform tailors (I can only speculate)

I could go on and on with the problems this kind of positional turnover creates. All teams have constant turnover in twenty-first century baseball, yet they don't have it at almost *every* position.

Andy MacPhail's failure with the Cubs (**Reason 92**) was not due to lack of effort. Professional baseball is a game of results. After eleven seasons MacPhail's Cubs had two play-off appearances, a couple of successful draft picks, five really lousy seasons, and perpetual change at almost every position. On October 1, 2006, Andy MacPhail stepped down from his position with the Cubs...it may have been his most accurate decision.

REASON 93

JIM HENDRY'S SECOND TERM

Jim Hendry became general manager of the Chicago Cubs on July 5, 2002. Hendry had previously served as assistant GM/player personnel director and director of player development. Hendry started working for the Cubs in 1995, after a brief tenure with the Florida Marlins and a successful run as head coach of Creighton University. Hendry worked as Cubs' GM until the summer of 2011. Hendry is one of the people who I find difficult to include on this list, that's why his reason comes with a qualifier.

By Hendry's final years with the Cubs, he was a much maligned figure. Based on some of the moves and results of post-2008, the fans disapproval of Hendry was warranted. Prior to that (no pun intended related to Mark) Cubs' fans had no reason to be disgruntled with Hendry. Consider:

- Hendry is the only Cubs' general manager to oversee three post-season appearances.

- Under Hendry, the Cubs reached the post-season in consecutive seasons for the first time since the 1930s.

- Even with seasons of 87, 91, and 96 losses (irrespectively) Hendry's Cubs' teams finished 749-748.

- Hendry is the third longest serving general manager in Cubs' history.

- Without a few of the key debacles in Game 6 of the 2003 NLCS (of which he had no control), Hendry would be considered the greatest GM in Cubs' history, and I am not writing this book in 2013.

Okay, I will quit *defending* Jim Hendry, but I know that if he's *not* included, many Cubs' fans will question the validity of the book. For all the success Hendry had, he made decisions that hurt the Cubs immensely. It's almost like there were *two* Jim Hendrys that worked for the Cubs. The first Jim Hendry made smart, solid moves, had the Cubs set with a stocked farm system, and had them on the brink of history. The second Jim Hendry, overspent (way, way overspent!), made short-term mistakes, and mortgaged the future. I often wonder if the NLCS loss to the Marlins ate at Hendry so much that he altered the way he did business. No matter the reason, there are moves Hendry made in what I am calling his "second term" that can be examined critically. Many of Hendry's "second-term" choices have had (and continue to have) a damaging effect on the team's efforts toward success.

After the 96-loss season of 2006, Hendry hired Lou Piniella to manage the Cubs. Over the course of the next few years, Hendry would make moves that would help the Cubs win in 2007-08, but came with huge long-term costs:

- Despite numerous red flags, Hendry re-signed Cubs' pitcher Carlos Zambrano to a five-year, $91.5 million contract. The Cubs paid Zambrano $15.5 million in 2012...to play for the Miami Marlins.

- Hendry signed Alfonso Soriano to an eight-year, $136 million contract in November 2007. While Soriano helped the Cubs in the 2007 and 2008 regular seasons, his post-season performance in each of those years was dreadful. Soriano's contract was front-loaded, meaning that even as Soriano's skills continued to erode, the Cubs were paying him more. As of 2013, the Cubs are still paying Soriano $19 million per season. Soriano has put up "decent" numbers as a Cub; yet far below the expectations of a $19 million a year player.

- After the 2006 season, Hendry re-signed third baseman Aramis Ramirez to a five-year, $73 million contract. Ramirez remained a productive player with the Cubs; nevertheless, his horribly slow start in 2010 coincided with the team's awful start...knocking the Cubs out of contention. Ramirez hit .152 in April and .173 in May with a total of four home runs.

- After the Cubs' 2007 season play-off disappointment, Hendry signed Japanese export Kosuke Fukudome to a four-year, $48 million contract. Multiple teams were interested in Fukudome's services; unfortunately for the Cubs, Hendry won the bidding.

- Perhaps Hendry's biggest blunder came with the 2008 signing of Milton Bradley to a three-year, $30 million deal. Bradley as a Cub was a disaster...on and off the field.

- Prior to the 2011 season, which would be Hendry's last, he traded four of the Cubs' top prospects for Tampa pitcher Matt Garza. Depending on the futures of those prospects, there is much time for this to develop into a long-term cost.

- Also prior to 2011, Hendry hired Mike Quade to manage the team. Quade's tenure as manager lasted one year; for the sake of brevity, I will simply state that Quade was *not* successful.

Jim Hendry's moves during the latter part of his time with the Cubs proved to be costly and detrimental to the long-term opportunities of the Chicago Cubs. Alfonso Soriano's contract with the Cubs does not expire until after 2014, three full seasons after Hendry's departure.

Here is what I believe to be a great analogy of Jim Hendry's time with the Cubs. Picture a man who goes into a Las Vegas casino to make a wager one year (choose any game of chance you want!). It appears he has won the greatest jackpot in the history of gambling. His winning is five minutes (say like *five* outs) from occurring. Then, in the blink of an eye…it's gone. This devastates the man, and after being so close…he vows to right the wrong.

The man keeps coming back to the casino year after year. He sometimes comes close to winning, yet most times misses entirely. And the man keeps upping his bet. He keeps coming back, throwing money at the chance to win the jackpot that once escaped his grasp. The man continues this cycle year after year and does things he wouldn't normally do. He mortgages everything. The man continues until he loses for the last time…he is broke. The man no longer has a chance to bet.

No casino will even let him in to play.

Jim Hendry (**Reason 93**) will get more opportunities in Major League Baseball. He came closer than any man has of bringing the Cubs a World Series title, but in the end he ran out of chances.

REASON 94

TOTAL INSTABILITY

I have stated throughout this book that the 1977 Chicago Cubs' season was the first I followed closely. The manager of the Cubs in 1977 was Herman Franks. As Dale Svuem began the 2012 season as Cubs' manager, he was the twenty-first different manager since 1977. Upon arriving at the number twenty-one, it seemed an excessive amount of managers in thirty-five years. I decided to do a bit of comparative research.

For the purpose of **Reason 94**, I only include men who managed twenty-five games with a Major League team. I did not count "interim" managers who may have only managed a few games. Since 1977, the Cubs have employed twenty-one managers in those thirty-five seasons, with the average manager lasting 1.6 seasons. My theory is that the Cubs' managerial instability is one of the 104 reasons why the team can't win a World Series title. If I am wrong, then I have already wasted time, ink, and paper writing this far.

Before totally delving into managerial stability and how I measured it, there are variables that cannot be reflected in my numbers. For example, managerial changes are far more common and frequent today than in the Major Leagues pre-1960s. Despite the dizzying popularity the game enjoyed during this era, the constant media scrutiny and news sources of today did not exist. Financial considerations cannot be accurately reflected in these numbers: Did some teams avoid changes because of the money involved? In the early part of the twentieth century, teams may have just avoided making changes based on comfort level.

Here is how I measure *managerial stability*. I compiled a list of all National League teams since 1908 (the last Cubs' World Series title). For teams that didn't exist in 1908, their first year in the league was used as a starting point. The comparative information included below: the total managers of each franchise, the average length a manager's term for the franchise, and the total number of World Series appearances and titles for that team. Here are the National League numbers. (Franchises will appear in their current inclination. For example, the Atlanta Braves will be referred to as the Atlanta *Braves*, not the *Milwaukee* Braves, *the Boston* Braves, Boston *Rustlers*, Boston *Doves*, or the Boston *Bees*…as they were previously named.)

TEAM	SINCE	TOTAL MGRS.	AVG.	W.S. APP.	TITLES
Chicago	1908	50	2.08	7	0
Arizona	1998	6	2.5	1	1
Atlanta	1908	35	2.97	9	3
Cincinnati	1908	42	2.47	9	5
Colorado	1993	5	4	1	0
Houston	1962	16	3.1	1	0
Los Angeles	1908	19	5.5	18	6
Milwaukee	1993	6	2.5	0	0
Miami	1993	9	2.2	2	2
NY Mets	1962	18	2.7	4	2
Philadelphia	1908	36	2.8	7	2
Pittsburgh	1908	26	4.0	6	5
St. Louis	1908	29	3.6	18	9
San Francisco	1908	22	4.7	16	5
San Diego	1969	15	2.9	2	0
Washington	1969	14	2.9	0	0

*Reminder: On this list we only included men who managed
at least twenty-five games for their respective teams.*

Numbers can be a bit confusing, scary, and manipulated. If you make sense of this chart, there are two conclusions that can be easily drawn.

1. The Cubs have had more managerial changes than any other team in the National League. The "college of coaches" years may skew the number a bit, but not enough to make a significant difference. Furthermore, that was the Cubs' silly idea so they should be doomed to have it count against them.

2. The teams with the most National League World Series appearances: Cardinals, Giants, and Dodgers have managers whose tenures *average* close to four and five years. The Cubs' average a turnover at the position every *two* years.

Now if we narrow the list to display just teams in the National League since 1908: **Dodgers 19, Giants 22, Pirates 26, Cardinals 29, Braves 35, Phillies 36, Reds 42, and the Cubs 50.** The Reds are the only team that comes close to the Cubs. The Reds' five World Series titles take the stink off of their relatively high number of managers. A fact that cannot be disputed: There is a correlation between the managerial stability of the **Cardinals, Giants,** and **Dodgers** and their successes in winning the National League.

Whatever reasons we may or may not try to apply to these numbers, there is one thing that cannot be denied: Since 1908, the Chicago Cubs have been the most unstable team in the National League in terms of manager tenure. During the same time, their competitor's leadership situations were more constant.

The Cubs' **Total Instability** of managers is **Number 94** of our 104 reasons; it also makes me feel better about the time, ink and paper I used working on this piece.

Chapter Summary

In this chapter we dealt with both field managers and general managers who may have contributed to the Chicago Cubs' astounding lack of success over a 104-year period. For the purposes of this prologue, I will divide the two positions.

Managers

In regards to this chapter, and all the managers mentioned in any of the reasons, there is a definite *self-fulfilling prophecy* that goes along with managing the Cubs. (Actually **anything** that has to do with the Cubs.) If you are not familiar with the concept, it means that when a certain outcome is expected people tend to act consciously and perhaps even subconsciously in accordance with that expected outcome. Let me try to explain that in *English*, with regards to the Cubs: If there are expectations that the team and thus the manager will fail, the people involved may unknowingly help reach those expectations. This is not to imply that anyone who ever managed the Cubs has *tried* to fail, more likely on some level they knew that it was a likely outcome and acted accordingly. Imagine then, a manager trying to manage against this; having a team, city, and even a *country* acting in accordance with an expected outcome.

All right, enough of the psycho-babble, let's get back to talking specifically about baseball. Cub managers over the years have not had much talent to work with, that's why there are very few specific managers mentioned in this chapter. Oh, there have been some seemingly unqualified people to fill the position, but in more years than not the Cubs' problems ran deeper than just the manager.

General Managers

A qualifier I wanted to include at the end of this chapter is that all of the decisions, both poor and good, attributed to these GMs are rarely total individual decisions. In regards to trades, drafts, and free agent signings, a baseball organization has many people that help come to some collective decisions. There is no way that the general managers listed in this chapter know all of the draftees that were taken during their tenure. The GMs have to rely on scouts, player development people, assistants, minor league coaches and many more voices when making these decisions. A general manager, like many positions of authority in this country, have a "Buck Stops Here" sort of label that goes with them. Regardless if the move was initiated by the GMs, the owner or top assistants and scouts, the deal goes on the ledger of the general manager. Some hypothetical/possibly factual examples:

Was Jim Hendry solely responsible for the length and amount of Alfonso Soriano's contract, or was ownership pushing for it?

Were the GMs of the team prior to the Tribune ownership forced to make deals on the merits of their economic value and not their baseball sense?

Were deals that were made like Brock for Broglio, based on poor scouting information?

How many of the bad drafts were driven by economics?

Were there better moves to be made by general managers of the Chicago Cubs that were nixed by ownership?

I can only imagine that there has to be some truth in some of the above scenarios, unfortunately for the general manager, he is the one that takes the bullet.

In the fall of 2011 Theo Epstein was hired as president of baseball operations of the Chicago Cubs. This move was predominately met with exuberance by Cub fans, and obviously I am hoping they are right. However there have been good baseball men like Theo Epstein who have tried and failed with this team over the last 104 years. A Cubs' World Series title would be the biggest mountaintop any executive could climb, and it has derailed many careers of men who have tried to scale it.

The men listed in this chapter in both capacities as field and general manager accomplished some good things in Major League Baseball. For some of them it is only during their tenure with the Cubs that poor decisions and mistakes were made and magnified. When a team is trying to break the longest championship in the history of all sports, no one attempting to get the job done comes in with a truly clean slate. One hundred and four years of previous failures, mistakes, and losses are automatically squarely on the person's back. With that much baggage, reaching the mountaintop has proven to be impossible.

CHAPTER 9

REASON 95—Not So Tough Image
If you were a pro athlete, would you rather be a bear or a baby bear?

REASON 96—Fan Favorites
Cubs' fans are passionate, loyal and have adored mediocre players for years.

REASON 97—A Lack of Aces
When the Cubs have had a true "ace" leading their staff, they contend...
unfortunately that is a very rare occurrence.

REASON 98—A Need for Speed
Quick trivia…how many players have stolen sixty bases for the Chicago Cubs...
and are alive to talk about it?

REASON 99—Green Goes Too Soon
Dallas Green lasted only five years with the Cubs,
but his positive imprints changed the franchise forever.

REASON 100—Don't Walk
The focus on drawing walks and OBP is now a vital baseball strategy…
the Cubs have been ignoring it for over 100 years.

REASON 101—LACK OF LEFTY POWER
Can you name a Cubs' left-handed power hitter
other than Billy Williams?

REASON 102—NO GOLD PART 1:
A LACK OF BACKSTOPS
Would you believe that teams with Gold Glove catchers win often?
The Cubs have had one.

REASON 103—NO GOLD PART 2:
"PUT ME IN, COACH!"…UNLESS HE CAN'T PLAY
Would you believe that teams with Gold Glove center fielders win often?
The Cubs have had one.

REASON 104—THE DECIMATION OF THE 2003 STAFF
Did the Cubs' short-sided pursuit of a title ruin the careers
of some of their most promising pitchers
…ever?

BLUNDERS
(PHILOSOPHICAL, HISTORICAL, AND JUST PLAIN STUPID)

In regards to the Chicago Cubs the term "blunder" can be used *so* many ways. In this book, I have examined numerous different types of "blunders:"

- a manager throwing a pitcher on only one day rest...after that pitcher threw numerous pitches over two consecutive days

- a physical error such as a shortstop booting a grounder that would have been a double-play...thus ending a potentially apocalyptic inning

- an eventual Hall of Fame left fielder being traded away for a sore armed pitcher

- year after year of really awful draft decisions

- financial blunders...such as allotting huge sums of money to players past their prime

Many of the previous ninety-four reasons fit nicely into the categories they were classified in. For our final chapter, I will be scrutinizing *blunders* that transcend a simple or easy qualification. These upcoming blunders may be some of the strongest *reasons* yet. Here is a brief attempt to describe the kinds of blunders that make up **Reasons 95-104**:

Philosophical

These will be blunders in which the Cubs made continued errors in judgment or a series of consistent bad decisions. These "philosophical" reasons will cover areas in which the Cubs made critical "wrong thinking" in short- or long-term capacities. I will give an example (and a preview) from an upcoming reason: How can you explain one team leading the league in walks just *three* times over a sixty-seven year period? Philosophically the Cubs have apparently either devalued the walk, or were unaware of their continued weakness in this area.

Historical

You may have heard the saying, "Those who fail to learn history are doomed to repeat it,"…or some other cliché that your history teacher tried to impress upon you to illustrate the subject's importance. Apparently many Cubs' decision makers never were educated in regards to this lesson. Throughout CHAPTER 9, I will demonstrate how the Cubs have historically either ignored or failed miserably at important positions like catcher and center field. The Cubs' lack of talent in these areas is explained by either ignorance regarding their previous poor choices at these positions…or by complete stupidity.

Just Plain Stupid

These reasons will concentrate on areas and decisions in which it appears there was little to no thinking taking place. Ideas or choices in which logic and rational thinking seem to be as absent and elusive as the titles the Cubs are pursuing.

How else can you explain a team taking *two* "once-in-a-generation" type starting pitchers and using them like they had bionic arms? Why would a team abuse these two pitchers over a short period of time with no apparent thought for their futures? Why would they inadvertently (I hope) assist in shortening and ending the careers of two of their most valuable pitching prospects ever? Stupidity and shortsidedness are the only answers I can assert.

One of the truly interesting aspects of **Reasons 95-104** is that multiple people at different times have been making many of these philosophical, historical and stupid blunders for the Cubs. It has not mattered who has been the owner, the team president, the general manager or the field manager; many of these mistakes keep getting *made…over and over* again! Perhaps there is a book of idiotic guidelines each of them follows as to how to keep the Cubs from attaining their World Series aspirations. What would that book of guidelines be called I wonder?

Reasons 95-104 will conclude our journey through the vast history of Cubs' failures and offer final logical reasons. The Cubs have historically found different ways to "blunder"…and they have been consistent in repeating them.

REASON 95

NOT SO TOUGH IMAGE

Are you familiar with the concept of *free-association*? The method of free-association is a technique developed by Sigmund Freud to examine and explore people's subconscious. The examiner states a word, phrase or concept; then the participant shouts out the first thing that comes to his mind. (I guess he doesn't have to *shout.*) The participant is instructed *not* to give the response any thought at all, nor should he edit or censor the reaction. Freud believed that this helped understand a person's subconscious wishes, desires, and innermost thoughts. Freud also believed young boys and girls rivaled their same-sex parent for the other parent's affection...yuck! (*Understanding Psychology,* Kasschau 2003.) Freud's method of free-association is commonly used today in analysis ranging from standardized tests to job interviews. If you are still unclear, here is a hypothetical free-association:

- EXAMINER: Red
- PARTICIPANT: Blood
- EXAMINER: Blue
- PARTICIPANT: Water

Yes...it can be just that exciting! Why am I explaining free-association and Sigmund Freud? Because I plan on using the method right now! Okay, clear your mind...what do you think of when I say the word...

Cub.

Now as a Cubs' fan, your first thoughts are probably regarding the team...you may have responded with Starlin Castro, Larry Bittner, or Mark DeRosa. Imagine if you *weren't* a Cubs' fan...what would pop in your head upon hearing the word "Cub?" The average person would possibly think of a young bear... perhaps a *baby* bear. A young animal or a baby...that's an image associated with the Chicago National League ball club. A *baby* is not going to instill fear in anyone, not even a baby bear; unless that baby's mother is in the general vicinity. "Cubs" just does not sound threatening; it's even worse that they are referred to as the "Cubbies." Growing up, the White Sox fans in my neighborhood constantly razzed my "*Cubbies*"...and damn it...I couldn't fight back. In retrospect I should have inquired about the strength of a White Sock...footwear inspires no intimidation or has any combative abilities. In terms of tough sounding mascot names, the *Red* Sox would rank ahead of the White Sox. I mean at least if you washed them together, the Red Sock could "bleed" on the White Sock...hence asserting its dominance. Why, even a young baby bear cub would tear that white sock to shreds! A White Sock's only hope would be to be choked on by one of the animals or other combatants.

Back to my point...here is the *dictionary.com* definition of a cub:

cub

1. the young of certain animals, as the bear, lion, or tiger

2. a young shark

3. a young and inexperienced person, especially a callow youth or young man

4. a young person serving as an apprentice

How strong would *you* feel playing for a team representing a young animal? I realize some may find this silly, yet in all seriousness, "Cubs" just sounds *so wimpy*...and "Cubbies?" Please. I know I have reiterated the importance that the previous ninety-four reasons were logical and rational, and **Reason 95** sounds contradictory to that premise...yet stay with me here.

If you remember from the CHAPTER 1: NEAR MISSES (1969-1945), the Chicago Cubs were once called the Chicago Colts. I honestly believe that the "Chicago Colts" would have won a World Series in the last 104 years. Laugh at me...I don't care, because I really trust that men playing for the Chicago Colts would feel a greater sense of self-esteem than those playing for the Cubs. Here are other animals, whose young are referred to as cubs:

Badger	Bobcat	Cougar	Fox	Leopard	Lion
Mink	Otter	Raccoon	Seal	Tiger	Walrus
Wolf	Woodchuck				

Now, you tell me which sounds tougher: Cubs or Badger-Cubs? Cubs or Lion-Cubs? Cubs or Tiger-Cubs? (I can't do much with Mink, Otter and Woodchucks) *Bear-Cubs* would sound much more intimidating than just regular old *Cubs*. If Bear-Cubs won't work for you, how about attaching a tough sounding adjective:

Fighting-Cubs	Killer-Cubs	Grizzly-Cubs	Sluggin'-Cubs
Running-Cubs	Deadly-Cubs	Roarin'-Cubs	Shark-Cubs

Okay, so they are not *ALL* good, and we give up the bear image with *Shark*-Cubs…but they do sound less wimpy.

I feel another image problem for the Cubs that attributes to their overall lousy play is their colors. The red is fine, but the only wimpier blue than the royal-blue the Cubs wear is baby blue. (Like the late 1970s pajama-type uniforms the Cubs wore.) Let's rank a few "blues" based on their tough appearance:

MIDNIGHT BLUE
Darkest shade, often mistaken for black, the bad-a$$ of colors

DENIM BLUE
Blue-jeans aren't tough, yet it's a nice, dark color

NAVY BLUE
Great looking color that maintains an edge

AIR-FORCE BLUE
Not as tough as navy, yet extremely tougher than…

ROYAL (CUBBIE) BLUE
Loses out to all other forms of the blue family except…

BABY BLUE
Only the San Diego Chargers can make this look cool

Here is my advice to the Chicago Cubs regarding their team colors... change them. However, traditional Cubs' fans would go bonkers at this suggestion! I could just hear Cubs' fans say, "I would rather *not* win a World Series than change our colors!" (Personally, the Cubs could wear polka-dots with stripes and I wouldn't care if they could get a World Series title.)

So what to do about these traditionalist Cubs' fans? Trick them. Here is what I suggest; each season darken the blue by a tiny increment. Year by year "Cubbie" blue will get darker and darker, and no one would have to know. By the year 2028, the Cubs will wear navy blue and red and no one will notice, especially if they happen to win a World Series by then! (...not bloody likely.)

I will admit that on my logical and rational journey to 104 reasons, **Reason 95** takes a whimsical detour. Yet I maintain the Chicago Cubs and their fans suffer from a bit of an inferiority complex due to their name and colors. Contrast the Chicago Cubs' image with that of the Chicago Bears? Does anyone ever question the toughness of the Bears? For the last fifty years the Bears haven't had phenomenal success...yet no one would ever question their image because an adult bear is much tougher than a *baby* bear.

...and the adults get to wear *navy* blue.

REASON 96

F AN FAVORITES

After the debacle that was the 2003 NLCS and other disappointments of the 2000s, a strange new phenomenon began to occur at Wrigley Field: Cubs' players getting booed...by Cubs' fans. I cannot quantify or source this information; it's just my personal observation. I have seen more Cubs' players booed in the last five years than in all of my previous years. Perhaps the collective psyche of the paying customer at Wrigley Field finally snapped? Maybe the cynical attitude of the outside world finally penetrated the force field of good feeling that had covered Wrigley for generations? I can't explain it; I can only state that it is a much different attitude than had customarily been portrayed by the "greatest fans in baseball."

I am not endorsing the booing. In fact, I have always felt booing or yelling at players is rather silly. Have you ever been at a professional sporting event and observed fans yelling at players? Have you observed it from the last row of the bleachers, the upper deck, or even from the rooftops? Have you ever thought how insignificant and ridiculous this is? Have you observed a situation like this?

LOUD FAN FAR AWAY FROM GAME TO ANONYMOUS PITCHER:
"Come on, (player's name)! Throw some bleeping strikes!!!"

MAJOR LEAGUE PITCHER:
"Thanks for the advice, sir. I am trying."

Right, you have never seen that happen. I realize it's a rather unrealistic and preposterous example. Yet it's not more ridiculous than the fan who is yelling to expect some kind of results from his rants. Perhaps I am being too logical; fans yell at players through their televisions.

This yelling and booing of our Cubbies (ugh) *is* something new. I don't think this new behavior is fruitful...it is a stark new reality. A reality that is quite different from fan behavior of **Reason Number 96: Fan Favorites.**

Cubs' fans have historically displayed an uncanny ability to adore marginal players. Fans have been unbelievably loyal and shower players with love and admiration...many times undeservedly, based on the player's production on the field. Cubs' fans are certainly not the only fandom guilty of this...just one of the greatest perpetrators.

You may question the validity of **Reason 96**, or ask why it matters if fans *love* their players? What is wrong with loyalty? I believe Cubs' fans' levels of appreciation have been so extraordinary that it has hindered the progress of the team on the field. Here are examples of what I mean:

Mark Grace was a very good baseball player for the Chicago Cubs. Grace played first base for the Cubs from 1988 to 2000. Mark Grace was most definitely a fan favorite. Very few fans would question Grace's ability to help the Cubs win, or dare to think he might be replaceable. Grace was a very solid player, yet the Cubs only made the post-season twice during his tenure with the team. I do not believe Grace was responsible for the team's lack of play-off appearances. In fact, in typical Cubs' fashion Grace would win a World Series with the Arizona Diamondbacks in his first non-Cubs' year. Grace would help win that World Series with Arizona by putting up numbers consistent with his previous thirteen seasons with the Cubs. Logically, had there been better players around Grace from 1988 to 2000, he certainly could have helped the Cubs win a World Series.

Nevertheless, the point I make is this: was Mark Grace's ability as a Cub worthy of the status he was given? Mark Grace had a career average of .303, had 2,445 career hits, won four Gold Gloves and made two All-Star games. Yet let's consider this about Grace; at the power position of first base, he never hit more than seventeen home runs and never drove in 100 runs. In his thirteen seasons, he led the league in a category just four times. Those categories were *at bats* with 619 in 1991, *doubles* with fifty-one in 1995, *grounded into double plays* with twenty-five in 1993 and *sacrifices flies* with ten in 1999. Grace's statistical prowess as a Cub can surely be questioned.

The Cubs replaced Grace in 2001 with Matt Stairs and eventually Fred McGriff. While Grace compared very favorably with both players in OPS and fielding, Stairs' and McGriff's power numbers were far superior. Stairs and McGriff were very capable replacements for Mark Grace, yet neither player lasted more than a season and a half with the Cubs. Stairs and McGriff were *not* fan favorites, even though they were comparable to Grace by most rubrics.

Here are some other Cubs who I would classify as *fan favorites*, akin to the case of Mark Grace:

Shawon Dunston

Dunston was the starting shortstop for the Cubs for twelve seasons, and fans famously displayed the *Shawon-O-Meter* at Wrigley to measure his batting average. Let's look at Dunston using WAR. A reminder, WAR numbers represent a player's value above a generic AAA or replacement player. A good player is considered between 2 and 3, a great player is 4-7, and a WAR of 8 is considered MVP material. Here are Dunston's WAR numbers with the Cubs: 1.3, 0.6, -0.4, 0.8, 2.2, 1.3, 1.6, 0.4, 0.0, -0.4, 0.5, and 0.0. Using this metric, Dunston was *good* in only one of his twelve seasons with the Cubs.

Kerry Wood

I LOVE Kerry Wood; he is one of *my* favorites. In my opinion Wood is one of the classiest, most team-oriented, and hard-working players I've observed. Wood struck out twenty Astros in one game, but was a victim of numerous unfortunate injuries throughout his career. Consider though (sorry, Kerry) in his thirteen seasons with the Cubs: Wood won ten games or more just four times, led the league in strikeouts *once*, started over thirty games *twice* and was converted to a reliever in order to continue his career.

Don Kessinger

Kessinger was a little before my time but was the Cubs' starting shortstop for twelve seasons. Kessinger was a six-time All-Star, regarded as an elite fielder. Kessinger won two Gold Gloves during his Cubs' career. Using the same WAR metric we used on Dunston, here are Kessinger's numbers: -0.2, -1.6, -0.5, 0.7, 1.5, 4.1, 1.0, 0.0, 2.8, -0.4, 0.3, and 0.1. According to WAR, Kessinger was good in two of his twelve seasons…not very good in the other ten.

For the purposes of **Reason 96**, I focused on players who played ten seasons with the Chicago Cubs. The fan favorite narrative for the Chicago Cubs can be seen in players with limited careers as well. I hate to do this, because after all I am a Cubs' fan and I **loved** most of these guys as well. So sorry, but here goes: Jody Davis, Ivan DeJesus, Bill Buckner, Bob Dernier, Randy Hundley, Joe Pepitone, and Jose Cardenal. Yes…I just trashed my childhood.

Having fan favorites is not a unique quality relegated to Cubs' fans, yet I would contest the level is higher than with most sports' franchises. Cubs' fans historically fall in love with mediocre to very good players. Those players then seem irreplaceable to the fans and perhaps even Cubs' management. A familiarity and comfort level grows, and rational criticism of these players disappears. The players have been given extended careers or numerous unearned chances since they are loved. Perception has trumped production for many years at Wrigley Field.

I may not like the booing, but perhaps it is a sign that this phenomena is ending. Although the booing is misguided and silly in my opinion, it may indicate Cubs' fans are holding players more accountable. The fandom may have finally reached its breaking or tipping point in continuing its undying love for a team such as the Cubs.

...104 years without winning a
World Series championship tends to do that.

Hope exudes from the new Cubs' management team led by Theo Epstein who took over in the fall of 2011. Epstein and current Cubs' general manager Jed Hoyer have stressed rational, logical, and long-term decision making at every turn. The trade of popular left-handed reliever Sean Marshall was met by some in the Cubs' universe with disgust. Hoyer and Epstein saw a chance to turn a short-term asset into multiple long-term assets, regardless of how much Marshall was loved.

Fan Favorites (**Reason 96**) can be positive for a team and its fandom. If those players can help sustain winning and perhaps assist in a World Series championship, they deserve love and admiration. Average (or below) players can certainly be liked by a team's fan base...within reason. If an average player helps his team win a World Series, heck yes! You can love him!

It's just never happened with the Chicago Cubs.

REASON 97

A LACK OF ACES

On November 5, 1955, Denton True "Cy" Young passed away. Cy Young holds the record for most wins by a Major League pitcher with 511 victories. Young pitched his final game in 1911 and certainly pitched in an entirely different era. The feats and legends of Young are so great that upon his passing, Commissioner Ford Frick began honoring the best pitcher with the Cy Young Award. From 1956-1966, the award was given to the best pitcher in the Major Leagues, as voted on by the Baseball Writers Association. Beginning in 1967, separate awards for the American and National Leagues were presented. For the purposes of **Reason 97**, I am only going to examine Cubs' pitchers from 1956 until today...the Cy Young Era.

The Chicago Cubs have won four Cy Young Awards: **Fergie Jenkins** in 1971, **Bruce Sutter** in 1979, **Rick Sutcliffe** in 1984, and **Greg Maddux** in 1992. The all-time leaders for Cy Young Awards for National League teams are the Dodgers with ten. The Braves and Phillies are next with seven apiece. Considering that Sutter was a reliever, the Cubs have had three *starting* pitchers since 1956 to win a Cy Young. The number of Cy Young Awards for the Cubs is not remarkably low; nonetheless, the lack of top-line pitching *is* an undeniable factor in the Cubs' dearth of success.

For the purpose of this piece, **Fergie Jenkins** is labeled as the Cubs' most prominent "ace." Here is why:

- The Cubs' record in the seven seasons *prior* to Fergie Jenkins' arrival was 472-646; a .422 winning percentage.

- The Cubs' record in their seven seasons (1967-73) *with* Fergie Jenkins was 592-533; a .526 winning percentage.

- Fergie Jenkins' win totals with the Cubs from 1967-73 were 20, 20, 21, 22, 24, 20, and 14.

- After Fergie's sub-par 1973, the Cubs traded him to the Texas Rangers for Bill Madlock. In 1974 with Texas, Fergie went 25-12 with a 2.89 ERA.

- Fergie's inning totals with the Cubs from 1967-73: 289, 308, 311, 313, 325, 289, and 271.

With Fergie Jenkins as their ace, the Cubs were a consistent contending team. Other Cubs' pitchers who could have potentially been long-term "aces" were either injured or became ex-Cubs. Here is who I would qualify:

Rick Rueschel (1972-1981, 1984)
Rueschel's only twenty-win season for the Cubs came in 1977 as they finished .500 for the season. The Cubs traded Rueschel to the Yankees in 1981. Rueschel briefly returned for part of the 1984 season. An interesting fact about Rueschel is after battling arm injuries for most of the early 1980s, he pitched extremely

well after the Cubs let him go the *second* time. In 1988 Rueschel was 19-11 with a 3.12 ERA for the Giants. In '89 Rueschel was an All-Star (17-8, 2.94) and helped San Francisco make it past the Cubs in the 1989 National League Championship Series.

Rick Sutcliffe (1984-1991)

Rick Sutcliffe went 16-1 with a 2.69 for the Cubs after being acquired from Cleveland in June. A series of injuries kept Sutcliffe from being a consistent number one starter for the Cubs. Sutcliffe finished second in Cy Young voting in 1987 after going 18-10 for the Cubs, and teamed with Greg Maddux to lead the Cubs to the 1989 Eastern Division Championship.

Greg Maddux (1986-1992, 2004-2006)

I think I have made my feelings clear on this subject in the previous ninety-five reasons. The Cubs had one of the greatest pitchers of all time and let him escape during his prime years...in which he won *three straight* Cy Young awards. (...after winning one with the Cubs!) Had Maddux stayed with the Cubs, he would have been the consummate franchise ace.

Kerry Wood (1998-2008, 2011-2012) and Mark Prior (2002-2006)

The Cubs had two pitchers with first-rate stuff at the same time...unfortunately they are forever linked due to their collective inability to stay healthy. It's no coincidence that in their mutually healthy season, the Cubs came closer than ever to the World Series.

Carlos Zambrano (2001-2011)

The enigmatic right-hander's ace-like stuff seemed to come and go in his latter career with the Cubs. I included him on this list because the Cubs made the play-offs three times with Carlos in the rotation. One knock against "Big Z"... he never won a post-season game for the Cubs.

The Cy Young has been awarded in Major League baseball for the past fifty-six years. I have included seven Cubs' pitchers that I would consider an "ace" during that period. (Rueschel may be a stretch, but he *did win* twenty games.) Instead of spouting another cliché about the importance of quality starting pitching, let's examine the last fifty-six years of Cubs' history in a simple way:

YEARS	COMMENTS
1946-1966	No real aces and the Cubs are awful for 20 seasons.
1967-1973	Jenkins leads them to 6 of 7 seasons over .500.
1974-1983	Yuck...20-win Rueschel gets Cubs to .500 in '77.
1984	Rick Sutcliffe leads Cubs to first play-offs in 39 years.
1989	Sutcliffe/Maddux lead Cubs to second play-offs in 5 years.
1990-1997	Maddux departs and this is a stretch of really dreadful teams.
1998	A dominant young Wood helps Cubs win wild card.
2003	The best Cubs' staff ever with a healthy Wood and Prior.
2007-08	Zambrano/Cubs in two straight play-offs; no play-off wins.

A correlation can be made after reviewing the last fifty-six years of Chicago Cubs' history; in the Cubs' six play-off appearances they had good to great pitching. The Cubs with Jenkins leading the staff were perennial contenders. Good pitching in baseball equals success...duh?! When you breakdown the Cubs' history, the Cubs' "aces" coincide with their rare contending years. Now, let's examine some starting pitching of the non-Cubs' variety. Here are the World Series Champions since 2000 and pitchers who led their staff:

YEAR	TEAM	TOP STARTERS
2012	San Francisco Giants	Matt Cain, Madison Bumgarner, Barry Zito
2011	St. Louis Cardinals	Chris Carpenter, Jamie Garcia
2010	San Francisco Giants	Matt Cain, Tim Lincecum
2009	New York Yankees	C.C. Sabathia, Andy Pettite, A.J. Burnett
2008	Philadelphia Phillies	Cole Hamels

2007	Boston Red Sox	Josh Beckett, Daisuke Matsuzaka, Curt Schilling
2006	St. Louis Cardinals	Chris Carpenter, Jeff Weaver
2005	White Six	Mark Buerhle, Freddy Garcia, Jose Contreras
2004	Boston Red Sox	Curt Schilling, Pedro Martinez
2003	Florida Marlins	Josh Beckett, Brad Penny
2002	Anaheim Angels	John Lackey, Kevin Appier, Jarrod Washburn
2001	Arizonda Diamondbacks	Randy Johnson, Curt Schilling
2000	New York Yankees	Roger Clemens, Andy Pettite

How many seasons would you like me to list? Wherever stopped, the World Series Champions would have one or two very good pitchers who showed flashes of dominance. Did you notice the number of pitchers whose names appear list twice? The types of pitchers listed are essential to winning a World Series.

The Chicago Cubs have *had* pitchers such as these: Fergie Jenkins, Greg Maddux, Rick Sutcliffe, Mark Prior and Kerry Wood. The dilemma is the Chicago Cubs have these "type" of pitchers infrequently…a continuing cycle and constant predicament that lands as **Reason 97** of 104.

REASON 98

A NEED FOR SPEED

Since I was an absolute baseball nerd growing up, I played a game called *Strat-O-Matic Baseball.* My friends and brothers were also baseball nerds, thus we all played "Strat." Actually as a baseball fan, there is a decent chance *you* may already be familiar with Strat-O-Matic. I remember one of Strat-O-Matic's marketing slogans from the 1970s was "So You Think You Are the Only One" to demonstrate that Strat was being played all across the country. Before I tell you a bit more about Strat and why I am including it in **Reason 98,** let me clarify one more thing about the game. If you are a baseball fan, you liked the game, but if you are a baseball stat nerd, you *loved* the game.

From Strat-O-Matic.com…here is "What it is?"

"If this is your first acquaintance with Strat-O-Matic, welcome to the hobby enjoyed by millions of sports fans since 1961. You will be welcomed enthusiastically by the many thousands of gamers (self-described 'Strat-O-Matic Fanatics') who connect in league play, online forums and national tournaments. This is the hobby showcased in the Baseball Hall of Fame, in a Spike Lee film, on Broadway, and in an award-winning book, *Strat-O-Matic Fanatics*. It is the hobby that helped inspire numerous big-league sports announcers. The ease of play, realism and statistical accuracy of our games earn us exceptional loyalty, as have our constant efforts to improve our games based on the experiences of our customers."

Now that you know Strat-O-Matic is a legit baseball board game that pre-dates fantasy baseball and video games, you can see why it was so influential to young stat-craved baseball geeks from the 1970s like me.

Now…why am I referencing it in **Reason 98**?

Each year when my brothers and I would get the new teams around early February, we would instantly check out the Cubs and see if they were good. (They usually weren't.) Each player had his own individual Strat-O-Matic card based on statistical information, in regards to hitting, running, and fielding. Pitchers had their own cards as well. Since it was the late 1970s and early 1980s, speed was an important factor in the game…thus, Cubs' players' speed ratings were one of our main concerns. Players had a stealing *and* running rating on a scale of 1-20 in accordance with a "split" deck of cards from 1-20. For instance, the fastest runners were 1-17, meaning if you drew any number between 1 and 17, they would be safe. The stealing numbers were based on the same scale, but the player was given a letter ranking. (Strat was smart enough to recognize that fast guys can't always steal bases, and slower guys sometimes can.) The best base-stealers are AA (1-17), then in descending order: A (1-15), B (1-13), C (1-11), D (1-9), and the dreaded E (1-7). On *rare* occasions there would be an AAA (1-18) base stealer; 1974 Lou Brock and Rickey Henderson from numerous years. This element of the game caused me the most angst as a Cubs' fan!

The Cubs *rarely* had guys that were As, let alone AAs. Stealing was such an important (and fun) part of the game...and the Cubs had very few guys that could run. The Phillies, Cardinals, Dodgers, and Pirates would have As and AAs up and down their lineups...yet not our Cubs. Do you know how frustrating it is to fill out your Strat-O-Matic batting order and not have any guys that could steal at the top? When Ivan DeJesus was an A in the late 1970s, I was giddy with excitement.

Not until the glorious 1984 Chicago Cubs (yes, I was still playing it in high school) was there some Strat stolen base satisfaction: Bob Dernier AA, Ryne Sandberg A, Gary Matthews B, Leon Durham B, and Larry Bowa C. Is it a coincidence that this Cubs' team was so close to a World Series with guys that could run?

Obviously, stolen bases are not the only way to measure speed in baseball. Stolen bases *are* accurate when it comes to "elite" speed. Elite speed, and even average speed, is something that has eluded the Cubs from generation to generation. Were there any really fast guys on the 1969 team? Other than Kenny Lofton in 2003 (ah...and he was older then), did the 2003 team have much speed? The back-to-back play-off teams of 2007 and 2008 had virtually *no* speed.

Aside from recent (yet rare) successful Cubs' teams, let's look at the Cubs' lack of speed from a historical perspective. Here are the top-ten single season stolen base totals for the Chicago Cubs:

RANK	PLAYER	STOLEN BASES	YEAR
1	Bill Lange	84	1896
2	Walt Wilmot	76	1890
3	Walt Wilmot	76	1894
4	Bill Lange	73	1897
5	Frank Chance	67	1903
6	Bill Lange	67	1895
7	Bill Lange	66	1894
8	Fred Pfeffer	64	1888
9	Bill Dahlen	60	1892

Courtesy of Baseballreference.com

Upon examining this list, there are two things you should notice: 1) these guys are all dead...*way* dead...and, 2) the Cubs have not had a player steal more than sixty bases in *100 years*. Obviously the game was different pre-1900, yet before embarking on this project, I would have thought the Cubs had at least *one* sixty stolen base guy since 1903. Nope. I was quite surprised by this.

Conversely, is this atypical? Would other teams' lists be skewed in this way? After perusing the single season top-ten stolen base leaders, there were teams that were skewed in favor of the late 1800s. To get a more accurate depiction of the Cubs' historical lack of stolen bases, I examined the top *fifty single season* stolen base years for each team. I included the eight teams that have been continuous National League franchises since 1908: the Cubs, Braves, Cardinals, Dodgers, Giants, Phillies, Pirates, and Reds. Here are the results in a convenient and easy-to-read chart:

Top-50 Single-Season Stolen Base Seasons
for Eight NL Teams

Team	Non-Dead Players in Top-50	Non-Dead Percentage
1. St. Louis Cardinals	28/50	.560
2. Brooklyn/LA Dodgers	25/50	.500
3. Philadelphia Phillies	20/50	.400
4. Pittsburgh Pirates	16/50	.320
5. Cincinnati Reds	14/50	.280
6. NY/SF Giants	9/50	.180
7. Boston/ATL Braves	9/50	.180
8. Chicago Cubs	7/50	.140

I present *another* historical list...and it's a*nother* last-place finish for the Cubs. I offer up an additional historical list...and the Cardinals and Dodgers (the two most successful National League franchises) are at the top of the rankings. The strategy of stealing bases in Major League Baseball reached its most recent apex in the 1970s and 1980s. Yet this list leaves little doubt that no matter the era, the Cubs have not valued the stolen base...or they are slow.

I stated early in this piece that stolen bases are just one rubric to measure speed in baseball. In attempting to find another valid measurement, I was led to a rather simple one: the eye test. Running speed is something observable for even a novice baseball fan. I have watched the Cubs enough, you have probably watched the Cubs enough…see if you disagree with my assessments. To truly be an "eye test" for me, I have to start around 1977:

Really Fast Cubs

Tony Campana, Shawon Dunston, Kenny Lofton (very limited time), Corey Patterson, Juan Pierre, Ryne Sandberg, Sammy Sosa (and then…), Bump Wills, and Eric Young

Fast Cubs

Mark Bellhorn, Starlin Castro, Ivan DeJesus, Leon Durham (for a few years), Doug Glanville, Lance Johnson, Dave Martinez, Gary Matthews Sr. and Jr., Brian McRae, Lenny Randle, Alfonso Soriano (for 1 year), Ryan Theriot, and Jerome Walton

Average Speed Cubs

Darwin Barney, Larry Bowa, Bill Buckner, Damon Buford, Ronnie Cedeno, Andre Dawson (really bad knees), Mark DeRosa, Kosuke Fukudome, Mark Grudzielanek, Ricky Gutierrez, Steve Henderson, Jaques Jones, Derek Lee, Mickey Morandini, , Rafael Palmeiro, Karl Rhodes, Benito Santiago, Dwight Smith, and Rondell White

Slow Cubs

Moises Alou, Jeff Baker, George Bell, Milton Bradley, Marlon Byrd, Blake DeWitt, Cliff Floyd, Joe Girardi, Luis Gonzalez, Alex Gonzalez, Greg Gross, Jose Hernandez, Dave Kingman, Jerry Martin, Derek May, Jerry Morales, Keith Moreland, Bill Mueller, Bobby Murcer, Matt Murton, Steve Ontiveros, Kevin Orie, Luis Salazar, Matt Stairs, Manny Trillo, Mike Vail, Todd Walker

Really Slow Cubs

Shane Andrews, Michael Barrett, Damon Berryhill, Tim Blackwell,
Jeff Blauser, Steve Buechele, Ron Cey, Jody Davis, Barry Foote, Gary Gaetti,
Mark Grace, Leo Gomez, Todd Hundley, Eric Karros, Vance Law,
Fred McGriff, Damion Miller, George Mitterwald, Carlos Pena, Dave Radar,
Aramis Ramirez, Ken Reitz, Henry Rodriguez, Rey Sanchez, Scott Servais,
Geo Soto, Rick Wilkins, Todd Zeile

Okay, so it's not an exact science…and certainly debatable, but I would say it's a fairly accurate assessment of the last thirty-five years of Cubs' speed (or lack thereof).

Whether using an eye test, stolen base totals, or a board game's rating system, the Chicago Cubs have historically lacked speed. **Reason 98** asserts that this lack of speed has been a factor in the team not winning a World Series since 1908.

***Any player or former players who disagree with my assessment of his running speed, please feel free to file an official protest with me. And if you really want to show me up, come to my house and race me.

REASON 99

GREEN GOES TOO SOON

Even in the technologically advanced world of 2013, I look forward to getting a pocket schedule for the upcoming Cubs' season. In a world where the Cubs' schedule can be pulled up on Cubs.com, MLB.com, or ESPN.com, there is something comforting about having that little schedule in my wallet. I will never forget the first time I saw the *1982* version of the Cubs' pocket schedule.

I was in my freshman science class and a kid whose dad had season tickets was looking at one of the schedules. The exciting element of the 1982 schedule was the phrase, "Building a New Tradition" which was written in green just below the Cubs' logo. Observing this schedule enhanced the feeling of anticipation that I held for the upcoming season. "Building a New Tradition" was the slogan put in place by the Cubs' incoming executive vice-president and general manager Dallas Green. (Hence the **green** writing on the cover.) In 1982, Dallas Green *was* Theo Epstein…just thirty-nine years prior.

Green was the field manager of the 1980 World Champion Philadelphia Phillies. The Tribune Company hired Green away in its first bold move of ownership. Green quickly exerted his influence by raiding the Phillies' coaching staffs and scouting departments, including hiring Lee Elia as his first Cubs' manager. Elia is famous in Cubs' lore for his profanity-laced tirade regarding Wrigley fans after a loss. If you have never heard Elia's rant, it does warrant a listen…just make sure there are no youngsters within a one-mile radius.

The Cubs struggled in both 1982 and 1983; then Green hired Jim Frey to manage in 1984. Frey had managed the Royals against Green's Phillies in the 1980 World Series. By the beginning of 1984, Green had placed his stamp on the Cubs' improved lineup and he continued to make deals as the team showed signs of contention. The Chicago Cubs would finish 96-65 and come one win away from representing the National League in the 1984 World Series. Here is a look at key players from the 1984 Cubs, and what Dallas Green gave up in order to acquire them:

1984 CHICAGO CUBS	ACQUIRED FOR…
1984 NL MVP Ryne Sandberg	Ivan DeJesus
1984 Cy Young Rick Sutcliffe	Mel Hall and Joe Carter
LF-Gary Matthews	Bill Campbell and Mike Diaz
CF-Bob Dernier	Bill Campbell and Mike Diaz
RF-Keith Moreland	Mike Krukow and Cash
3B-Ron Cey	Dan Cataline and Vance Lovelace
SS-Larry Bowa	Ivan DeJesus
SP-Steve Trout (with Warren Brusstar)	Scott Fletcher, Pat Tabler, Dick Tidrow and Randy Martz
SP-Scott Sanderson	Craig Lefferts and Carmelo Martinez
SP-Dennis Eckersley	Bill Buckner

In his third year with the Cubs, Green had built a contending team, had the Cubs on the threshold of history, and gave up marginal players in most cases. The trading of Joe Carter was the only loss of this group but without the addition of Sutcliffe, the 1984 Cubs probably don't win the division.

Green may have been a victim of his own success; the Cubs weren't *supposed* to win that fast. After the Cubs suffered through three straight ('85-'87) losing seasons, Dallas Green resigned his post in the fall of 1987. Green and the Tribune Company cited the proverbial "philosophical differences" to explain Green's departure. Green's impact on the Cubs was far from finished.

After not making the post-season for thirty-nine years, the Cubs won a second National League Eastern Division title in 1989...just five seasons after 1984. Jim Frey was (technically) the general manager of the 1989 team, but let's look at how the 1989 team was built:

KEY PLAYER FOR '89 CUBS	HOW AND BY WHOM PLAYER WAS ACQUIRED
Ryne Sandberg	acquired by GREEN via trade
Rick Sutcliffe	acquired by GREEN via trade
Andre Dawson	signed by GREEN as a free agent
Greg Maddux	drafted under GREEN's tenure
Mark Grace	drafted under GREEN'S tenure
Jerome Walton	drafted under GREEN's tenure
Dwight Smith	drafted under GREEN's tenure
Shawon Dunston	drafted under GREEN's tenure
Scott Sanderson	acquired by GREEN via trade
Les Lancaster	signed as amateur free agent under GREEN
Damon Berryhill	drafted under GREEN'S tenure

The only significant players from the 1989 team acquired by Jim Frey were pitchers Mike Bielecki and Mitch Williams. Frey *had* to acquire Williams as a closer to make up for his dreadful trade of Lee Smith and the subsequent signing of Goose Gossage. The players Frey traded for Williams?...Rafael Palmeiro and Jamie Moyer...both drafted under Green.

The 1989 Cubs were still Dallas Green's team. Anyone who says otherwise does not understand baseball...or is related to Jim Frey.

Dallas Green's impression on the Cubs surpassed the teams he placed on the field. When Green became GM of the Cubs, he was the first in his position to openly state the Cubs needed lights at Wrigley Field. The subject of lights at Wrigley was a taboo topic that Green challenged. Green changed the debate from "lights or no lights" to "Cubs in Chicago or Cubs in the Chicago Suburbs." Green famously said, "If there are no lights, there will be no Wrigley Field." (**Baselllibrary.com.**) Green had completely altered much of the fan base's perception, and by August of 1988, Wrigley Field held its first ever night game.

Dallas Green's Cubs' tenure includes another disregarded attribute. The image has persisted throughout the 1990s and 2000s that Wrigley Field is just a beer garden…where baseball happens to be played. The theory is, just open Wrigley's doors and people will flock there no matter how bad the Cubs are. Here is an interesting fact that often goes unnoticed:

1981	ATTENDANCE	AVERAGE LEAGUE RANK
Chicago Cubs	9,752	11th of 12

No, that number is not a misprint…in 1981, the year *before* Green's arrival, the Cubs averaged less than 10,000 fans per game. It may have been a beer garden in 1981 at Clark and Addison…but it was an empty one.

In my humble opinion, had Dallas Green stayed with the Cubs, the probability of a World Series title would have been significantly enhanced. In five years Green built two play-off teams, helped lure the Cubs and their fans out of the dark ages (awful, awful pun) and transformed Wrigley and the Cubs into the amazing, money-making machine they have been for the better part of the last three decades…long after Green's departure.

The incredible feat that was the 1984 Cubs harmed Green in the end. Coming close to the World Series may have hastened the impatience of Green's superiors at the Tribune Company. After the success of 1984, the Cubs were besieged by injuries in 1985 and 1986. Green deserved a better fate with the team, and the Cubs' players, management, and ownership since do not realize the debt they owe to this man.

Reason 99 is the premature departure of Dallas Green from the front offices of the Chicago Cubs. Green's tenure may have been short, but the imprints he made on the franchise positively altered Cubs' history.

REASON 100

D ON'T WALK
"Swinging at the first pitch, Dunston pops out to short left field."
It drove me crazy when Harry Carry would frequently say things like this.
Harry was clearly frustrated with the Cubs' lack of patience at the plate.
Many times he would break out that preface of "*Swinging at the first pitch.*"
I viewed it as Harry being negative, and I didn't like it. Apparently, I didn't
feel anything was wrong with swinging at the first pitch as a younger man…
so *naïve*.

"*A walk is as good as a hit,*" is one of the most overused clichés in baseball.
There is a viable argument to make that a *walk* is not as good as a *hit*; as in a
hit that goes over the fence. A *walk*, opposed to a *hit*, can only knock in one
run. A *walk* is not near as exciting or sexy as a *hit*. Walks might not be sexy,
but Harry understood their value. Twenty-plus years later, I have come to a
conclusion regarding this matter: I was *wrong*, and Harry was *right*.

As I aged and started to understand the game more, I began to notice the
Cubs' unwillingness to take walks. With the 2003 book release of *Moneyball*
by Michael Lewis (which detailed Billy Beane and the Oakland A's success
with high on-base percentage players), organizations began putting more
emphasis on the ability to draw a walk. Yet the Chicago Cubs continued
their poor aptitude at taking walks and it became apparent to those paying
attention. It seemed that no matter the manager, hitting coach or players, the
"don't walk" philosophy appeared to be in place. When I decided to embark
on this long journey to 104 reasons, I hoped I could find some research to
back up this seemingly consistent approach. I examined the sixty-six seasons
since the last Cubs' World Series in 1945. Before drawing (no pun intended)
any conclusions, here is the raw data I compiled. (Included is the *year*, the
Cubs' National League *rank* in walks, and if the Cubs were *above or below* the
league average.)

Year	Rank in NL	A/B Lge Avg	Year	Rank in NL	A/B Lge Avg
1946	3RD OF 8	ABOVE	1947	7TH OF 8	BELOW
1948	7TH OF 8	BELOW	1949	8th OF 8	BELOW
1950	8th OF 8	BELOW	1951	7TH OF 8	BELOW
1952	8TH OF 8	BELOW	1953	5TH OF 8	BELOW
1954	7TH OF 8	BELOW	1955	8TH OF 8	BELOW
1956	6TH OF 8	BELOW	1957	5TH OF 8	BELOW
1958	6TH OF 8	BELOW	1959	3RD OF 8	ABOVE
1960	1ST OF 8***	ABOVE	1961	2ND OF 8	ABOVE
1962	7TH OF 10	BELOW	1963	9TH OF 10	BELOW
1964	2ND OF 10	BELOW	1965	2ND OF 10	BELOW
1966	4TH OF 10	ABOVE	1967	5TH OF 10	ABOVE
1968	6TH OF 10	BELOW	1969	3RD OF 12	ABOVE
1970	4TH OF 12	ABOVE	1971	3RD OF 12	ABOVE
1972	3RD OF 12	ABOVE	1973	5TH OF 12	ABOVE
1974	3RD OF 12	ABOVE	1975	2ND OF 12	ABOVE
1976	8TH OF 12	BELOW	1977	7TH OF 12	BELOW
1978	3RD OF 12	ABOVE	1979	9TH OF 12	ABOVE
1980	9TH OF 12	BELOW	1981	6TH OF 12	AVG.
1982	8TH OF 12	BELOW	1983	12TH OF 12	BELOW
1984	1ST OF 12***	ABOVE	1985	3RD OF 12	ABOVE
1986	10TH OF 12	BELOW	1987	10TH OF 12	BELOW
1988	12TH OF 12	BELOW	1989	12TH OF 12	BELOW
1990	12TH OF 12	BELOW	1991	12TH OF 12	BELOW
1992	12TH OF 12	BELOW	1993	12TH OF 14	BELOW
1994	9TH OF 14	BELOW	1995	12TH OF 14	BELOW
1996	9TH OF 14	BELOW	1997	13TH OF 14	BELOW
1998	6TH OF 14	ABOVE	1999	12TH OF 16	BELOW
2000	6TH OF 16	ABOVE	2001	5TH OF 16	ABOVE
2002	6TH OF 16	ABOVE	2003	14TH OF 16	BELOW
2004	14TH OF 16	BELOW	2005	16TH OF 16	BELOW
2006	16TH OF 16	BELOW	2007	15TH OF 16	BELOW
2008	1ST OF 16***	ABOVE	2009	6TH OF 16	ABOVE
2010	14TH OF 16	BELOW	2011	15TH OF 16	BELOW

There will be a quiz over all of these numbers later. (Not really.) I felt it was important to show *all* of the years before I summarized the data… to illustrate just how consistently futile the Cubs are at walking! Over a sixty-six year period, there are several extended stretches where the Cubs are below (…*well below*) the league average in walks. For a team to be this consistently poor at drawing walks…with different coaching staffs, players, and management…is astonishing. Let's summarize some truly amazing stats pulled from the raw data:

- The Cubs finished below the league average in forty-one of the sixty-six seasons (62 percent), twenty-four times above the league average (36 percent) and right at the average once.

- Twenty-nine times the Cubs finished in the bottom three in walks, as opposed to only fourteen times in the top three.

- Twenty times the Cubs finished in the bottom two, as opposed to only seven times in the top two.

- The Cubs have finished dead last in the league in walks eleven times, as opposed to leading the league only three times.

- From 1969 to 1972 the Cubs were above the league average in walks…during this stretch the Cubs finished .500 or better in all four seasons.

Perhaps the most *important* statistic…*two* of the *three* seasons the Cubs led the league in walks: *1984* and *2008*. These are the *only* seasons in which the Cubs won ninety-five or more games in the last sixty-six years…and *both* times they led the league in walks. That is one astounding *coincidence*!

I started the research at 1945, the last time the Cubs appeared in a World Series. Looking a little deeper into Cubs' history and including *all* six times the Cubs have won ninety-five games since 1908…the correlation between rare Cubs' successful seasons and rare Cubs' walks is astounding:

YEAR	RECORD	LEAGUE RANK IN WALKS
1910	104-50	3RD OF 8
1929	98-54	1ST OF 8
1935	100-54	1ST OF 8
1945	98-56	3RD OF 8
1984	96-65	1ST OF 12
2008	97-64	1ST OF 16

The *only times* that the Chicago Cubs have won ninety-five games or more…they have been one of the top National League teams in drawing free-passes…quite a coincidence!

The statistics above prove there has been considerable value to drawing walks in the infrequent historic successes of the Chicago Cubs. When Theo Epstein took over as president of baseball operations for the Chicago Cubs in the fall of 2011, he arrived with a history of constructing teams built upon the importance of on-base percentage. This approach may be one of the most important elements Epstein could possibly bring to the Cubs. (In 2012, the Cubs finished fifteenth out of sixteenth in the National League in walks and lost 101 games, so the philosophy has not taken root…*yet.*)

Reason 100 out of 104 is simple and convincing; the Chicago Cubs historically just don't *walk* enough.

REASON 101

LACK OF LEFTY POWER

Let me ask a question. Have you ever watched a Cubs' game on television? Of course you have, you would not be reading this book if you hadn't. Another question: have you ever seen a game in which a player hit a home run *out* of Wrigley Field? If you answered yes to that inquiry, then how often have you heard one of these home runs described as "Out onto Waveland Avenue?" Have you seen the camera zoom in on people waiting on Waveland Avenue for a potential home run from Dave Kingman, Andre Dawson, or Sammy Sosa? Now let me ask you this: Can you remember a home run call "Out onto

Sheffield Avenue?" As a knowledgeable Cubs' fan, you know that Waveland Avenue is beyond the left field bleachers, and that Sheffield Avenue is outside the right field bleachers. What you may not have realized, is that in the history of the Chicago Cubs, balls rarely make it onto Sheffield Avenue.

In the off-seasons of 2007, 2008, and 2009, Cubs' general manager Jim Hendry was nearly vilified for trying to "balance out" the Cubs' lineup by adding left-handed power. Truly, Hendry had the right idea, most of the Cubs' lineup; Alfonso Soriano, Aramis Ramirez, Geovany Soto, Mark DeRosa, Ryan Theriot, and Derek Lee *were* right-handed. Hendry's mistake and a measure of his subsequent downfall was selecting Kosuke Fukudome, Jaques Jones, Cliff Floyd, and Milton Bradley to be those left-handed bats. While those four choices of left-handed hitters were not the answer, Hendry was correct in identifying an integral problem. The Cubs' lineup *was* uneven and extremely vulnerable to strong right-handed pitching. This is a maddening Cubs' shortcoming that has historically transcended the Hendry era. Right-handed hitters just seem to be the Cubs' modus operandi…throughout their *entire history*. Even in the glorious season of 1984, the Cubs only had one left-handed hitter in Leon Durham and one switch-hitter in Larry Bowa. I often wonder if Goose Gossage would have been able to dispose of the '84 Cubs had he faced just *one* more lefty bat?

When I started this project, I knew I wanted the Cubs' lack of lefty hitters as one of the 104 reasons. My only concern was finding the proof and making correlations between the lack of lefties and the lack of titles. It wasn't a problem. Here are some simple ones, using both "old" and new statistics:

- There is only one lefty in the all-time Cubs' top ten for OPS… Billy Williams at number nine.

- Of the Cubs' all-time top-ten slugging percentage seasons, *none* were accomplished by a left-handed hitter.

- In career *slugging percentage*, Billy Williams (number seven) is *once again* the lone lefty. Of the top ten single-season home run totals by a Cub, *none* is by a left-handed hitter.

- Of the Cubs' all-time top-ten home run hitters, there are only two lefties; Billy Williams at number three and Bill Nicholson at number eight.

- Of the top ten Cubs' seasons of *runs batted in,* none have been by left-handed hitters.
- Of the *all-time* Cubs' RBI leaders there are three lefties: Billy Williams, Mark Grace and Phil Caveretta.

There are not many left-handed hitters on the above lists, especially left-handed hitters *not-named* Billy Williams. In terms of Cubs' power statistics, it's a fact that the players holding the marks are predominately right-handed. Three out of ten was the highest number of left-handed hitters, and that was only in one category (all-time RBIs).

These are significant numbers, but a question remains: Is there any proof that these numbers correlate with the Cubs' lack of World Series titles or other National League teams' ability to win World Series titles? A comparison needed to be made between the Cubs and the other teams in the National League. I took the *top-ten home run hitters* for each National League team and compared them by right-handed hitters, left-handed hitters, and switch hitters:

TEAM	RH	LH	SWITCH	RH-HRs	LH-HRs	DIFFERENCE
Cardinals	4	5	1	1,184	1,384	+200 LH
Giants	6	4	0	1,669	1,742	+73 LH
Diamondbacks	5	5	0	545	600	+55 LH
Padres	5	4	1	682	594	+88 RH
Pirates	6	4	0	1,117	982	+135 RH
Mets	5	2	3	939	721	+218 RH
Phillies	5	5	0	1,485	1,149	+336 RH
Rockies	7	3	0	1,083	730	+353 RH
Reds	6	4	0	1,645	917	+728 RH
Marlins	8	2	0	1,058	196	+862 RH
Dodgers	8	2	0	1,654	750	+904 RH
Astros	8	1	1	1,741	424	+1,316 RH
Expos/Nationals	9	1	0	1,463	115	+1,348 RH
Braves	8	1	1	2,618	854	+1,762 RH
Cubs	8	2	0	2,534	597	+1,947 RH

Sorry Brewers, you still have more seasons in the AL

Of all the National League teams, the Cubs have the biggest discrepancy in their top-ten home run leaders between left-handed hitters and right-handed hitters. Not even the Braves with right-hander Hank Aaron's 733 can match the Cubs. So we have proven that in this select category the Cubs finish last... again.

Yet, does this prove any correlation between winning and losing? Let's take a look at this:

TOP-FIVE ALL-TIME WORLD SERIES CHAMPIONS:

1. New York Yankees—27
2. St. Louis Cardinals—11
3. Oak/Phil/KC A's—9
4. Boston Red Sox—7, S.F/New York Giants 7
5. LA/Brooklyn Dodgers—6

The Cardinals have more championships than any other National League team and are one of only three teams that have more left-handed home runs in their all-time top-ten than right-handed home runs. It is certainly not the only factor, but the presence of left-handed power is at least *relevant* to winning. Just for the fun of it, let's take a look at this:

TEAM	RH	LH	SWITCH	RH-HRs	LH-HRs	DIFFERENCE
Yankees	3	5	2	1,182	2,583+1,401

Hmmm, so the greatest baseball team of all time has a very significant amount of more left-handed home runs in their top ten than right-handed home runs. Yes, they had Babe Ruth, and all inclinations of Yankee Stadium with short right field lines, but there is no denying the left-handed power of the Yankees has made a difference.

The newest "new" Cubs' regime led by Theo Epstein has declared that acquiring left-handed power will be one of their foremost priorities. Epstein and GM Jed Hoyer backed this up by making prized prospect and left-handed hitting Anthony Rizzo one of their first additions. Perhaps they will succeed where Hendry and others have failed by fielding a lineup with more than just one left-handed power threat. Maybe Epstein and Hoyer can add hitters more equipped than Fukudome, Jones, Floyd and the one and only Milton Bradley. Perhaps we will start to hear Sheffield Avenue mentioned as often as Waveland Avenue. Possibly, in future summers, the people waiting on the street for home runs will have to move back and forth between Waveland and Sheffield.

Reason 101 is the Chicago Cubs' historic lack of left-handed power hitters. A historical pattern that has followed the Cubs through numerous eras, and is unique compared to their opposition. Billy Williams is the *only* consistent left-handed power hitter the team has ever had...and it has been almost forty years since he played for the team.

REASON 102

No Gold Part 1: A lack of Backstops

Clichés in baseball are rather abundant. Many of these clichés are painfully obvious and simplistic: "It's not over until it's over," "Wait for your pitch," "Ducks on the pond," "Insurance runs," "You can't steal first base," and "Take them one game at a time," etc., etc., and etc.! Nevertheless there are differences; there are clichéd *sayings* and there are clichéd *ideas*. A clichéd idea that I decided to investigate was the notion that a baseball team needs to be "strong up the middle" defensively for success. The basic premise is that a baseball team needs to be strong at catcher, the middle infield positions and center field. That leads to two essential questions: is there any correlation to strength at these positions and winning...and if there is...how do the Cubs compare? As expected, the Cubs fail *disappoint* when it comes to delivering *disappointing* results.

One of the underlying themes I have discussed is the numerous new metrics and statistics that are being created for baseball. These innovative methods of measurement have found their way to the defensive side of the game. *Range Factor*, *Defensive WAR* and others are now used to evaluate how truly beneficial a defender is. For the purposes of **Reasons 102 and 103:** *No Gold Parts 1 and 2*, I am going to go a bit "old-school" and just use Gold Gloves as a measuring stick.

Beginning in 1957, Rawlings and Major League Baseball began awarding the Gold Glove to each defensive player. The award is voted on by managers and coaches, who *cannot* vote for their own players. Gold Glove winners may not always be quantified as the absolute best fielder at his position; yet I think we can agree that if a player wins the award, he *is* one of the top defensive players at his position. Simply put, the Gold Glove may not be universally agreed upon to represent the league's best fielders, but it will serve our purpose.

Since the inception of the Gold Glove, the Cubs have had two catchers win the award: Randy Hundley in 1967 and Jody Davis in 1986. First, let's compare that to the rest of the National League teams, as well as the number of Worlds Series appearances and titles for that team during the time period:

	GOLD GLOVE CATCHERS	W.S. APPEARANCES	W.S. TITLES
Cardinals	12	9	4
Reds	12	6	3
Braves	5	5	1
Pirates	4	3	3
Marlins	4	2	2
Dodgers	3	9	4
Phillies	3	5	2
Astros	3	1	0
Expos/Nats	3	0	0
Padres	3	2	0
Cubs	2	0	0
Giants	1	4	2
Mets	0	3	2
D-Backs	0	1	1
Rockies	0	1	0

Surprise, surprise…the Cardinals are at the *top* of another one of my lists again! The truly relevant correlations we can make from this: the Cardinals and Reds success *can* be related to their good defensive catching and the Cubs (again) are near the *bottom*. I would like to note that in each of the *Marlins'* championships they had Gold Glove catchers in Charles Johnson and Pudge Rodriguez. After compiling this list, I felt a bit unsatisfied. The compilation displays that the Cubs aren't good at drafting/acquiring/trading for solid defensive catchers, yet I felt it only told part of the story.

What I decided to do next was to scan all of the National League World Series representatives since 1958, and see how many teams had a Gold Glove-winning or *former or eventual* Gold Glove-winning catcher on their team. The years listed below are years in which the National League representative *had* a Gold Glove-winning catcher on their team. The years in bold represent those in which the Gold Glove winner for that season was on the team:

1958 1959 1963 1964 1965 **1966 1970**
1972 1975 1976 1980 1986 1987 1989
1997 2002 2003 **2004** 2005 2006 2010
2011

Now, in summation the information listed above shows further that the Cubs' *lack* of Gold Glove-winning catchers emphatically qualifies as a reason for the 104 year lack of World Series titles:

- Out of fifty-two World Series teams from the National League during this period, twenty-two had Gold Glove-caliber catchers on their team...a pretty impressive 42 percent.

- Notice the apparent recent trend toward the importance, seven out of the last ten National League World Series representatives had Gold Glove-winning catchers on their teams.

- In each of the dreaded Cardinals' recent World Series appearances they had a Gold Glove caliber catcher... either Mike Matheny or Yadier Molina.

- One outstanding catcher like Johnny Bench can help a team dominate for a decade.

I also found that in years when teams did not have a Gold Glove defender, they had an elite, or very good offensive performer at catcher: Mike Piazza, Javy Lopez, Mike Scioscia, Buster Posey, etc. Regrettably for the Cubs, they rarely have a catcher who qualifies in either of these categories.

Jody Davis in 1984 *was* this type of catcher, not coincidently in a year that was one of the Cubs' greatest near misses. However, for every Jody Davis-type the Cubs have had, there has been: Barry Foote, Tim Blackwell, Damian Miller, *old* Jason Kendall, Scott Servais, and Todd Hundley (yuck). With all the constant criticisms the Cubs receive, the topic of their continued lack of quality catching rarely gets broached. Cubs' fans constantly hear about the lack of pitchers developed, position players established or the Cubs' shortage of overall prospects. Nevertheless, a position of such importance as catcher seems to get glossed over by both the Cubs *and* their critics.

At the beginning of **Reason 102**, I listed some oft-used baseball clichés. "The tools of ignorance" is a cliché that is used to describe catcher's equipment. The idea being that one has to be ignorant to want to take the beating associated with catching. The Cubs' lack of attention to this important position has been truly *ignorant*. With an organization that has a history as depressing and dismal as the Cubs, there are many areas that lack proper detail. The Cubs' weakness at catcher is **Reason 102** and it absolutely deserves to be on our list of 104.

REASON 103

No Gold Part 2: "Put Me in, Coach!"…Unless He Can't Play

I was playing baseball in high school when the song "Centerfield" by John Fogerty became popular and thus synonymous with baseball for the next twenty-seven years. Most people can now recognize the beginning, which has a rhythmic sound of a ball hitting a bat like a drum beat. Fogerty could not have picked a better position to lionize in his catchy ode to America's National Pastime. Center field has historically been home to the greatest names in baseball. Willie Mays, Mickey Mantle, and Joe DiMaggio are just three of the all-time greats that immediately come to mind. These three players would be in the Hall of Fame of

Hall of Famers, if there were such a place. Surprisingly (sarcasm implied), center field has *not* been a position of strength for the Chicago Cubs.

Since 1957, the first year a Gold Glove was awarded at each position in the NL and AL, the Cubs have had only *two* outfielders win the Gold Glove award. Bob Dernier won a Gold Glove in 1984 while playing center field and Andre Dawson won in 1987 playing right field. As the data I am about to share will demonstrate, it's not surprising the Cubs were a near World Series team in 1984 with Dernier patrolling center. I will use the same method used in **Reason 102** for catchers and apply it to center fielders. In the years listed below, the team that represented the National League in the World Series had a Gold Glove or former Gold Glove winner playing center field. The years listed in **bold** indicate seasons in which the actual Gold Glove winner was playing for the eventual World Series representative.

1961	**1962**	1963	**1964**	1965	1966	**1967**
1968	1969	**1975**	**1976**	**1980**	1982	1983
1985	1987	1990	**1995**	**1996**	1997	1998
1999	2001	**2004**	2006	**2008**	2009	2010

This data shows that in twenty-eight of the fifty-five seasons since 1957 the team that plays in the World Series for the National League has a center fielder who has won a Gold Glove. Twenty-eight out of fifty-five equates to a surprising 51 percent. The actual Gold Glove-winning center fielder for the National League has played in the fall classic fourteen times, or 27 percent of the time. There are very simple conclusions that can be drawn from this: if you have a good defensive center fielder, you have a much greater chance of playing in the World Series. In 1984, one of the paramount Cubs' near misses, the team had their one and only Gold Glove-winning center fielder. This data illustrates that this was *not* a coincidence.

While researching center fielder facts, I came across something that was pretty amazing. Other than Dernier, Andre Dawson is the *only* other Cubs' Gold Glove-winning outfielder. When we include left fielders and right fielders, here are the *only* years in which the National League World Series team did *NOT* have a Gold Glove-winning outfielder in one of their three outfield spots:

1973	1981	1986	1988	1989	1991	1992
1993	2000	2003	2005	2007	2011	2012

In only fourteen of the last fifty-three seasons has the National League World Series representative fielded an outfield void of any current or former Gold Glove winners. Therefore, in thirty-nine out of fifty-three seasons, or 75 percent of the time, one of the outfield spots was manned by a Gold Glove defender. Those statements denote a very strong correlation, but also consider:

- Since the inception of the Gold Glove in 1958, it took twenty-four years before a team represented the National League *without* a current or former Gold Glove winner.

- The connection seems to be very consistent, as in at least every decade, six out of ten seasons include a team with at least one Gold Glove-winning outfielder.

With this information presented in front of us, it makes the Cubs' total of *two* outfield Gold Gloves seem pathetic. I have belabored the point that in 1984, the Cubs won ninety-six ballgames and were one game away from the World Series with a Gold Glove-winning center fielder. Here are more points along that same line of thinking:

- In 2003, (you remember...when the Cubs were five outs away from the World Series) who was the Cubs' center fielder for the second half of the season and the play-offs? Why, it was Kenny Lofton, a former Gold Glove center fielder.

- In 2008, the only season other than 1984 in which the Cubs won ninety-five games since 1945, who played center for the Cubs down the stretch? That would be none other than Jim Edmonds, winner of eight Gold Gloves as a center fielder for the Angels and Cardinals.

At the beginning of this reason, I mentioned the names of Willie Mays, Mickey Mantle and Joe DiMaggio…two of whom are actually featured in John Fogerty's "Centerfield." A "Cubs' Centerfield" song would be more like "We Didn't Start the Fire" by Billy Joel:

Tuffy Rhodes, Brian McRae, Marlon Byrd and Felix Pie

Damon Buford, Lance Johnson, ancient Willie Wilson

Scot Thompson, Carlos Lezcano, even Fonz Soriano

Ty Waller, Joe Wallis, really hard to say who is worse

Sammy Sosa and Leon Durham before he went to play first

Walton was a flash in the pan; Kosuke came from Ja-pan

Corey Patterson hurt could never play, Davey Martinez traded away

What else do I have to say!

Okay, I am sorry if that was embarrassing for *you* to read (embarrassed for me), but I couldn't resist the feeble attempt to make light of Cubs' center fielders. Regardless of what you thought of my lame attempt at being a lyricist, the point remains: the Chicago Cubs have lacked quality defensive outfielders for most of their existence…a trait that World Series teams do not exhibit.

Reason 103 states that the Cubs' astonishing low number of Gold Glove-winning center fielders (one…*cough*) is a strong reason why the Cubs have not been in a World Series since 1945. Considering the fact that the Cubs have had only two Gold Glove outfielders *ever*…is astounding! That surprising lack of quality defenders in the outfield demonstrates why the Cubs rarely contend.

…and my lame attempt at "Cubs' Centerfield" is why I rarely write lyrics.

REASON 104

THE DECIMATION OF THE 2003 PITCHING STAFF

In September of 2012, the Washington Nationals made one of the most controversial decisions in recent baseball history. The Nationals decided to "shut down" their ace Stephen Strasburg after 159.1 innings pitched. Strasburg, who turned twenty-four in 2012, was only one year removed from reconstructive surgery on his elbow. Strasburg was one of the preeminent pitchers in the National League with a 15-6 record, a 3.16 ERA and 197 strikeouts. At the time of Strasburg's "shut down," the Nationals had a comfortable division lead and appeared headed to the play-offs. The Nationals rolled the dice on the side of caution and the long-term health of Strasburg. Nationals' general manager Mike Rizzo has placed the future value of Strasburg to the Nationals ahead of a 2012 World Series title. The Nationals did not win the 2013 World Series, leaving Rizzo's choice to shut Strasburg down to endless debate. I have never heard Rizzo say it publicly, but his decision may have been based on the history of the Cubs and their "aces."

When Theo Epstein and Jed Hoyer took over the Cubs in the fall of 2011, they spoke eloquently of the need for the Cubs to acquire "assets." Undoubtedly Epstein and Hoyer would love to have an asset like Strasburg, a twenty-four year old who throws a fastball in the mid-nineties. *Every* team in baseball would give up quite a bit to acquire an asset such as a rare arm like Strasburg. The Nationals have decided to take extreme care of Strasburg's unique talent. When presented with similar assets in the early 2000s, the Chicago Cubs' organization did the opposite.

As a Cubs' fan, I don't think I was ever as excited as when the Cubs had Kerry Wood (26), Mark Prior (22), and Carlos Zambrano (22 – with a constant question mark regarding his actual age…but still young) in their rotation. Rounding out the rotation was Matt Clement (28), who could still be as dominant at times as Wood, Prior and Zambrano. Even the most cynical of Cubs' fans had to feel the Cubs were on the verge of pitching dominance like that of the 1990s Atlanta Braves. Regrettably, the Cubs treated these four assets much differently than Rizzo and the Nationals treated 2012 Stephen Strasburg. If these four Cubs' pitchers were "assets" like classic cars, then here is what the Cubs did:

- They never got their oil changed.
- They ran them into the ground regarding mileage.
- They drove them on just the axles without tires.
- They let all the exterior rust.
- They never even took these "classic cars" to get washed.

The Cubs burned up these players' careers, they scorched up money, and they threw away any chance at sustained success. Throughout **Reason 104**, I will constantly reference pitch counts. I cannot universally proclaim 100 pitches as being too high, particularly with strikeout pitchers like the Cubs had. However, I can question pitch counts that exceeded 110, 120 and even *130* throughout **Reason 104**.

Let's take a look at each pitcher individually:

Matt Clement

Though not quite as dominant as fellow members on the Cubs' staff, Clement at age twenty-eight was showing flashes of brilliance. Clement was spared the 2003 abuse his fellow rotation members absorbed as far as pitch counts. In 2004 though, Clement started thirty games, and threw over 100 pitches twenty times. In nine games Clement threw over 110, and he twice threw over 120. The Cubs let Clement leave via free agency after 2004. Clement pitched another year and a half for the Boston Red Sox, and had initial success in Boston. However by 2006, Clement had pitched his last game in the Major Leagues due to shoulder injuries. He attempted comebacks with the Cardinals and Blue Jays before officially retiring in 2009.

Kerry Wood

Kerry Wood had already missed the entire 1999 season with Tommy John surgery before he began to re-establish himself as a force in the Cubs' rotation. Teamed with Prior, Wood gave the Cubs two top-flight arms to lead the staff. In 2003 Wood started thirty-two games for the Cubs, and in twenty-five of them threw 100 pitches or more. Once again, due to control issues Wood was destined for high pitch counts, yet there are at least two stretches of the 2003 season that are inexcusable. Wood threw over 100 pitches in nine of his first eleven starts of the season. These games were to *start* the season…not the stretch drive. Here is a pretty surprising four-game stretch from April and May 2003 of Wood's pitch counts: **120, 124, 121, and 141.** Kerry Wood threw *141* pitches in a game on May 10, 2003! Let me repeat that…on May 10, in game thirty-six of the season in a 3-2 win over the Cards, one of the Cubs' most valuable resources threw an *staggering 141 pitches!* Wood did not get the decision in the game, left after seven innings, and we can only wonder if taking Kerry out after 100 or so pitches really would have mattered to the outcome of an early season game.

In the last ten games down the stretch of the 2003 season, Wood threw **118, 95, 75 (in two innings), 71 (four innings), 125, 120, 122, 114, 125, and 122.** The Cubs needed Wood down the stretch, and they rode him to the play-offs.

In the 2003 National League Divisional Series against the Braves, Wood was dominating in games 1 *and* 5. Kerry went 2-0, allowed only seven hits over fifteen innings, and struck out eighteen. Wood threw 124 pitches in Game 1 and 117 in Game 5. Kerry Wood started Games 3 and 7 against the Marlins in the NLCS. In the deciding Game 7 he was not the same Kerry Wood. This Wood allowed seven hits, four walks and seven earned runs in just over five innings. As we examined in CHAPTER **2, Reason 20**, *Was Kerry Wood's arm toast by this point?*

In 2004 Kerry Wood made twenty-two starts for the Cubs, but was shut down for almost two months from mid-May to mid-July. Apparently the Cubs had very little concern regarding the 2003 workload's effects on Kerry as he threw over 110 pitches in *four of his first six* starts. Included in those first six starts of 2004, Wood threw a **131** pitch outing on April 17! This, the Cubs eleventh game of the year, Kerry's third start in twelve days, he threw **131** pitches! (I wish there was something stronger than an exclamation point.) Wood threw over 110 pitches over his next three starts; two in April and one on May 5. In his next start on May 11, Wood left the game early and would not start again until July 11.

Kerry Wood made only fourteen starts over 2005 and 2006 combined, and by 2007 was pitching entirely out of the bullpen to protect his partially torn shoulder. Wood had great success as the Cubs' closer in 2008 before leaving as a free agent. Wood returned in 2011, before retiring mid-season in 2012.

Throughout his Cubs' career, Wood was labeled as injury-prone, an assertion that I obviously disagree with. The contrast between how the Cubs handled Kerry Wood, and the 2012 handling of Strasburg by Rizzo and the Nationals could not be starker. Perhaps the case study of Wood was enough to convince the Nationals how to handle their young ace. Troublingly for the Cubs, Wood was not their only example of ruining a young arm.

Mark Prior

Mark Prior came out of USC as one of the best pitching prospects ever! Mark Prior fell into the Cubs' collective "lap" when the Minnesota Twins selected Joe Mauer with the first pick in the 2001 amateur draft. Prior quickly asserted his dominance in the Major Leagues and by 2003 he and Kerry Wood provided the Cubs with their finest top-two pitchers in team history. Prior was flat out awesome in helping the Cubs to the 2003 play-offs, going 18-6 with 245 strikeouts in 218 innings. Prior's remarkable 2003 came at a costly price:

MARK PRIOR 2003 GAME BY GAME PITCH COUNTS

90 OR LESS	95-99	100-105	106-110	111-119	120-129	130+
1	3	3	4	10	6	3

Mark Prior was twenty-two years old in 2003, and in nineteen of the thirty games he started for the Cubs he threw over 110 pitches, and nine times he threw over 120.

Prior started 2004 on the disabled list with an apparent Achilles tendon injury, although there were constant whispers that his arm was actually hurting. When Prior did return, he started twenty-one games and struggled early, yet finished the year strong striking out sixteen Reds in his final start of the year.

An elbow strain delayed the start to Mark Prior's 2005 season, and upon his return, a freak injury would add to his list of woes. Prior was struck by a line drive estimated to be at 117 mph to his pitching elbow...and missed a month. He was able to make twenty-seven starts over 2005, and finished the season 11-7 with a 3.67 ERA.

The 2006 season would essentially be Prior's last year pitching for the Cubs. The shoulder problems he struggled with in spring training of that season portended what was to come. *Fangraphs.com* records and compiles pitchers average velocity, and it shows that Prior's fastball in 2006 averaged around 91 mph. During his dominant 2003 season, Mark Prior's fastball averaged around 93 mph. At first glance, this 2 mph difference may not seem significant. I ask you to remember just how an *average works*. In 2003 Prior's fastball would bottom out around 91 to 92 mph and top out around 95-96 mph. By 2006, Prior would be topping out at 93-94 mph and his bottom numbers would touch the high 80s. For a strikeout pitcher like Prior, that bit of velocity drop is crucial. Prior's numbers in 2006: a 1-6 record with a 7.21 ERA. Prior allowed a hit per inning for the first time in his career, and his strikeout rate dropped by 20 percent.

Exploratory surgery found Prior to have a "loose" shoulder, which the Cubs attributed to the basic weakening of Prior's shoulder joints. The injury essentially ended Prior's career with the Cubs, and his continued comeback attempts have fallen short.

I have yet to place any blame in **Reason 104**; the most obvious target has always been Dusty Baker. There can be no argument that Baker believes in allowing his starters to pitch long into games. When Baker took over the Reds, some of the same concerns voiced about the Cubs' young pitchers were echoed in Cincinnati. Blaming Baker is the most convenient, and Dusty does deserve much of the culpability. But if we are attempting to charge Dusty with the first degree murder of Mark Prior's and Kerry Wood's careers, the evidence does not completely hold up. Dusty may be an accessory to the crime, but there are many other people and factors to blame:

- Baker's superiors such as Jim Hendry and Andy MacPhail are just as responsible as Baker. If they felt Baker was ruining their young pitchers, they could have easily stopped it.

- The high school, college, and little league coaches of these pitchers contributed as well. Youth sports' culture is at fault, as young pitchers simply play many more games than they used to.

- With coaches and managers trying to win at each level and with the advent of "showcases," young pitchers are rarely *not* pitching.

- You have to excuse Baker, Hendry, and MacPhail in some sense; the ultimate achievement of being the "ones" who brought that first title to the Chicago Cubs since 1908 would cause anyone shortsightedness.

This *Reason* was actually the inspiration for this entire book. I woke up one morning, wondering just how different the 2000s might have been if these pitchers had stayed healthy. I came to the conclusion that the Cubs would have definitely had a much greater chance at winning a World Series....duh?

Kerry Wood, Matt Clement, and Mark Prior are not the first or last pitchers to have their careers cut short by arm injuries. However against a backdrop of 104 years of futility, the poor choices and bad luck that led to these injuries get lumped in with other "Cubbie Occurrences"...as Lou Piniella called them. The compounding of all of these factors leads fans to abandon logic and reason, and start talking about ridiculous things such as curses.

According to **Reason 104**, Mark Prior and Kerry Wood were not cursed. Nor did a goat affect their pitching abilities in any way. Each of them threw too many pitches at a young age...and their promising careers and a great chance at a Cubs' World Series were wiped away.

EPILOGUE
YEAR 105?

I did my student teaching in the fall of 1990 at Peoria Central High School in Illinois. Among the teachers and coaches that I attached myself to there was a Cubs' fan with a distinctly different perspective; *Mr. Boyle rooted for the Cubs to lose*. Mr. Boyle took constant razzing and befuddled questioning from other Cubs' fans, yet he stuck to his position and never wavered. His rationale was simple; the Cubs were only "the Cubs" *because* of their losing ways. In Mr. Boyle's eyes that's what set his team apart…that was the Cubs' unique quality. I was twenty-two years old at the time; Mr. Boyle was a man in his mid- to late-fifties and I thought he was just a crazy old man. After just a few more years of perspective (twenty-two), I still would never adopt his philosophy. I want the Cubs to win as much as I always have. Yet, I wonder if there wasn't just a touch of wisdom in Mr. Boyle's unique philosophy.

The 2013 Major League season is about to begin…yet it began on *Bleacher Nation* (the awesome Cubs' blog run by Brett Taylor) in late February. When the Cubs played insignificant inner squad games, the response on *Bleacher Nation* was as intense, as if the Cubs were in the middle of a pennant race. The lineups for the games were analyzed and scrutinized by Brett's impressive cadre (known as BNers in the blogosphere). These BNers are extremely passionate and incredibly knowledgeable. Most of them are not casual fans…they can recite to you at least twenty of the Cubs' top prospects and describe them. When Cubs' prospect Jorge Soler crushed a homer in his first inner squad at bat, legions of them watched it on *Bleacher Nation*. Okay…I watched it, too.

This passion displayed for a meaningless inner-squad game is astonishing. This type of obsessing will occur on *Bleacher Nation* daily until the end of the 2013 baseball season. Perhaps that's why Brett uses the phrase "Obsessing since 2008" (the year he began the site) printed below the logo on his *Bleacher*

Nation T-shirts. Cubs' fans are *obsessed*…we are infatuated with the idea of our team actually winning a World Series title. We devour any information we get that may give us hope of that impending World Series. When Jorge Soler hits that mammoth home run in a pointless game, we make a cognitive leap…"this guy's gonna finally do it for us"…we see it for much more than it really is. This in itself is not a negative quality, it's just generational conditioning. Cubs' fans are different from any other fandom…we are the definition of *obsessed*.

Years and years of living this fanatical following of the Cubs, and observing it in so many others, has given me a different perspective. There was some truth to what Mr. Boyle believed. What would a post-Cubs' World Series world look like for Cubs' fans? More importantly, what would it feel like? In 2003, after the Cubs beat the Braves in the NLDS, I had a hard time wrapping my head around it. My thought process was askew, my Cubs' perceptions off-kilter…it was difficult for me to process. I can only imagine what a Cubs' championship might do to the psyches of millions of people. What *would* we do?

Road Runner cartoons were very popular when I was a youngster, but perhaps you are familiar with them. Every episode would feature Wiley Coyote trying to catch the Road Runner. (I imagine he was trying to eat him, but they really never told us that part.) Did you ever see Wiley Coyote actually *catch* the Road Runner? Of course he was never caught! Yet we watched intently anyway…just for the possibility…even though we knew the outcome. That poor coyote was never going to catch his prey…and what if he had? There would be no reason to watch.

Peanuts was also a significant cartoon influence on a kid growing up in the 1970s. Have you ever seen Charlie Brown attempt to kick a football with Lucy Van Pelt as his holder? Charlie barrels full speed ahead toward Lucy, ready to finally kick that ball…only to have Lucy pull it away time after time after time. And every time Charlie goes flying into the air and lands squarely on his back. (I imagine Charlie Brown dealt with some serious lower back issues later in life.) Charlie Brown *never* gets to kick that football. He never attains his goal. Lucy wins every time.

Actually, Charlie Brown has much in common with the Chicago Cubs.

In both of these examples the thrill or anticipation of the pursuit of the goal is what grabs us. The Cubs' faithful heavily invests psychologically, emotionally and behaviorally year after year in this team. Year after year we are disappointed; we have a symbolic Lucy Van Pelt who pulls the ball away from us. Like Good Ol' Charlie Brown that doesn't stop us from trying again. Even when the hurt is monumentally tough (1969, 1984, 2003)...we *still* come back.

But...what if? If the Cubs win the 2013 World Series (no bleeping way!), what are we going to do? Generations and generations of Cubs' fans have emulated Charlie Brown and Wiley Coyote their entire lives and repeated the same behavior year in and year out. Would a Cubs' World Series title force all of us to think and act differently? In 2003, one Cubs' play-off series victory scrambled my thought processes. I can't even fathom what a World Series would do.

Perhaps Mr. Boyle was on to something.

Fortunately (or unfortunately, depending on your perspective), there does not appear to be any immediate threats to our Cubs' perspectives being thrown for a collective loop by a World Series title. 2014? 2015? 2068? (I would be 100.) Who knows...we may have to deal with a new reality. I have spent a great deal of time here pointing out the many mistakes of the Chicago National League ball club, yet please don't misconstrue...I love the Chicago Cubs. I hope to live to see a World Series title. I will deal with my psychological issues after the fact. Perhaps I will take any money I may accrue from sales of this book and wager it yearly on the Chicago Cubs.

That's probably not a good idea.

C.N.
March 2013

ABOUT THE AUTHOR

This is me in March of 1978...
and I look exactly the same today.

CHRIS NEITZEL has been a teacher and coach for 23 years in his hometown of Oswego, Illinois. He still lives in Oswego with his wife, Krista, of 21 years and their three children, Kara, Olivia, and Scott. A lifelong Cubs' fan, Chris began contributing to the Cubs' blog, *Bleacher Nation*, in 2011. While he has always aspired to be a writer, Chris credits his exposure to Brett Taylor's *Bleacher Nation* for giving him the forum and the audience to get his creative juices going. This is his first book.